Mighty Fine Words and Smashing Expressions

Mighty Fine Words and Smashing Expressions

MAKING SENSE OF TRANSATLANTIC ENGLISH

ORIN HARGRAVES

OXFORD
UNIVERSITY PRESS
2003

OXFORD
UNIVERSITY PRESS

Oxford   New York
Auckland   Bangkok   Buenos Aires   Cape Town   Chennai
Dar es Salaam   Delhi   Hong Kong   Istanbul   Karachi   Kolkata
Kuala Lumpur   Madrid   Melbourne   Mexico City   Mumbai   Nairobi
São Paulo   Shanghai   Singapore   Taipei   Tokyo   Toronto

Copyright © 2003 by Orin Hargraves

Published by Oxford University Press, Inc.
198 Madison Avenue, New York, New York, 10016
http://www.oup-usa.org

Library of Congress Cataloging-in-Publication Data

Data available
ISBN: 0-19-515704-4

EDITORIAL AND PRODUCTION STAFF
Copyeditor: Carol-June Cassidy
Jacket designer: Leah Lococo Ltd.
Designer: Irving Perkins
Editor: Erin McKean
Assistant Project Editor: Abigail Powers
EDP Director: John Sollami
Publisher: Karen Day

Printing number: 9 8 7 6 5 4 3 2 1

Printed in the United States of America
on acid-free paper

This book is dedicated to
MARIA AND YADI,
my home (away) from home

Contents

List of Tables

CHAPTER FOUR
The Government and the Law

CHAPTER FIVE
Education

CHAPTER SIX
Sickness and Health

CHAPTER SEVEN
Food, Clothing, and Shelter

CHAPTER EIGHT
Transport(ation)

Preface

The idea for this book developed naturally out of two circumstances. First, my off-and-on residence in Britain that has filled up about half of the last fifteen years: that has provided me with the opportunity for intermittent total immersion in British English. Second, my full-time work in lexicography for the past dozen years, which began in Britain and which continues today as a transatlantic undertaking. As is the case with any American spending time in Britain I have had occasion to note the subtle but pervasive differences between British English and my own native American English. As a lexicographer it is my job to be aware of these differences, to keep track of all of their finer points and exceptions, and finally to document them in dictionaries and other reference works.

There came a time when all of this material—that is, the differences between British and American English—began to seem like a kind of monster. The monster that might best represent this perception is The Blob. There are so many areas of difference, and most of them are much more complicated than mere equivalences, like American *diaper* and British *nappy*. There came a time when it was no longer possible for me to retrieve from memory when I needed them all the distinctions I had noted at various times. The possibility of successfully retrieving them from some other place—where I had written them down, printed them out, or remembered seeing evidence of them—was even more remote. So it made sense to collect them in a book, where they could reliably be found all in one place.

Of course no one in his right mind writes a book only for himself; or if he does, it is unlikely that he will find anyone to publish it. Therefore I have

1

tried to create a book that will be of interest and use to many speakers of English, both native and cultivated, and whether speaking the American or British variety. The book should also be a helpful tool for many different kinds of English users: readers, writers, editors, visitors to the US or the UK from across the Atlantic, and students of language. I have tried to keep the needs of all of these groups in mind as I set about organizing and writing this book.

Many readers of and listeners to English may be unaware of the great deal of Americanizing and Briticizing that goes on to render transatlantic language palatable to its final consumers. There is at present no reliable or comprehensive guide for doing this kind of editing; I hope that this book may go some way toward filling that void. Speakers and listeners on both sides of the Atlantic are, however, aware when this editing hasn't been done, and when the lack of it presents an obstacle to understanding. It is hoped that this book will address that obstacle by providing readers and listeners with the translations they need. Every American and every Briton who is fully engaged by today's world can see the benefit for full fluency in the other's dialect: Americans who limit their grasp to American English may miss out on the subtleties in the rich cultural offerings from Britain in all the narrative arts. More importantly, they miss out on the critical perspective offered by British news organizations and correspondents on matters of international importance. All of Britain's "quality papers"—they are called that to distinguish them from the tabloids, but the term is also a very accurate descriptive one—are available online and their easy availability is an excellent opportunity for Americans to enlarge the narrow perspective on world affairs presented them by the media at home; that the writing doesn't always quite sound right need not be an obstacle.

A few might argue that the stakes are somewhat lower for Britons in their need to acquaint themselves with American English. Failure to do so may amount to no more than running the risk of being not altogether with-it at a cocktail party by failing to understand all the obscure cultural references in the latest episodes of imported sitcoms. On the other hand, no one can deny that the language driving the Internet and technical innovation is American English, and resistance to its hegemony is not likely to avail. It is hoped that this book will open a window on the American dialect for British speakers who may have found themselves continuously in the dark about particular terms and usages.

Finally, there is a wealth of material here for the millions of people whose first language is some other variety of English, or whose second language is English. For the first group, this book can provide some new perspectives about the relationship of their dialect to the world's two foremost varieties of English, as well as filling in gaps in their knowledge of them. For the second group, it is hoped that this book will shed light on many of the little confusions that arise in the acquisition and mastery of another language, insofar as those confusions arise from there being two major dialects that in some cases compete for the "correct" version of a particular area of English.

What's In This Book

Anyone who has looked into the differences between British and American English in a sustained or systematic way discovers early on that at any given time, you only see the tip of the iceberg. It is a subject that you never quite get to the end of. A completely exhaustive treatment of the differences would be beyond the scope of practicality, as well as nearly impossible to organize. What I have attempted here is more or less the shape of the whole iceberg, with a lot of its substance filled in, and it is hoped, no gaping cracks that are points of possible collapse. In putting together the book as I have done, and deciding what to put in and what to leave out, I have been guided by two principles: first, to organize the book by subject as much as is possible and practical. While many distinctions between British and American English transcend nearly all subject categories, my experience has been that people seeking vocabulary in the other dialect are not typically after just one word; they want a number of words in the same field, in order, for example, to understand an article about a given subject that contains unfamiliar terms, or as an aid to writing or editing for readers of the other dialect, when it is helpful to know where those readers might be coming from with regard to a particular subject. The result of this is the broad subject categories that form the chapters and the appendices in this book. Introducing words in the context of the subjects they mainly belong under also has the benefit of providing them with mnemonic hooks, thus promoting their convenient storage in the reader's memory.

My other guiding principle has been to include as much as possible that is useful for the general reader, writer, editor, speaker, and listener, and thereby to make a book that will hold interest for a great many readers, but at the same time to avoid filling the book with material that will be of interest to only a few specialized researchers, linguists, and trackers-down of arcane references. In many cases I have trusted my instincts and my experience in lexicography in deciding what to include and what to cut. But in many more instances I have relied on the opinions of practitioners in various fields (law, education, medicine), and I have also enjoyed access to many of Oxford University Press's unsurpassed language resources. This has given me an opportunity to check, for example, the actual frequency of a word or construction in either dialect (usually as a number of instances per 10,000 words of language, a standard measure in lexicography for how important a word or phrase is). As a result of this exercise, I have found it practical to leave out (a) the majority of archaic, obsolete, and dated terms, unless they are found in older literature that is still widely read; (b) most slang and a great deal of informal language, unless it is so well established as to appear frequently in journalism without special treatment. I have also generally avoided going into the historical context in which various differences in usage have arisen, unless this has a bearing on contemporary meaning. Although it is endlessly interesting to students of language, adding this dimension to the book would have doubled its length and the amount of time it took to write it.

I have also not included any material in this book on pronunciation, which is, in the end, a technical subject, and for the most part has little bearing on comprehension of the written word. Finally, I have tried to avoid pointing out what, though possibly unfamiliar, would be perfectly obvious to any reasonably competent speaker of English in its context. But as an incurable "word nerd" I am sure that I have strayed into this territory from time to time, and I trust that readers, particularly those suffering this same affliction, will be forgiving.

The table of contents and the list of tables in the front of the book provide a cursory look at what you will find within; the subject index in the back gives a more detailed look at the range of subjects covered. For those who are looking only for the discussion of a particular word, it is recommended that the extensive "word index" is the best place to start. And of course I hope that the book will reward browsing on any given page.

Notes on Terminology

Throughout this book, I have used *dialect* in its broadest sense, that is: "a variety of a language that is distinguished from other varieties of the same language by features of phonology, grammar, and vocabulary, and by its use by a group of speakers who are set off from others geographically or socially." This admirable definition is from the *Random House Unabridged*

Dictionary and I have quoted it wholesale, seeing no way to improve upon it. *Dialects* can be taken to mean American English (AmE) and British English (BrE). In the few instances where I refer to other local English dialects it is noted in the context.

It is convenient, because of their frequency, to abbreviate United States to US and United Kingdom to UK. I apologize for the lack of periods after each initial to any American readers who may think they belong; the two forms I have used are much faster to type. *Britain* is used interchangeably with UK. The individual countries that constitute the UK are identified by name when reference is limited to them: England, Scotland, Wales, Northern Ireland.

Every attempt is made to keep the discussion straightforward and not unnecessarily technical, but at the same, the most direct route to clear description is usually to call a thing by its proper name. Thus the following short glossary, which the dedicated student of language will already be familiar with.

Collocate: a word that is typically found juxtaposed with another word. For example, *mutually* is a frequent collocate of *beneficial* and *intelligible*. Another way of saying this is that *mutually* collocates with *beneficial* and *intelligible*. The phenomenon of words habitually keeping the company of other particular words is called *collocation*. Discussions about it figure frequently in the analysis of language, and many important differences between American and British English can be seen in collocations that are extremely common in one dialect and hardly known in the other.

Countability: a feature of English nouns that affects whether they are used in a singular or plural form, and has some bearing on when and how articles are used with nouns. It is a bugbear for all who learn English as a foreign language. Most nouns for concrete things are *countable* or *count* nouns (five golden rings, four calling birds, three french hens). Most abstract nouns are *uncountable* or *uncount* nouns (*liberty, equality, fraternity*). A considerable number of nouns have both count and uncount senses, with related but still distinct meanings.

> uncount: Give me *liberty* or give me death.
> count: He has taken considerable *liberties* with the text.

Many concrete things also behave as *mass* nouns: they aren't referred to in the plural even when multiple units of them are under discussion: five pounds of *broccoli*, an acre of *wheat*. For the purposes of this book, countability is a feature of some usage differences between American and British

English. Most of these are discussed in chapter 2, with other miscellaneous references throughout the book.

Retronym: a term, nearly always a compound noun of recent vintage, that is coined to designate something whose former name has lost its specific designation. *Snail mail* is an example of a retronym for what used to be called just *mail*.

Variant: a word or a form of a word that does not uniquely represent the thing it denotes. Two types of variants are talked about in this book: an *orthographic variant* is a word that is merely spelled differently in one dialect than in the other: *color* and *colour* are orthographic variants. They are the same word etymologically, and the variation in spelling is historical convention. The vast majority of orthographic variants between American and British English, which mostly answer to rules, are discussed in chapter 1. *Lexical variants* are pairs or larger groups of words that denote exactly the same thing, though the words are unrelated to each other etymologically. A familiar examples are the already mentioned *diaper* and *nappy*; *aubergine* and *eggplant* is another one.

A related idea that is used in this book regularly (though it is not strictly a linguistic phenomenon) is *functional equivalency*. This is a handy category for encompassing items that are more or less the same thing, and more importantly, items that fulfill the same or an analogous function in the two countries, even though they go by different names and aren't in fact identical. A simple example is the size of paper (and their names) used for letters: A4 in the UK and $8\frac{1}{2}$ x 11 or letter size in the US. A more complicated example is the US National Guard, and the UK Territorial Army: of course they are entirely different organizations with different histories and no relationship to one another, but they serve more or less equivalent functions in the two countries.

Conventions Used in This Book

A list of tables appears at the front of the book. The tables are mainly of two kinds. Two-column tables are used for presenting lexical variants, alphabetized by the American entry in the left-hand column. An arrow ($\rightarrow$) in either column indicates that the term has some currency in the other dialect. Three-column tables are used mainly for presenting terms unique to each dialect in particular subject areas that may require explanation for speakers of the other dialect. These are alphabetized by entry; the explanation of the term appears in the right-hand column in language geared to the other dialect's speakers. Within tables, parentheses are used to indicate optional parts of a compound word or idiom; material in square brackets is explanatory. Tables that vary from these formulas are explained as they appear.

The abbreviation *sth* is used for *something*; *sb* stands for *somebody*.

A Note on Regional and National Variation

A great deal of linguistic variation between the UK and the US arises out of the differences inherent in being a small country, as opposed to being a large country. This results in differences in the pattern of uniformity in certain areas of language, some of which figure in this book. It is reasonable and sensible to apply uniform systems of administration in a country that consists of 60 million people squeezed into an area of 95,000 square miles. It is impractical or impossible to do this with 287 million people spread out over more than 3.5 million square miles. It must also be borne in mind that the UK is not one country, but really three or four for administrative purposes. England and Wales share many institutions with regard to law, education, healthcare, and social services, but Scotland goes its own way, and Northern Ireland may have another way still. By comparison, a number of public and government institutions that are handled nationally or transnationally in the UK are completely under the control of the fifty individual states in the US. It would be impossible in a book of this scope, and really not very useful in a book of any scope, to deal with all possible linguistic differences that arise from such a welter of overlapping or analogous systems. What is attempted here instead is to give, for the US, a picture of language that is used and encountered generally in the subject areas covered in the chapters of this book; and for the UK, a similar picture of language that can be held to apply to the greatest number of cases, though it may not apply to all areas. For terminology relating to institutions of the kind noted above, that is law, education, healthcare, and social services, the de facto standards in the UK are the systems in use for England and Wales.

Acknowledgments

I am grateful to Erin McKean of Oxford University Press who hitched her considerable locomotive to this project early on, and without whose enthusiasm it might not have happened. The book benefited considerably from the copyediting of Carol-June Cassidy; her experience as a lexicographer and familiarity with both dialects of English, along with her editorial expertise, made her the best possible choice for the job, and she deserves a big credit for many additions and revisions that are now incorporated into the text. I am very grateful to my friends and colleagues in the small, friendly, and truly transatlantic world of English lexicography: many have provided or alerted me to material that I would otherwise not have seen; others have willingly allowed me to pick their native-speaker brains when I wasn't confident about my own memory or instincts. In particular I would like to thank Faye Carney, Paul Heacock, Dana Johnson, Elizabeth Knowles, Ken Litkowski, and Fraser Sutherland. Other friends outside the world of lexicography but steeped in various professional fields performed similar services and also did critical readings of various chapters, which were of tremendous help. Among these I thank Erroll Bowyer, Neil Pavitt, Dr. Paul Pierron, Libby Walker, Frances Webber, and Kathy Wildman. I also thank Nate Weir for his valuable assistance in compiling the indexes.

I am fortunate to benefit from the excellent Carroll County, MD, Public Library system, with its extensive resources and bargain Internet service that allow me to experience many of the fruits of civilization while living in the back of beyond.

Finally, I am very grateful to all the powers—and there are many—who have made it possible for me to spend part of my working life in

Britain. Living there has been the fulfillment of a childhood dream. I think I share with many others the belief that the existence of a special relationship between the United States and the United Kingdom is more than political rhetoric; it is a phenomenon that can be experienced quite meaningfully on a personal level. I hope that my book makes a small contribution toward sustaining and building upon that relationship.

Introduction

How amazing that the language of a few thousand savages living on a fog-encrusted island in the North Sea should become the language of the world.

— NORMAN ST JOHN-STEVAS, former MP
and leader of the House of Commons

Language has always had the ability to cross international borders and oceans; it only requires a medium. The original, and still today the most compelling medium, is the human voice. In the very earliest crossings it is safe to assume that the human had to accompany the voice. Now, millennia after those first bold transgressions, language crosses borders in a staggering variety of media that continues to grow as technology develops. We take completely for granted the easy flow of language-encoded information around the world in forms that would have seemed extraordinary or inconceivable to our grandparents: e-mail, the Internet, satellite broadcasting, and international teleconferencing, to name a few. The digital age has turned the physical and other substantial barriers that might once have impeded the flow of language into permeable membranes through which traffic is completely unimpeded and unmonitored. Today language from anywhere can go anywhere else, traveling with equal facility to destinations where it is perfectly understood, and where it is not understood at all.

This easy flow of language, particularly language in a code that we already know, sometimes disguises the fact that words carry baggage. Words arriving at our door or on our screens may look and sound in every way like the words we already know and love, and in many cases they are. But language nearly always carries the mark of its maker, in the form of usage preferences and cultural bias. These markers give readers and listeners hints as to national origins of language. In the case of written English, such markers may very often be camouflaged. It is the preeminent language of the world, and nearly everyone can use at least a few words of it. The easy portability of language and the ubiquity of English give rise to three possible situations when English crosses borders, in particular when that border is the Atlantic ocean. Any of these possibilities can result in imperfect transatlantic communication, even between native speakers of English:

1. an unfamiliar word appears, comfortably ensconced among known words but giving no clue to its meaning
2. a familiar word appears, used in a way that is clearly not familiar
3. a familiar word appears, used in a way that seems familiar but in fact means something entirely different

This book is mainly concerned with fleshing out the contexts in which these situations arise between the two major dialects of English in the world today: American English and British English.

There was a time long ago when the language was only called *English*, and a relatively short period after that when it seemed reasonable to add a qualifying adjective—such as American—to a variety that deviated from the source. But the source from which all of today's major dialects sprang is now itself a historical dialect, and the English used in Britain today is one among many dialects of English that continues to evolve on its own ground. While it is still possible, and in fact it is usual, to speak of English as a single and unified language, the differences among the dialects are a required object of study for anyone who would penetrate the inner core of the language.

The Dialects Today

No one disputes that English today is the closest thing we have to a world language. Throughout the nineteenth and early twentieth centuries the British Empire succeeded in propagating it around the globe to speakers on every continent. Today the cultural, electronic, and economic empire of the United States has largely taken over the business of maintaining the vivid presence of English in nearly every corner on earth. English is the first language of 380 million people, and the second language of another

250 million. Today, 750 million people are learning English; by the year 2050 it is expected that half the world's speaking population will be proficient in it. Eighty-five percent of the world's international organizations use English as an official language; three-quarters of Europeans think that everyone in the EU should be able to speak it.

Behind these monumental figures is a many-headed creature comprising the English dialects used around the world today. Many of these dialects have developed sufficiently to be recognized as distinct and worthy of study as individual subjects. Certainly Australian, Canadian, Indian, Irish, and South African English would fall into this class, but only two dialects can be regarded as international standards: British English and American English. British English has the undisputed claim to the prestige of tradition among dialects: its record in literature is likely never to be surpassed, and the legacy of Britain's colonial period has given British English an authority, in the Commonwealth of Nations and beyond, that does not appear to be weakening today, many decades after Empire collapsed. American English has also claimed a very large territory. Its progress and power are fueled by the unrivaled economic power and technological leadership of the United States. These two major dialects are the medium of nearly all internationally recognized English language teaching. They are also the only two dialects that are given comprehensive coverage in learners' dictionaries—that is, dictionaries of English with simplified vocabulary and a limited headword list, geared to learners of the language. They are generally also the only dialects that are given comprehensive coverage in major bilingual dictionaries in which one of the languages is English.

Given their historical development, it might seem natural and proper to regard British English and American English as being in a sort of parent-child relationship. But such a cozy and simplistic picture works only with considerable modification: you have to regard the parent as something of an enfeebled aristocrat and the child as an insatiable and selfish—some would even say heedless—leviathan. Consider these statistics:

- Native speakers of American English make up about 70 percent of people in the world whose first language is English.
- The amount of American English that fills newspaper columns, even though it may be wrapping fish or lining litter boxes the next day, accounts for two-thirds of the total volume of English appearing in newsprint every day worldwide.
- Seventy-five percent of syndicated television programming and a majority of internationally distributed films are of American origin.

- More than 90 percent of websites that are linked to a secure server (for
  the purposes of e-commerce) are sites written in American English.

The American tongue today penetrates far more frequently and persistently (and to the minds of many, insidiously) into the ears and minds of all English speakers than British English can ever again hope to do. The child has not completely usurped the place of the parent, but the child has succeeded in reducing the parent to an emeritus competitor in the world marketplace of English.

Mutual Regard

The very different ways in which English from the "other side" is regarded by native speakers in the US or the UK reflects to some degree the course that the dialects have taken since they split. Given the way in which demographics, politics, and geography have pushed American English to the forefront of the language, and at the same time relegated its parent to secondary status, it is perhaps understandable that American English is today regarded as daughter gone bad by some speakers of the mother tongue. This attitude is not new: the idea of regarding American English as inferior arose immediately following the independence of the US from England, and since then the idea has never been without champions. Regular readers of the British press today will come across an article every few months by a British columnist or correspondent, lamenting the unfortunate effects that American English exerts on "the Queen's English."

British English on the other hand, to many an American, is today not considered to be anything much more than a funny accent. But unlike the British, who have been more or less historically consistent in their stance with regard to the language of their failed colony, Americans have not always been so disinterested in the mother tongue. Opinion leaders in the fledgling United States regarded British English as a force to be resisted and rebelled against, and this very resistance resulted in many of the differences between the dialects, particularly in orthography, that are evident today. From the very earliest times Americans have preferred to follow their own path in the development of their dialect, rarely taking account of what was considered proper by British standards. Over time, because of distance, demographics, and changing national fortunes, the influence of British English on the American variety, early on regarded as a force to be contended with, ceased to be a concern at all. Accidents of history have given undisputed precedence to American English in numbers and in influence. Because of this, there is no need today for Americans to regard the British version of the language as threatening in any way; it is more fashionable for Americans to regard it merely as quaint.

Consider the situation of two native speakers of one dialect or the other in conversation, when one becomes aware that a Transatlantic usage has appeared in an otherwise native context. The American who notes that one of her fellow citizens is using a Briticism assumes either (1) that he is putting on airs, or more simply (2) that he has made a mistake. The Briton, on the other hand, who is a bit careless in letting his speech be infiltrated by Americanisms, is likely to be accused by his fellow subject of dragging down the language, letting down his side, failing to defend the national honor, and so forth. This suggests that Britons regard their tongue as under attack somehow, and barely able to withstand the barbarian at the gate. The tendency on the part of Britons to regard American English as inferior, as already noted, is combined with regarding it as almost dangerous. This is probably partly attributable to the "sour grapes" phenomenon: once it was determined that the colonies were impossible to rule and keep, it became expedient to decide that they were not worth having. The ink on the US Constitution had hardly dried before English media pundits (they existed, even in those days!) decried "the corruptions and barbarities which are hourly obtaining in the speech of our trans-atlantic colonies."[1]

Of course, it didn't help matters that early Americans consciously tried to throw off the mantle of authority of the King's English almost from the beginning. This was the exception to nearly every other colonial export of British English; everywhere else the English of the Crown was regarded as the inviolable standard. But in the fledgling United States, the attitude was quite different. The great lexicographer Noah Webster wrote in his *Dissertations on the English Language* in 1789, the same year in which the US Constitution went into effect:

> Great Britain, whose children we are, and whose language we speak, should no longer be our standard; for the taste of her writers is already corrupted, and her language on the decline. . . . [L]et reason and reputation decide, how far America should be dependent on a transatlantic nation, for her standard and improvements in language.

A very early English visitor to the colonies seemed to support Webster's contention that English in the motherland had lost its former glory. Writing

1. Quoted in H. L. Mencken, *The American Language*, p.15. New York: Alfred A. Knopf (1937).

in 1777, Nicholas Creswell observed that "though the inhabitants of this country are composed of different nations and different languages, yet it is very remarkable that they in general speak better English than the English do."[1] This view, however, did not long prevail, and soon gave way to a view that is more commonly held today. An early nineteenth-century British traveler in the United States remarked that "I very seldom, during my whole stay in the country, heard a sentence elegantly turned and correctly pronounced from the lips of an American. There is something either in the expression or the accent that jars the feeling and shocks the senses."[2]

Mutual Influence

Under the influence of economic, technological, and population dynamics today, it is only natural that Americanisms will creep into every dialect of English—including British English—far more successfully, and without even trying, than Briticisms can ever do into other dialects. Speakers and writers of American English exercise their irresistible influence successfully without even intending to do so. The dominance of American broadcast and other language media result in the dialect appearing in many more forms and contexts than any other; the sheer numbers of people whose preference is for American English ensure that original appearances of the dialect are propagated repeatedly, whether this is in the form of syndication, reprinting, or even forwarding of e-mails. These repetitions have a way of fixing usages in their place, just as repeated strokes of a hammer fix a nail in wood.

Such incursions of American language into other dialects eventually become naturalized, and at that point they cease to be recognized as invaders at all, thereby ceasing to cause irritation to the old guard. H. W. and F. G. Fowler, writing in 1908, noted that "every one knows an Americanism, at present, when he sees it; how long that will be true is a more anxious question."[3] In the same discussion they identify several Americanisms that have either already passed out of American usage altogether, or that the British speaker of today uses with complete ease and fluency, and in most

---

1. Quoted in Guy Jean Forgue, "American English at the Time of the Revolution," *Revue des Langues Vivantes* 43:253–269 (1977).

2. Frances Trollope in her *Domestic Manners of the Americans*, originally 1831 (New York: Penguin, 1997).

3. *The King's English*, 3d. ed. (1908; reprint Oxford: Oxford University Press, 2002), p. 35.

cases with no awareness that they were once considered Americanisms. This is true of many other words as well that were clearly marked as American when they first made appearances in other English dialects. What English speaker today could use *caucus* or *lengthy* or *eventuate* with the intention of evoking their American origins?

Television programming and movies aside, it is arguable that one of the most fertile areas today for mutual influence between the dialects, indeed a very hotbed of that activity, is the community of English-speaking news professionals around the world who are responsible for filing audio and video reports for broadcast. Happily, this is one profession in which the proportion of Britons is disproportionately greater than their numbers in the world English population, and an area where their influence may at least equal or even outstrip the American-to-British influence. Thirty years ago most Americans would have found it quite jarring to hear a news dispatch on television or radio delivered in a British accent, but now they can hear it every day. British correspondents don't in general edit their speech for the American outlets that pick up their reports, and this gives Americans a chance for exposure to constructions that would not otherwise come into their view. But even more successful than that is an indirect route by which this mutual influence takes place among foreign correspondents: the intensely social nature of their small community results in a degree of mutual language influence that may find its way into the reports that they file. How else to account for the occasional Briticism that slips into the text of a report filed by an American correspondent?

As an example of this, a *New York Times* correspondent filing an audio report from Zimbabwe in early 2002 mentioned events taking place there "in the run-up to the election." A perusal of US dictionaries yields several senses of the compound word "run-up," but if there is a mention of the sense used here, i.e., "period leading up to a notable event," it is labeled *chiefly Brit.* Why would an American correspondent use this phrasing? Probably because she had heard it among her colleagues in journalism in Zimbabwe, who may be disproportionately British, or read the phrase in the press there, which can be assumed to be in the thrall of British English. And it's a useful locution, firmly established in British English and having no concise equivalent in American English. Why shouldn't she use it? And why shouldn't any American, when he has a need for it, use it as well? After all, if a *New York Times* correspondent uses it on the radio, it must have something going for it.

The Road Ahead

The current status of the dialects, and the way in which they have gotten to where they are, give a pretty good indication of where they are going. Opportunities for mutual influence, arising out of globalization and information technology advances, will continue to increase. The hegemony of American English in the world of English generally does not look threatened; for that reason, its influence will probably increase, even as its advance is consciously resisted in many quarters, and many of those quarters can be found on the island of Great Britain. There is no likelihood that a world standard of English will emerge, and there is no reason that such a thing is desirable: language, like an organism, has many adaptive mechanisms, and these mechanisms do their work best when they are allowed to respond without undue stress or force to local conditions. If there is a case for increased standardization it can be made most convincingly in the area of orthography, or to put it more simply, spelling. Chapter 1 of this book serves as a pillar for that argument. For the many other areas in which English manifests itself differently, according to the differences in the environments where it is used, there is every reason to believe the glorious diversity evident today will continue. All the other chapters of this book are exhibits in evidence of this, and the reader is invited to partake of the delights.

CHAPTER ONE

The Arrangement of Letters

It is now nearly four hundred years that British and American English have been separated and evolving independently, although never during that period without mutual influence. Today even the simplest samples of written language are likely to carry markers that identify their probable origin in one place or the other, and that is where we will begin our investigation: by cataloging the systematic—and occasionally random—differences in spelling, and punctuation that give written language its American or British credentials.

In matters of style, writers are given some license for variation. Choosing a word, turn of phrase, or way of expressing an idea that is not standard for one's dialect is usually interpreted as conscious on the part of the writer; the worst charge the writer might be subjected to is that of putting on airs (in the case of an American using a Briticism), or dumbing things down (in the case of a Briton using too many Americanisms). Not so, however, with spelling. Except in the cases of variant spellings that occur with some frequency in both dialects, a writer who uses a spelling not standard for his own dialect is assumed to have made a mistake. For editors then, this is the part that has to be put right before all else.

The vagaries and inconsistencies of English spelling are notorious and a bane to native speakers and learners of the language alike. There have been persistent and ongoing attempts to reform spelling on both sides of the Atlantic throughout history; these have been spotty in their results at

19

best. None of these efforts has been international in scope, and that is the reason that systematic differences now appear in the two major varieties of English: no broadly based British attempt at spelling reform has ever succeeded in the period of modern English, but Americans simplified the spelling of many classes of words in the nineteenth century. The motive force behind this event was the lexicographer Noah Webster, who introduced systematic, simplified spellings in his dictionary of 1828. The majority of these were accepted by the US government later in the century, and they have been standard in American English since then. The systematic differences described in the following sections are mostly the results of Webster's spelling reforms.

Disappearing U

This large group of words ending in *-our* (*BrE*) and *-or* (*AmE*) mostly entered Middle English with a *u* following the *o* intact, mostly from Old French or Anglo-French and ultimately from Latin. The British spellings today all retain the *-our* ending:

-OR VS. -OUR

arbor	demeanor	glamor	parlor	succor
ardor	disfavor	harbor	pavior	tumor
armor	dishonor	honor	rancor	valor
behavior	dolor	humor	rigor	vapor
belabor	enamor	labor	rumor	vigor
candor	endeavor	misbehavior	sapor	
clamor	favor	misdemeanor	savior	
clangor	fervor	neighbor	savor	
color	flavor	odor	splendor	

The unschooled might be tempted to treat *languor, pallor, stupor, torpor,* or *tremor* in this category, but they do not belong, and have the same spelling in both dialects. Likewise with *pompadour, tambour,* and *troubadour,* all of which are properly spelled with the *u* in both dialects. *Rigor mortis,* directly from Latin, also has identical form. *Glamour* is a special case in being an equally acceptable spelling in American English, particularly in glamorous contexts.

A trap lies waiting for the American who would predict the spelling of derivatives of *-our* words in British English. Note that the *u* disappears in the British spellings *armorial, colorimeter, humorously, odorous*, etc. (that is, in all derivatives in which Latin lurks in the deriviative suffix, particularly *-(i)ous*, *(i)ously*, and *-(i)ousness*), but not in *colourful, favourite, honourable, odourless, rumoured* (in all other derivatives formed by inflection or by the addition of other non-Latinate suffixes).

The letter *u* disappears from a few other American spellings in predictable ways: *balk, mold, molt*, and *smolder* are the preferred American spellings of British *baulk, mould, moult*, and *smoulder*. *Caulk* is the preferred spelling in both dialects, though *calk* appears in American. *Gauge* (noun, verb, and inflections) is still largely preferred in both dialects, though *gage* appears in American, especially in technical use. *Moustache* appears in both dialects though Americans prefer *mustache*.

Words Ending in *-re* (BrE) and *-er* (AmE)

This group of words are also mostly French imports and mostly entered Middle English with the *-re* habit, retained in British but systematized in American English by Webster to end with *-er*. Later additions, such as *epicenter*, conform to the established pattern in each dialect.

-ER VS. -RE

acouter	liter	ocher	somber
caliber	louver	reconnoiter	specter
center	luster	saber	theater
fiber	meager	saltpeter	titer
goiter	miter	scepter	
lackluster	niter	sepulcher	

Additionally, all of the compounds of *liter* and *meter* (*deciliter, hectometer*, etc.) fall into this category, though the spelling of *meter*, when it means *measuring device*, is the same in both dialects. *Maneuver* is a special case, being subject to two transformations from the British spelling *manoeuvre* (see Latinate Ligatures, below). The mainly British spelling *theatre* appears frequently in the names of particular theaters and theater companies in the US, either because they predate the spelling reform, or perhaps because they wish to enhance themselves with an air of refinement. Because of this, the spelling *theatre* cannot really be considered incorrect in American English. In American dictionaries *ocher* is the preferred spelling, but *ochre* is still far commoner in usage.

Words Ending in -*ce* and -*se*

There are four that follow roughly the same pattern: *defense, license* (noun and verb), *offense,* and *pretense* are the American spellings; the *s* persists in derivatives. The British spellings are *defence, offence, pretence,* and *licence* (noun only); the *c* is persistent in derivatives. The British verb is *license,* and all verb derivatives have the same spelling as the American ones (*licensor, licensee, licensable*). Note that *offensive, defensive, pretension,* and *pretentious* have the same spelling in both dialects. The noun *licensure* is an Americanism and doesn't occur naturally in British English.

Following a pattern of its own is *practice.* Noun and verb have identical form in American English; British has *practice* for the noun, *practise* for the verb.

S and Z in suffixes

Webster's idea was that wherever a word's origin could be traced to a Latin and Greek spelling using z[1] or the Greek letter zeta, z ought to be used in the American spelling. The cases in point are words ending -*ize* (e.g., *hypnotize*) and -*ization* (e.g., *democratization*). These spellings are also acceptable in British English and in fact are now the preferred spellings in most British dictionaries, though most British newspapers persist in preferring the -*ise* and -*isation* spellings that entered English through French. The -*ize*/-*ise* suffix is one of the most productive in English, and is appended to many words that have no discernible roots in Greek (e.g., *bowdlerize, randomize*), but the spelling conventions remain the same in the two varieties of English.

Though they lack the credentials for this treatment (because not derived from Greek roots), the forms *merchandize, televize,* and *advertize* sometimes appear in American English; however, the preferred forms for these words are with -*ise* in both dialects, with the *s* persisting in derivatives. *Recognize* is preferred in American English despite its lack of Greek roots, though -*ise* forms also appear, especially in older writing.

By a curious extension of the -*ize* rule, verb forms derived from nouns in which the Greek root *lysis* appears (e.g., *analysis*) are formed by conversion of the *s* to *z* in American English.

1. Remember, that's "zed" in British English and "zee" in American English.

-LYZE VS. -LYSE

ammonolyze	cryptanalyze	hydrolyze
analyze	dialyze	paralyze
autolyze	electrolyze	photolyze
catalyze	hemolyze	psychoanalyze

This group of words, which could be made lengthier by the addition of more obscure scientific terms, are all spelled with a terminal *-lyse* in British English.

Two other words show 'z' in the American spelling and 's' in the British; the easy one is American English *cozy*, British English *cosy*. The complicated one is *czar*, or *tsar*. Except in academic writing, American uses *czar* for both the former Russian rulers and the latter-day high officials (e.g., drug czar, housing czar, etc.). British English (and American academic writing) uses *tsar* for the Russian rulers, but *czar* otherwise.

The Behavior of *L*

No letter better illustrates the desirability of internationally standardized spelling rules in English. In American English, verbs ending in an unstressed syllable (with the schwa sound, represented by /ä/) and followed by *l* form all their inflections and derived forms by simple addition of a suffix: *travel, traveled, traveling, traveler*. In British English, the *l* is doubled to form the past tense, past participle, and agentive noun: *travel, travelled, travelling, traveller*. These double *l* spellings are not incorrect in American and they are preferred by some American publications, notably the *New Yorker*, but the general rule is a single *l* for American inflected and derived forms, and double *l* for British ones. The commonest words affected by this rule are:

-L- VS. -LL

apparel	chisel	drivel	grovel
bedevil	council	duel	hovel
bejewel	counsel	empanel	imperil
bevel	crenel	enamel	initial
bushel	cudgel	equal	jewel
carol	devil	fuel	level
cavil	disembowel	funnel	libel
channel	dishevel	gambol	marshal
chapel	dowel	gravel	marvel

-L- VS. -LL *(continued)*

medal	peril	rowel	towel
metal	pummel	shovel	travel
model	quarrel	shrivel	trowel
nickel	ravel	signal	tunnel
outgeneral	revel	snivel	unravel
panel	refuel	spiral	yodel
parcel	remodel	stencil	
pedal	revel	swivel	
pencil	rival	total	

Dial, trial, vial and *phial* (an alternate British spelling of *vial*) are similarly treated when used as verbs. Inflections of the adjective *cruel* have *ll* in British English, *l* in American English.

A different, small group of verbs end with *ll* in American English, and with only a single *l* in British English. This *l* is doubled in the inflected and derived British forms, except where a derivational suffix begins with a consonant. Thus, American *install, installed, installing, installer, installment,* and British *instal, installed, installing, installer, instalment.* The *ll* infinitive and derivative forms are acceptable, though not standard, in British English. The small group of words in this category is:

> *appall, distill, enroll, enthrall, fulfill, install, instill* (AmE)
> *appal, distil, enrol, enthral, fulfil, instal, instil* (BrE)

Two words not in this category though with confusingly acceptable credentials for it are *extol,* (preferred with one *l* in both dialects, double *l* in inflections), and *forestall* (two *ls* in both dialects). Both dialects have *thrall,* but American has *thralldom*; British, *thraldom.*

Other *l* disparities between American English and British English include the following:

MISCELLANEOUS DISPARITIES WITH *L*

American	British
caliper	calliper
calisthenics	callisthenics
chili	chilli
jewelry	jewellry
skillful	skilful
willful	wilful
woolen	woollen

Other Consonant-Doubling Anomalies

A general pattern of a single consonant in American English, and a double in British English, prevails in the preferred spellings of the following words:

CONSONANT-DOUBLING ANOMALIES

American	British
pita bread	pitta bread
whir	whirr
worshiped, worshiping	worshipped, worshipping

Wagon is preferred in both dialects, though the spelling *waggon* is seen in British English. The spelling goes the other way with AmE *raccoon*, BrE *racoon*, and AmE *granddad*, BrE *grandad*.

When spelling aloud words that contain double letters, the fixed British habit is to say, for example, "double g." This is acceptable but not standard in American English, where speakers normally say, "g g."

Words Ending in *-gue* or *-g*

Words historically ending in *-agogue* (Greek root *agein,* to lead, drive) and *-ologue* (Greek root *logos,* a word, thought, speech) have become the target of various spelling reform programs with the aim of eliminating the terminal and silent *-ue*. This campaign has succeeded to the extent that some of the commonest words fitting this description—*analog, catalog, dialog*—are now preferred with the simplified form in American English. British English prefers the *-ogue* endings for all words in this camp but increasingly does not blink at the simpler *-og* endings for the commonest words, viewing them as one of the more harmless American imports. The words in this category listed below are still oftener found, and listed in dictionaries, with the *-ogue* ending. As a group they can be viewed as being in transition, and the writer wishing to avoid the taint of seeming old-fashioned may wish to choose the *-og* endings, though it is unlikely that *eclogue*, *ideologue*, and *synagogue* will ever make the leap.

-OG VS. -OGUE

apologue	demagogue	emmenagogue
cholagogue	duologue	epilogue
decalogue	eclogue	grammalogue

homologue	mystagogue	synagogue
hydragogue	prologue	theologue
ideologue	protologue	travelogue
isologue	secretagogue	trialogue
monopolylogue	sialagogue	

Shortened Phonetic Spellings

Simplified spellings of some common words containing what were thought to be many unnecessary silent letters have been championed by various spelling reformers throughout history, particularly the *Chicago Tribune,* which used the simple forms for a sizable chunk of the twentieth century. It abandoned them in 1975 and they currently have no official status in American English, never being found in edited or formal writing; however, they appear widely in informal communications, in advertising, and in modern compounds in which the idea of speed, ease, or convenience is salient (*drive-thru, all-nite,* etc.). British English has little use for them. The commonest are *altho, donut, lite, nite, rite, tho, thru,* taking the place of *although, doughnut, light, night, right, though,* and *through.*

Words Ending in *-gram* or *-gramme*

Under the influence of French, some old-fashioned forms still appear from time to time in British English for words that Americans invariably spell with terminal *-gram,* but in general the simpler ending prevails in both dialects, with the singular exception of *programme,* still preferred in British English for all contexts except computing. A sheet of folding paper with pre-printed postage for international letters is officially called an *aerogramme* in both countries, though the spelling *aerogram* is common in the US.

Latinate Ligatures

A large class of words derived from Latin, or from Greek via Latin, first appeared in English with the ligatures æ or œ. These words are still spelled with an *-ae-* or *-oe-* combination in British English; American English, except as noted below, has uniformly simplified these to *-e-*. Since words in this category are overwhelming found in the field of medicine, a fuller treatment of them is given in chapter 6. The following words and classes of words outside the field of medicine show spelling differences: Words beginning with

levo- (AmE) and *laevo-* (BrE), e.g., *levorotation*
paleo- (AmE) and *palaeo-* (BrE), e.g., *paleobotany, Paleocene*

Many other common words show these predictable variations between the two dialects, with the longer traditional spellings occasionally appearing in American English, and the simplified spellings more rarely appearing in British English:

Cesium and *Caesium*
encyclopedia and *encyclopaedia* (but *Encyclopaedia Britannica* in both countries)
eon and *aeon*
maneuver and *manoeuvre*
peony and *paeony*

Note, however, the following words in which the *-ae-* or *-oe-* spelling is preferred in American English, though forms without the *a* or *o* are also found: *aesthete, aesthetic, archaeology, caeoma, caesura, onomatopoeia,* and *paean*. Both dialects use *medieval*, though *mediaeval* turns up with fair regularity in British English.

Different Treatments of Silent *E*

A bugbear for spelling reformers through the ages has been the silent, usually terminal *e* in various English words that does not have the conventional job of lengthening the vowel found two letters back in the word. Phonics taught us that *site* has a long *i* and *sit* a short one because of the *e* on the end of *site*, but the rule doesn't apply uniformly, and most glaringly, in *have* and *give*; thus spelling reformers would prefer *hav* and *giv*. The eminent good sense of this proposal has never prevailed. There are, however, many words and derivatives in which American spelling has done away with a silent and functionless *e*. These fall into some predictable classes:

1. Words ending in *-dge* and adding the suffix *-ment* lose the terminal *e* in preferred American spellings but keep it in British: *abridgment, acknowledgment, judgment, lodgment* (AmE); *abridgement, acknowledgement, judgement, lodgement* (BrE)

2. Words, mostly verbs ending in silent *e* and adding the suffix *-able*, are inclined to lose the silent *e* in American spellings but keep it in British; thus *blamable, likable, lovable, sizable, unshakable, usable* (AmE); *likeable, loveable, sizeable, unshakeable, useable* (BrE).

   This list is not exhaustive but indicative, and dropping the silent *e* is not mandatory in American English; it is just commoner. Note that the silent *e* does not disappear in words whose last consonant is *c* or *g*, the presence of the *e* indicating that pronunciation of the consonant is soft: *manageable, noticeable*.

3. Words from French and ending in *-ette* have sometimes been simplified in American by dropping not only the silent *e*, but also the redundant consonant. This is apparent mainly in *epaulet* and *omelet*. The forms *cigaret* and *curet* are sometimes seen in American English, but not preferred.

Other words in which American English has dropped a silent *e* that British clings to are

DISAPPEARANCE OF SILENT *E*

American	British
adz	adze
ax	axe
gelatin	gelatine
glycerin	glycerine
phony	phoney
story [of a building]	storey
tartar sauce	tartare sauce

Whiskey is the American spelling used for the distilled liquor when it is made in the US or in Ireland, and the British spelling used for Irish whiskey. *Whisky* is the accepted British spelling for all varieties except the Irish one, and the American spelling for the liquor made in Scotland or Canada. Contemporary usage notwithstanding, *Whisky Rebellion* is as acceptable as *Whiskey Rebellion* to designate the 1794 farmers' uprising.

Different Ways of Spelling the *F* Sound

American English uses the spelling *sulfur* for the yellow nonmetallic element that the British spell *sulphur*. The *f* (AmE) and *ph* (BrE) difference is preserved in the many derivatives of this word (e.g., *sulfate, sulfide, sul-*

fite and other words in which sulfur lurks eytmologically). Similarly, Americans like *draft* for all senses, a spelling that Britons use only for a preliminary version of a piece of writing (noun and verb), for a bank draft, and for the verb sense (to select a person for a particular purpose). All other meanings have the spelling *draught* in British English.

Different Ways of Spelling the *K* Sound

American spelling prefers *k* to *c* in *disk* in nearly all forms except *compact disc* and *disc jockey*. British English uses *disc* uniformly. Other differences involving the *k* sound appear in

DIFFERENCES WITH THE *K* SOUND

American	British
check	cheque
checker *n, v*	chequer
checkered	chequered
karat	carat
licorice	liquorice
smart-aleck	smart-alec →

But to ensure that the pattern shouldn't apply universally, American has *curb*, British has *kerb*.

Anomalies Without Rule

Finally, a small group of words show variation in form between the two dialects without the advantage of conforming to a pattern for easy classification and retrieval from memory. For the spelling perfectionist, these must be assigned their own brain location.

ANOMALIES WITHOUT RULE

American	British
airplane	aeroplane[1]
aluminum	aluminium
behoove	behove
carburator	carburettor
gray[2]	grey

ANOMALIES WITHOUT RULE *(continued)*

American	British
jail	gaol
novitiate	noviciate
pajamas	pyjamas
peddler	pedlar
plow	plough[3]
pudgy	podgy
scalawag	scallywag
soy	soya
tire	tyre

[1] It is perverse that British English clings to this spelling
when it quite happily uses *airbase, airline, airport, airstrip,*
and *airspace.* Some UK newspapers now prefer *airplane.*

[2] Although note: *greyhound.*

[3] *The Plough* is the British English name for the constellation
that American English dubs the *Big Dipper.*

Compounds: Open, Closed, and Hyphenated

Unlike in German, where writers are free to tie up words that may
never have seen each other before into a seamless unit, English requires
some circumspection in the uniting of words that suddenly acquire a
reason to spend time next door to each other. There are three choices for
such marriages, called the open compound (e.g., *beauty parlor*), the
hyphenated compound (*artsy-craftsy*), and the closed or solid compound
(*drugstore*). American English generally is far quicker and more ready to
adopt solid compounds, and to eliminate hyphens, than is British English;
it is for the sociolinguists to debate whether this is revealing of cultural differences. For our purposes the differences are best treated under the general topic of hyphenation.

Questions about the use of the hyphen very often send writers and editors to the dictionary or style manual for guidance; it impossible to keep in
mind handy categories for the use of this small word divider when it appears to answer to no authority other than usage. Happily there are some
clearcut differences in usage between American and British English that
are easy to master. In general, British retains the hyphen in many compound words where American has eliminated it and closed up the gap.

ELIMINATION OF THE HYPHEN

Word class	AmE	BrE
Compounds beginning *anti-*	antinuclear	anti-nuclear
Compounds beginning *non-*	nonproliferation	non-proliferation
Compounds beginning *semi-*	semiautomatic	semi-automatic
Compounds ending in *-like*	eellike	eel-like
Compounds formed from points of the compass	southwest, northeast	south-west, north-east

The general rule in American English with regard to the above prefixes and suffixes is that the hyphen is used only to prevent the doubling of a vowel or the tripling of a consonant, but even the vowel rule is usually let go with the shorter prefixes, such as *co-*, *de-*, *pre-*, *pro-*, and *re-*. British English keeps the hyphen in an unpredictable group of such words, for which a dictionary or style guide is the only reliable reference: *prepolymer*, *preamplifier*, and *prewire*, but *pre-cook*, *pre-shrunk*, and *pre-eminent*. American English has forgone the hyphen in compounds beginning with *sub-* and *multi-*; British English retains it unpredictably in these words, or perhaps more accurately, different authorities have adapted different rules with regard to these prefixes.

There is also considerable variation in the spelling of compounds made up of two complete words, with no easy basis for predicting how they will be presented in either dialect. A general pattern prevails in which American English is more ready to go from open to closed once usage has been established, foregoing the hyphen stage altogether; and for British English to go immediately to a hyphenated form and never depart from it. But this is not a fast rule, and dictionary consultation is the only remedy for doubters: British English has *film-maker, night-time, newly-wed*, which are all closed compounds in American English. *Running mate* and *oil tanker* are the acceptable American forms, but these compounds can be found hyphenated in British English. A dictionary consultation would suggest that *earthmover* is preferred in American English, *earth mover* in British English, yet both forms can be found in large language samples of both dialects.

The pronoun *no one* is now largely found as an open compound in both American and British English, but the form *no-one* still occurs with some frequency in Britain, particularly in older writing. *Insofar* is written as one word in American English, three in British. Some British dictionaries don't even give *underway* as a headword, insisting that it must always be two words, but in fact the solid form of this adjective is as common in British writing as in American. Finally, *per cent* is written as an open compound in British English but as *percent* in American English.

This rather wearying catalog is strong evidence for the desirability of a world standard for English orthography, though it is debatable how compelling a proposal for such a standard could be made to the reading and writing public, or more importantly, to anyone in a position to actually effect the changes required. The sytematic and sensible spelling reforms proposed by Webster and gradually accepted by Americans were to some degree an expression of national identity; Webster himself said "a national language is a band of national union," and he saw the implementation of his spelling reforms as an encouragement for the printing of books in the United States, noting that the English "would never copy our orthography for their own use."[1] Resistance to spelling reform today stems in part from this very same assertion of national identity: American spellings would most likely prevail in any logical reforms because they are easier, more consistent, and often truer to etymology; but wholesale adoption of them would undoubtedly be seen as an unwanted advance of American hegemony. In 2000, a directive of the British Qualifications and Curriculum Authority said that students should use "internationally standardized" scientific terms, such as *sulfate* instead of *sulphate* and *fetus* for *foetus*. Science teachers, it was reported, reacted with disbelief, calling it cultural imperialism by America. Teachers also noted an advantage they would retain by insisting on British spellings from their pupils: American spellings in scientific papers were a dead giveaway that the material had been merely cut-and-pasted from the Internet. So until such time as flag-waving gives way to logic, it is likely that the current dual system will prevail.

Punctuation

There are important differences in general style of punctuation, and some minor differences in punctuation terminology, between American and British English. An American *period*, the dot placed at the end of a sentence and in various other places, is a British *full stop*. *Quotation marks* or *quotes*, sensibly so called in American English because they set

---

1. Both quotations are from *Dissertations on the English Language: With Notes, Historical and Critical, to Which is Added, by Way of Appendix, an Essay on a Reformed Mode of Spelling, with Dr. Franklin's Arguments on That Subject* (Boston, 1789). The entire text is widely available on the Internet.

off quotations, are sometimes called *inverted commas* in British English. The marks ( ), [ ], < >, and { }, are called respectively *parentheses, square brackets, angle brackets,* and *braces* (or *wavy brackets*) in American English. In British English the first are *round brackets* (or simply *brackets*), and the last may be called *curly brackets* as well as braces. The mark / is called a *slash* in American English and a *stroke* in British English when reading or dictating; both dialects use *virgule* (preferred in American English) and *solidus* (preferred in British English) as technical terms for it. Under the influence of computer usage, the mark \ is called a *backslash* in both dialects, and its frequent usage in computer contexts has given rise to the retronym *forward slash* for / in American English. The mark #, in the absence of any particular context, is called the *pound sign* in American English and the *hash mark* in British English. Its specialized uses and names are discussed at their places later in this book.

The accepted American style of punctuation is used throughout this book and observes the following conventions:

1. Commas and periods go inside a closing quotation mark, even if a single word is all that is set off by the marks: *Her recommendation was for something "a little more punchy."* British usage puts the comma or period outside the quotes unless the quoted material would require the punctuation even in absence of the quotes; e.g., if it is a full sentence: *Her recommendation was for something "a little more punchy"*.
2. Prevailing American style is to use double quotes to set off actual quotations, and for various specialized purposes, for example, to indicate that a word is being discussed as a word: *"Sweet" seems to be replacing "cool" as a term of general approval.* Single quotes are used inside a set of double ones. British usage prefers single quotation marks (inverted commas, if you will) to set off quoted material and nearly everywhere else, using double ones only inside a set of single ones.
3. British English typically shows the time in numbers by separating the hours and the minutes with a period, e.g. *10.05am*; note that no space intervenes between the last number and *am* or *pm*. American English typically uses a colon and a space: *10:05 a.m.*

Abbreviations

Except for acronyms that have come to be treated as words in their own right, American English usually has a period indicating that a form is an abbreviation: thus *Dr., Mr., Mrs., St.* (for saint or street), *etc., mgr.* (for manager, monseigneur, monsignor), *Jr., Sr., Inc.* These same forms are normally used without the period in British English: *Dr, Mr, Mrs, St, etc, mgr, Jr, Sr, Inc.* A rule fairly consistently observed in British English is that an abbreviation composed of the first and last letters of a word does not require a period; others may or may not use one. People whose names are typically written with one or two initials and a surname are generally styled with periods in American usage (*H. L. Mencken*) and without them in British usage (*HW Fowler*).

Variation in Capitalization

AIDS has been the preferred American spelling for the autoimmune disease since it was first identified, and seems to be gradually supplanting *Aids* in British use. Both dialects seem to prefer *NATO*, though *Nato* is equally acceptable in British English. Finally, British English is more inclined to put an initial capital on *Earth*, the planet, than is American English, which normally does so only in a context of a discussion of other named planets.

CHAPTER TWO

A Choice of Words

The success of English as a world language relies partly on its flexibility and richness of vocabulary; there are always numerous ways of saying almost the same thing, and there is the possibility of making almost infinite discriminations of meaning and connotation by choosing carefully among the dozens of ways of expressing a particular idea.

All of that notwithstanding, language is a matter of habit, and habits widely observed have a way of becoming usage rules. Some of these rules of usage are the distinguishing factors between British and American English: a particular word, phrase, or way of arranging words, though found on both sides of the Atlantic, is often so strongly preferred on one side as to become a marker of the English used in that country; the failure to use the form of words preferred by the natives can be jarring to readers and listeners. This chapter will examine the main areas where this phenomenon can be observed: cases of the strong, almost dictatorial preference for a form of language in one country that is little used, or perhaps even regarded as incorrect (or at the very least, foreign) in the other country.

The general categorization of these matters is usage and style, and it should be noted at the outset that even within one dialect, many rules are not fixed but vary by region, by institution, or by genre of writing. The observations made here are reliable in a general way, but anyone who is editing or rewriting English to appear in the other dialect with the view of conforming to a particular style should consult the pertinent style guide or manual. Some notes about these are given in the bibliography.

This chapter is organized by parts of speech; the important differences between American and British English affecting nouns, verbs, adverbs, and so forth *as a class* are treated in the sections that follow. Individual words are treated only insofar as they exemplify a pattern of difference between the dialects. Cases of lexical variation—in which each of two words designate essentially the same thing and each of them is more at home in one dialect than the other—are treated in chapters that follow under various subjects that subsume them, and in the appendices.

NOUNS

Variability of Number and Countability in Nouns

The distinction between count nouns and mass (or uncount) nouns is a bane for many a learner of English, since the distinction is either unimportant or handled differently in most other modern languages. Native speakers of English master the concept unwittingly by the age of five or so, enabling them to quickly spot deviations from the rule they are used to in other speakers. There is some variability in the countability of some nouns between British and American English, and while these generally do not result in misunderstanding, the differences in usage are distinct enough to require editorial attention. The general, though not invariable pattern, is for British English to treat certain nouns as uncountable that Americans treat as countable, which can be seen in the following cases:

- It is preferable in British English to say *She's got stomach ache/headache/toothache/cramp.* The equivalent American expressions are *She's got a stomach ache/a headache/a toothache/a cramp*, or in the case of menstrual distress, *She's got cramps.*
- Americans typically use *accommodations* as a plural noun when it refers to a place to stay or sleep: *a city with inadequate accommodations for tourists*; in British English it is usually an uncount noun: *The price includes accommodation and some meals.*
- Various foods are subject to mass noun treatment in British English when they are an ingredient in a dish or considered strictly in their capacity as food, rather than as, e.g., a discrete vegetable. In these cases Americans are more inclined to treat the items as countable, with the

plural supplying the general reference. Thus it is usual for a Briton to enquire, *Has this got carrot in it?* where an American would more likely ask *Has this got carrots in it?* All countable vegetables—that is, ones for which singular and plural forms are used—are in this category. All vegetables that are usually treated as mass nouns in American are treated the same in British English: *broccoli*, *spinach*, *lettuce*, etc. *Egg* is also typically a count noun in American, and uncount in British when considered as a constituent of some other food.

- Contrary to the pattern noted above, *coffee* and *tea* are usually treated in American English as mass nouns (*Would you like some coffee/tea?*); individual servings of these are countable in British English (*Would you like a coffee/a tea?*), but not usually in American (*Would you like a cup of coffee?*) The nearly endless variety of coffee-based beverages that now exists are countable in both dialects: *cappuccinos*, *lattés*, etc.

The following table sets out some other nouns that differ in number between the two dialects.

NOUNS DIFFERING IN NUMBER

American	British	Notes
compass	compasses	instrument for describing circles
main	mains	major conduit for water, gas, electricity, etc.
overhead	overheads	cost of doing business; BrE adjective is *overhead*
scale	scales	device for weighing
woods	wood	a small forest

Group Nouns

A group noun is one that, though usually singular in form, can be understood to represent a large number of things, usually people. The commonest example of these are proper nouns denoting the names of companies (British Aerospace, Wal-Mart), but many common nouns also fall into this category, such as *family*, *committee*, *department*. American English nearly always treats these nouns as singular: *Sears has everything*; *The family was elated at the news.* This treatment is acceptable in British English, but the preference is to attach a plural verb to group nouns, thus emphasizing the fact that such nouns represent many, and thus: *The British Medical Association were opposed to it*; *A committee are now studying the proposal.*

Preference for Variable Forms

A handful of word pairs sharing a (mostly or putatively) common ancestry appear in one or both dialects, in each of which one form is preferred so strongly over the other that the variant form can be jarring, or seem downright wrong to the transatlantic native when encountered in speech or text. Since most of these words are nouns, they are treated here. The commonest forms of the words are given in the table, but it can be assumed, unless otherwise noted, that each dialect also uses the derivatives, if any, of the preferred word.

VARIANTS WITH COMMON ANCESTRY

American	British
bridge loan	bridging loan
candidacy	candidature
centennial	centenary
costumer	costumier →
cut [for passage of a train or road]	cutting
deviltry	devilry
doodad	doodah
edgewise	edgeways
elasticized	elasticated
expiration	expiry
furor	furore[1]
hauler	haulier
hodge-podge	hotch-potch
hydroplane	aquaplane
jimmy [crowbar]	jemmy
math	maths
mom, mommy	mum, mummy
normalcy	normality
orient *vt*	orientate *vt*
part [of someone's hair]	parting
persnickety	pernickety
plunk down	plonk down
polyethylene	polythene
putter around	potter around
raise [in pay]	rise
sailboat	sailing boat

VARIANTS WITH COMMON ANCESTRY *(continued)*

American	British
sequester [money or property]	sequestrate
snicker [*n, v*]	snigger →
specialty [in medicine, academia, law, etc.]	specialism, speciality
syllabify	syllabicate
tidbit	titbit
turn [place where a vehicle can do this]	turning

[1] Discussed separately in chapter 11 under "The Media."

Sanatarium and *sanitorium* appear to have the credentials for inclusion here but are in fact separately derived and are discussed under "Peculiar Pairs" in chapter 11.

Verbal Nouns from Infinitives

English abounds with nouns that are identical in form to the infinitive, with the meaning of a single act or instance of the action described by the verb: a five-mile run, a long talk with my neighbor, a left-hand turn. British English has a few more of these in common usage than does American English, and is also more comfortable with inventing. Examples include *bathe* (*lying in the sun after a bathe*), *think* (*I need to have another think about that*), *clean* (*Those rooms could do with a clean*), *lie-down* (*A little lie-down right now would be just the thing*). American readers or listeners understand such uses without difficulty but would find other ways of expressing the same ideas (*I need to think about that some more; Those rooms need cleaning*). No rule can be supplied for translating these differences, and even spotting them is largely a matter of native-speaker instinct.

VERBS

Modal and Other Auxiliary Verbs

The interesting group of verbs in English called modal auxiliaries, along with a few others that do not express mood but in fact function like the modals, are rich ground for picking apart the distinctions between

British and American speakers and writers. While the forms for all of these, and their contractions, exist in both dialects, certain of them are so rare in one dialect or the other (usually American English) that their presence marks a passage or speech immediately as to origin.

American children are taught (or they used to be; these days it's not clear that they're instructed at all in these matters!) that *shall* is the proper future of *be* for the first person, but otherwise is used for emphasis, expressing a rather stronger or more determined future than *will* does. This flies in the face of American usage, because in fact nearly all Americans use *will* as the future of *be* for all persons, when they don't simply use a contracted form. Not so in British English, where *shall* for the first person singular and plural is common. Even rarer in American English is the contraction of shall not, *shan't*. Use of it by an American is an immediate sign of either fawning imitation, or putting on airs; *won't* takes its place in American English.

Britons are comfortable using *must* and *mustn't* for expressing necessity (*I must get the car fixed this week*), prohibitions (*You mustn't go to any special trouble*), demands (*She must bring it to me personally*), and strongly urged suggestions (*You must come and see us next time you're in town*). None of these usages is completely foreign to Americans and they certainly present no obstacle to understanding, but Americans are more likely to use *have to* or *have got to* for necessity and demands (*I've got to get the car fixed this week*; *She has to go now*), the more direct *don't* plus infinitive for prohibitions (*Don't go to any special trouble*), and *should* or *ought to* plus infinitive for strongly urged suggestions, in cases where they don't simply use a straightforward imperative (*Come and see us next time you're in town*).

What grammarians call a negative inferential sentence is constructed with *can't* in British English: *It's a very thorough survey, she can't have left out anything important.* American English subdivides such sentences into two classes. (1) Those where doubt is impossible and the conclusion is based on necessity use *must not*: *This is the first I've heard of it, I mustn't have been at the other meeting.* (2) Those where logic impels only one conclusion but doubt may linger use *could not*: *The report says that the injuries couldn't have come from the fall.*

Would as a polite modal in statements is usual in American English (*I would be happy to answer your questions*) where British English is as comfortable, if not more so, with *should* in this construction: *I should be happy to answer your questions.* In speech, inflection would probably make the meaning clear to an American, but the choice of *should* here would be unexpected in American English and without contextual markers, the sentence would probably be interpreted from an American speaker to mean "I ought to be happy to answer your questions but I am not." The same preference for *would* over *should* in American English appears in two other uses: (1) advice accompanied by a spoken or implied "if I were you," e.g., *I would tone down the reference to the Clintons,* and (2) the "putative" use, where a general assumption is indicated on the basis of a particular instance: *I'm shocked that they would just drop in unannounced. Should* would be the first choice of most British speakers in these two sentences.

Dare as a modal verb preceding an infinitive is used with or without *to* in both dialects, but Americans are more inclined to omit the *to,* and Britons to include it. The contraction *daren't,* for *dare not,* does not flow naturally from the lips or pen of any red-blooded American, who would only use *don't dare,* or formally *dare not.*

In speech Americans are more inclined to use *don't have to* rather than *needn't* as the negation of a *need to* plus infinitive construction; thus in response to the question *Do I need to show you these again before sending them off?* the preferred American answer is *you don't have to,* and the British is *you needn't.*

Britons frown on the use of *let's don't,* preferring *let's not.* Haughty Americans would also do away with *let's don't* but it is common in speech: *Let's don't stay till closing time.*

Alternatives to the Subjunctive

American English is fairly consistent in using a subordinate clause that uses the unadorned subjunctive after nouns, verbs, and adjectives of requiring or demanding: *It is imperative that he be detained, They demanded that the hostages be released, an order that the bombing stop immediately.* This elegant and simple construction is also widely found in British English, which allows other constructions as well, such as modal constructions: *It is imperative that he should be detained;* and simple finite tenses, in a construction that might be called the mangled subjunctive: *an order that the bombing stops immediately.* The fact that the subjunctive form is identical to the infinitive, and indistinguishable from all inflections but the third person singular in most verbs, makes this construction an unnecessary and burdensome puzzle on learners of English, and the freer constructions found in British English are likely to prevail in both dialects eventually.

Variable Ellipsis of Verbs

English has a handy (to native speakers, anyway) system of eliding predicates from one clause or sentence to another by repeating only the finite parts of the verb with the understanding that the reader or listener will supply the missing main verb that is not repeated. A difference between British and American English is that Britons generally use *do* or *done* as a placeholder for the main verb in addition to the finite constituents of compound moods and tenses, where Americans are content to supply only the finite parts of the verb. If asked to combine the two sentences, *I didn't visit the exhibit* and *I could have visited the exhibit if I'd known it was there,* an American is likely to respond: *I didn't visit the exhibit, though I could have if I'd known it was there.* The Briton responds: *I didn't visit the exhibit, though I could have done if I'd known it was there.* Similarly, in response to the question, *Could we stay and watch the second feature?* the amenable American would answer *We could* while the amenable Briton would answer *We could do.*

Differences In the Use of Tenses

There is a marked difference in the use of the present perfect tense between American and British English that is variously interpreted. One take on it is that American English treats the simple past tense as a genuinely perfect (in the grammatical sense) tense, and uses it for actions that are actually finished, whether or not they have a continuing effect on the present, whereas British English takes into account the continuing effect of certain finished actions, and therefore uses the present perfect for certain recent actions that are in fact finished when the reporting of them has an immediate bearing. Another and far simpler (though less charitable) take on this phenomenon is that Americans are simply sloppy and lazy in their choice of tenses and opt for the simpler simple past when they should be using the present perfect. Whatever the explanation, these differences can be observed. Americans are comfortable using the simple past with temporal adverbs *already, ever, just,* and *yet,* where a British speaker would be more inclined to use the present perfect.

PRESENT PERFECT VARIATION

American	British
I just saw him walking out.	I've just seen him walking out.
We already ate.	We've already eaten.
Did we ever go there together?	Have we ever gone there together?
Did you do your homework yet?	Have you done your homework yet?

It should be noted that this difference is far from invariable; that most American language authorities would agree that the perfect forms are more proper; and that as a result of the "corrupting" influence of American popular culture, the American forms are not completely unheard of in Britain, especially among younger speakers. But all that notwithstanding, the distinction exists.

Gerundive Constructions

British English has idiomatic uses for gerunds following *want, need,* and *look like* that American English normally handles by the use of clauses with finite verbs or with other constructions. A British English sentence along the lines of *It looks like being cold on Saturday* would be rendered *It looks like it will be cold on Saturday* in American English. In a few such constructions the *being* would simply drop out in the American English equivalent: *Both packages for under £200 looks like being a very good deal* doesn't require the gerund in American English. Similarly, something that *needs doing* in British English more likely *needs to be done* in American English.

Transitivity Matters

A few verbs with more or less identical meaning in both dialects are treated differently with regard to syntax:

agree. BrE allows a transitive use not found in AmE: *They agreed a five-point agenda* would be rendered in AmE, *They agreed on* (or *to*) *a five-point agenda.*

appeal. Intransitive only in BrE: *The families affected appealed against the decision.* In legal contexts, AmE permits direct objects with the same meaning as the BrE intransitive use: *appeal a ruling/decision/conviction/sentence/case.*

approximate. Transitive in AmE: *a frequency curve that approximates a relationship between duration and intensity,* and intransitive in BrE: *a frequency curve that approximates to a relationship between duration and intensity.*

bath/bathe. BrE has the transitive verb *bath,* meaning "give a bath to": *bath the baby.* This is absent in AmE, which uses *bathe* intransitively, or rarely transitively (*bathe the baby*), though it prefers a different construction altogether: *give the baby a bath.*

catch up. With the meaning "succeed in reaching a person who is ahead," British English allows a strict transitive use: *He called after her and ran to catch her up.* This doesn't exist in AmE, which would have it *... and ran to catch up with her.*

give. Both dialects support the various ditransitive constructions that can be made with *give: He gave her the book, he gave the book to her, he gave it to her.* Informally, BrE allows *He gave it her* but AmE does not, while AmE allows *He gave her it,* which probably wouldn't come naturally to a British speaker.

impact. It is nearly impossible now to avoid the transitive AmE use of this once-happy intransitive verb, as a journalistic or marketing-speak equivalent of *affect* or *influence: Each department must report on how the initiative has impacted it.* This is rightly regarded in BrE as a reeking Americanism. That notwithstanding, *impact on* with this same meaning is increasingly common in BrE.

loan/lend. BrE prefers *lend,* but doesn't object to the use of *loan* as a transitive verb for money and tangible objects. AmE uses *loan* more often in this sense; both dialects use only *lend* for abstract expressions (*lend me your ears; the government lent its support to the campaign*).

notify. The direct object (or in passive constructions, the subject) in AmE is always personal: *They notified the teachers immediately of the developments; We weren't notified in time to respond.* BrE allows an impersonal direct object (or subject + passive): *We must notify all births and deaths to the Registrar; The merger was notified to shareholders in advance.*[1]

protest. Britons will protest their innocence, but otherwise protest *against, at,* or *to* everything else: *nurses who protested against the new regulation.* Americans will protest anything, without an intervening preposition: *nurses who protested the new regulation.*

provide. Strict ditransitive construction, as in *The letter provides us all the motivation we need,* is found in AmE but not in BrE, which would

---

1. This results in the more frequent use of *notifiable* as an adjective in British English, meaning "that must be brought to somebody's attention": thus, *notifiable diseases/offences.*

have *The letter provides us with all the motivation we need* (equally acceptable in AmE).

write. A personal or impersonal object is acceptable in AmE: *Write me next week* or *Write me a letter next week.* BrE takes only an impersonal object and would use *Write to me next week,* in place of the second example, which is equally acceptable in AmE.

American English generally more readily accepts new verbal uses of nouns, and new transitive uses of intransitive verbs, than does British English: *impact*, as described above, is perhaps the most unfortunate example of this. Others gaining ground in American English are *transition*, as a verb meaning "make a transition," and *disappear* as a transitive verb meaning "make something disappear." Many of these start off as government or marketing jargon and soon make their way into general usage; perhaps provenance such as this in British English is not respectable enough to give a word credentials for widespread usage.

Double Imperatives

American English permits *come* and *go* to be followed by a second imperative verb in informal commands: *Come sit by my side if you love me*; *Go see who's at the door.* British English is more comfortable with an *and* intervening between the two verbs.

Variable Conjugations

When all variants are taken into account, and notwithstanding spelling differences, there is no verb in English whose principal parts are different in British and American English. But there are a handful of verbs where the preference for one variant of the past or past participle dominates in one country, to the near exclusion of the other.

GET

A case familiar to many speakers and readers is that of *get.* The past participle *gotten* is not found in contemporary British English (*got* is used instead), but it is preferred for most meanings of *get* in American English. *Gotten*, however, is not universally used as *get's* American past participle, and the distinctions may not be entirely clear to Britons. You can certainly get away with using *got* for all past participle needs in American English, but you will not sound quite native. Americans prefer *got* to *gotten* only in the sense meaning "possess" (*I haven't got enough money*), and "have as an obligation" (*You've got to be back here by midnight*). Note, however, that *gotten* appears in the compound *ill-gotten*, as common in British as in American English.

It is worth noting here a small difference in the use of *have* and *get* that is often misreported or at the very least overemphasized as a difference between American and British English. Speakers of both dialects naturally produce sentences such as *Have you got any money?* and *I haven't got any relatives in this area.* It is however rarer for British speakers to say, *Do you have any money?* and very unlikely that an American speaker would spontaneously produce *Have you any wool?* unless she were reciting a nursery rhyme. Americans would likewise regard a sentence such as *We haven't any need for such things* as British-sounding, and a Briton would regard *We don't have any need for such things* as American-tainted. Happily no obstacle to understanding arises from any of these variations, and those aiming for perfect mastery of the distinction need only note the general pattern.

-T FOR -ED

A small group of verbs conjugate regularly in American English, but British English uses the past and past participle forms ending in -*t*: *burn, lean, learn, smell, spell, spill, spoil,* all regular in American English, usually have *burnt, leant, learnt, smelt, spelt, spilt, spoilt* as the past and past participle in British English. Americans are quite comfortable, however, with *burnt* and *spilt* when used adjectivally, especially in fixed phrases (*a burnt offering, spilt milk*). Three other verbs show a preference for the -*t* inflections in both dialects, but American English has instances of regular inflections as well that would be regarded as incorrect in British English. These are *dwell* (*dwelt* or AmE *dwelled*), *kneel* (*knelt* or AmE *kneeled*), and *leap* (*leapt* or AmE *leaped*).

OTHER VERB ANOMALIES

British English uses *pleaded* as the past tense of *plead.* American English sometimes uses *pled* as the past tense, especially in legal contexts, but is equally happy with *pleaded. Proven* is the preferred past participle of *prove* in American English, though *proved* is also acceptable. *Bust* is an acceptable past and past participle form of *bust* in British English, but American uses *busted.* Finally, *spat* is the preferred past and past participle form of *spit* in both dialects, though *spit* also appears in American English.

ADVERBS

The Submodified World

There are a handful of high-frequency words in English that many readers will have learned to call intensifying adverbs. A current vogue term for these is *submodifiers*, and it is useful term because all of these words, though technically adverbs, function to qualify an adjective—which is itself already a modifier. Along with the modal verbs, discussed above, usage preferences governing this class of words is one of the readiest markers between American and British English that any listener or reader will seize upon immediately as evidence of transatlantic origin.

Though encountered with appreciable frequency on both sides of the Atlantic, the adverbs *rather*, *quite*, and *very* play different roles in the language of Britons and Americans. Some uses of these adverbs in one dialect are very obvious dialect markers to speakers of the other, such as the ordinary use of *rather* as a submodifier in British English: a sentence along the lines of *We found it rather warm on the verandah so we went inside* has British written all over it for most American speakers. An American speaker would be inclined to use *pretty*, *fairly*, or *too* in place of *rather* in this sentence. Other usage differences may result in slight misunderstandings, since the sentences embodying them are as likely to occur in one dialect as the other, but not with exactly the same meaning, as will be seen in the following discussion.

Some British uses of *rather* are cultural rather than strictly semantic and the best American "translation" of them is simple elimination. One expression of the British tendency to understatement is the habit of mitigating any statement that might suggest culpability on the part of the listener, subject, or some other implied culprit, by qualifying it. The preferred way of doing this is simply by dropping a *rather* in before the offending word. Thus, the American translation of *The food was rather cold* is *The food was cold*.

British English has a largely uncorrected habit of using the submodifier *very* without any good reason, and an American editor can almost get away with striking through such instances willy-nilly without fear of altering the meaning for American readers or listeners. Consider these examples from British newspapers:

[T]he Church still has some 24 million souls it can count as, formally speaking, members: people who, without very much thought, will write C of E on official forms and turn to their local vicar for births, marriages and deaths. (from a letter to the editor in the *Independent*)

[H]is drift—which is that we could save a lot of money bringing the third world out of poverty rather than dropping bombs on it—was extremely well received, and won him a real standing ovation from a very tough audience. (from a columnist in the *Guardian*)

Neither *very* adds meaningfully to the sentence or the passage that contains it, and its use in instances such as these is more a habit of the chattering classes, as they are called, than anything else. In the second passage, the same thing could be said of *real*, which suggests here that a false standing ovation would have been considerably less convincing.

Quite presents a slightly more complicated case. American uses are mainly idiomatic with fixed syntax patterns: *She's quite the romantic*; *The answer isn't quite right*; *That was quite a thunderstorm last night*. All of these patterns are also found in British English. The use of *quite* as a strict submodifier, occupying the slot in a sentence that could be filled as easily by *pretty*, *fairly*, *very*, *really*, *moderately*, *rather*, or *somewhat*, is commoner in British English, as well as being more specific. Most British speakers would recognize *quite* as denoting a degree of intensity falling between *rather* and *very*. This degree of specificity is lacking for American speakers, who are more likely to regard *quite* as a slightly formal alternative to the more popular *pretty* or *really*.

Mighty as an informal submodifier is mainly American English, and a marker of it to Britons, who normally don't let it rise above its original adjectival duties. *Way* has a respectable record as a submodifier of fixed prepositional and adjectival phrases (*way over the top, way below normal, way too much*). It is gaining ground in informal American English as an ordinary submodifier, especially in the phrase *way cool* (*a Los Angeles boutique that is way cool with a funky decor that includes chandeliers made of hats*). This is not seen in British English except among the frightening avant-garde of American wannabes.

SUBMODIFICATION WITH -*ISH*

Considerable variation in usage preferences for various adjectives can be found in the section "Peculiar Pairs" in chapter 11. Aside from these, there is no systematic difference in the use of adjectives between American and British English. There is, however, a facility for making adjectives ending in *-ish* from existing adjectives or numbers in British English to give a finer shade of meaning, or sometimes merely to affect one, that does not exist in American English, where the adjectives would be jarring. Those adjectives modifying the colors (*reddish, greenish*) are common in both dialects, but British English typically modifies times of day, making them less imprecise, by the addition of -ish: *What time should I come? Sevenish.* There are many other nonce usages that don't appear in dictionaries: *She wasn't very tall, five-sixish I should say; a saddish recollection.* The American approach to such shades of meaning is to submodify using words: *around five-six, a fairly/somewhat sad recollection.*

Too and As Well

The use of *as well* as an adverbial phrase meaning "in addition" is regarded as slightly formal in American English and is more likely to occur in writing than in speech, where Americans prefer simply *too;* thus *Are they going too?* instead of *Are they going as well?* British English uses *as well* in both formal and informal contexts. "Too" at the beginning of a sentence, an odious stylistic device in American English, is way beyond the pale in British English: *She found it difficult to settle into the new house. Too, the climate didn't suit her.*

Terminal -s in Adverbs

Toward (AmE) and *towards* (BrE) exemplify an area of variant usage in which no clear rules prevail, but happily one in which not a great deal can be lost in meaning by not following preferences. There is a general preference in British English for such adverbs to end in -*s* (i.e., *backwards, downwards, upwards*), but even British dictionaries vary in their opinion as to which form to lemmatize (that is, alphabetize as a headword entry). American dictionaries generally prefer the forms without -*s*, but include the -*s* forms as variants, and the -*s* forms prevail in some idioms (*upwards of, bend over backwards*). Unless the intention is to remove all traces of national origin, these adverbs can generally be left in their original form when Americanizing or Briticizing text. The related adjectival forms of these adverbs (*backward, upward,* etc.) are uniformly without the terminal *s* in both dialects, but the *s* sometimes occurs in informal contexts.

All Right and Alright

A notion persists that *alright* is the American version of the British adjective and adverb phrase *all right*, and some bilingual dictionaries provide the two variants as such. In fact *alright*, though frowned upon by arbiters of "good usage," is equally common in both dialects and will probably win acceptance before long like the well-established *altogether* and *already* before it, which started their lives as separate compounds with *all*.

Supplementary Conjunctions

Directly and *immediately* are mainly adverbs in both dialects but British English allows them cameo roles as subordinating conjunctions with the meaning "as soon as"; American English does not. Thus, when Grace Kelly (as the charmingly naïve Mrs. Wendice) is asked by Chief Inspector Hubbard in *Dial M for Murder*, "Why didn't you call the police immediately this happened?" the suspenseful pause that follows may be due only to her trying to parse the syntax.

Momentarily in British English means "for a moment." In American English it means "for a moment" or "in a moment." Thus, *She'll be with you momentarily* might suggest to the untrained British listener that he does not merit very much of her time.

PREPOSITIONS

It is unlikely that a misunderstanding will arise in the variable use of prepositions between British and American English, but the preferred use in many cases is a clear marker for the origins of speech and writing, and these need to be scrutinized carefully when text is being edited for presentation in the other dialect. This table presents some of the commonest differences.

VARIABLE USE OF PREPOSITIONS

American	British
aside from →	apart from →
different than	different from[1], different to
enroll in [a course, etc.]	enrol on
in (good) form	on (good) form

VARIABLE USE OF PREPOSITIONS *(continued)*

American	British
in (good) form	on (good) form
in a pinch	at a pinch
in school	at school
on the street, on South Street	in the street, in South Street
in tow [of a vehicle]	on tow
on the weekend	at the weekend

[1] Americans are not entirely averse to *different from* and use it with appreciable frequency but rarely use *different to*; the use of *different than* is rare in British English.

Around **and** Round

The use of *round* and *around* as both adverb and preposition is a clear usage marker between the dialects. American English uses *around* in all cases: *He came around to our point of view; The ropes are tied the wrong way around; There has to be a way around this obstacle.* The only exceptions are fixed expressions such as *round the clock,* (*the*) *year round,* and *round and round,* all more frequent in American English than their *around* counterparts. British English is more comfortable using *round* in nearly all cases (*He came round to our point of view; The ropes are tied the wrong way round; There has to be a way round this obstacle*), but *around* works in these equally well and doesn't raise eyebrows. *Around* is preferred in British English when it means "approximately" (*It costs around £100*) and other cases, typically modifying a verb, in which there is a notion of vagueness or indefiniteness: *We wandered around for ages; Have a poke around in the fridge.* By extension, *all-around* is the preferred American form of the adjective and *all-round* is British.

Around **and** About

There is a general pattern of difference in phrasal verbs in which *around* is more commonly used in American English and *about* in British English, with identical meaning. Examples include *mess around/about* (engage in nonproductive activities); *lie around/about* (pass time lazily, or be left carelessly out of place); *hang around/about* (loiter). This pattern persists in various idioms: *beat around/about the bush, throw one's weight around/about,* etc. The *around* versions of these are probably less jarring to the British ear (owing to the continuous din of American English) than the *about* versions are to the American ear, but the preferences in each dialect persist. A difference where the pattern breaks down is in the common British phrasal verb *mess sb about*. American English does not have a corresponding *mess sb around*, and would render it has *mess around with sb* or *play games with sb*.

Amidst, Amongst, Whilst

British speakers use *whilst* and *amongst* interchangeably with *while* and *among*, which are the only forms that are commonly found in American English. *Amidst* is a poetic and literary variant in both dialects.

Other Minor Differences

In general British English is not as comfortable with *inside of* followed by a personal pronoun, when the meaning is *within*: *I'm sure she has a very thin person buried deep inside of her.* This usage is unremarkable in American English. There are a few other prepositional differences noted in the section "Expressions of Time" in chapter 11, and in particular idioms, noted in appendix 2.

ARTICLES

Britons omit *the* in some common phrases where Americans use it: *in hospital, to hospital, at table*. American English uses *in the future* generally for its two principle meanings, "at a time in the future" and "from now on." For the second meaning, British English uses *in future*. Britons bring water (or other liquids) to *the boil*; Americans bring them to *a boil*. Once it has reached this state, it is *on the boil* in British English, simply *boiling* in American English.

Though now falling out of fashion, a few countries in the Middle East were characteristically prefixed with *the* in British English, perhaps reflecting a translation of the Arabic article missing in the English rendering: thus *the Yemen, the Sudan, the Lebanon*. These usages are now mainly regarded as historical; the article is not so used in American English.

A sports broadcast that could not be confused with any other may get an article in British English that American listeners would find adventitious: *We're going to stay home and watch the cricket; Did you see the snooker last night?* These usages would be regarded as quaint at best in American English, where the article would only be used if the noun were followed by another noun, such as game or tournament.

British English treats *nonsense* as if it were a singular, countable noun by prefixing the indefinite article: *a secret deal that makes a nonsense of privatisation.* American English omits the article.

Appendix 2, dealing with idioms, notes a few other instances where use of an article differs between American and British English.

PRONOUNS

Relative Pronouns: That, Who, and Which

H. W. Fowler summed up the situation admirably in his *Modern English Usage:* "The relations between *that, who,* and *which* have come to us from our forefathers as an odd jumble, and plainly show that the language has not been neatly constructed by a master builder who could create each part to do the exact work required of it, neither overlapped nor overlapping."[1] In the same article he makes a compelling case for the use of *that* for defining (or restrictive) relative clauses (*the man that I marry*) and *which* for nondefining (or nonrestrictive) relative clauses (*The birds, which mate for life, have both migrant and sedentary populations*). This informal rule of usage is more widely followed by Americans than Britons, who have largely ignored their esteemed countryman's excellent advice. British writers largely prefer *which* for both defining and nondefining clauses; Americans are more inclined to use *that* for defining clauses, though *which* occurs often in writing.

Americanizing editors can usually do no wrong in systematically changing *which* to *that* in defining clauses of British English, judiciously avoiding the transformation when euphony would dictate the use of *which.* This normally only occurs in a sentence with two clauses depending on the same noun, one of which can only use *which*: most readers would agree that "*a region of cytoplasm from which the asters extend during cell division and which contains the centrioles*" would not benefit by changing the second *which* to *that.*

Both dialects are comfortable using *who* where the antecedent is not strictly a person but an entity composed of persons: (*a company who lobbied for the change*) but American English generally uses *that* in such

1. *Modern English Usage,* 2d. ed., p. 625. Oxford: Oxford University Press (1965).

cases. It should also be noted that British English would follow such a construction with a plural rather than a singular noun: *the chairman of the GFA coaching committee, who organise the courses.*

Antecedents at War

English pronouns in both dialects are in a state of confusion at present because of an attempt to serve two masters. The older, and in the minds of many, decrepit and obsolete master, is grammar, which insists politely that pronouns agree with their antecedents in number. The newer, and because of that more energetic and demanding master, is political correctness, which has riveted attention on the fact that male gender has reigned for too long as the uncrowned representative of both sexes, and therefore demands that it be removed from this position of authority at any cost. This has resulted in long-established usages being deemed unacceptable. The problem can be illustrated with a saying that, as far as I know, is anonymous, and as such has the advantage of already existing in many forms, and being completely untraceable to its original form. It first came to my attention as

> There is no limit to the amount of good a man can do if he doesn't care
> who gets the credit.

Whether this is the thought as originally expressed may never be known. In any case, nearly everyone would agree that there is no reason to limit the capacity to do good to men. Therefore *person* can be harmlessly substituted. But that is where the trouble begins.

> 1. There is no limit to the amount of good a person can do if he
> doesn't care who gets the credit.

is seen to discriminate against women, because *he* is a masculine pronoun that is no longer considered adequate to include women in its reference. The politically correct (and grammatically offensive) substitute for this is

> 2. There is no limit to the amount of good a person can do if they don't
> care who gets the credit.

This is objectionable because *person* is singular and *they* is plural. It is not initially even obvious that *they* refers to *person* and the reader is startled to discover that new actors have entered the sentence unbeknownst until the trick is discovered. Of course the whole saying can be recast, as it sometimes is, in the plural, as

   3. There is no limit to the amount of good people can do if they don't care
   who gets the credit.

This sentence is unobjectionable politically and grammatically but does not
in fact express the original idea; it suggests, alarmingly, that people must
always act in concert, rather than individually, to do any good. The entirely
correct though little used solution to the problem is

   4. There is no limit to the amount of good a person can do if he or she
   doesn't care who gets the credit.

Writers and speakers rightly and instinctively reject this solution because it
is unwieldy and flouts the natural economy of language. British English, if
starting from scratch to express the idea of the sentence, might give it as

   5. There is no limit to the amount of good one can do if one doesn't care
   who gets the credit.

American English, because of its resistance to the use of *one* as a cold and
remote Briticism, would not find this solution agreeable; *one* as a pronoun
does not really belong in a sentence that dispenses homespun wisdom, in
American speech anyway. American speakers of an earlier era, as well as
approving 1 above, would also be comfortable with

   6. There is no limit to the amount of good one can do if he doesn't care
   who gets the credit.

But this usage, with the banished *he*, would be found unacceptable today,
and in any case would never have been welcome in British English. An
American setting out to express the original idea and offend no one would
probably put it as

   7. There is no limit to the amount of good you can do if you don't care who
   gets the credit.

This solution is probably acceptable to all, except for a traditional remnant
of British English speakers who would find the use of the second person singular to mean *anyone* too folksy and familiar for expressing general wisdom.
   It is likely that no good has been done at all in laying out all of these alternatives (for which I take all the credit) because there is in fact no solution to the general problem: there are sentences in which what is wanted
is a general third person singular pronoun and English doesn't have one
that works uniformly. The fashion among contemporary educators on both
sides of the Atlantic, and in countries around the world where teaching

English is an industry, is to accept solution number 2, at the expense of centuries of grammatical correctness. Most people would agree that *they* is satisfactory when the antecedent is *anyone, someone,* or *no one* (*If anyone thinks they can do better, they should try*), but when the antecedent refers to an individual (e.g., *person* or any agentive noun such as *teacher, cook, administrator*) it is jarring to introduce *they* because it is not immediately obvious that it in fact has a singular antecedent. There is no satisfactory solution to the dilemma, and no advice is offered here, except perhaps by way of another anonymous saying: "If you bend, you will break."

CHAPTER THREE

Money, Business, and Work

This chapter begins a long departure from the two that precede it. Material covered in the first two chapters represents what we might call the mechanical differences between American and British English: differences that apply in nearly all contexts, and that can be reduced in many cases to simple substitutions of letters, words, or phrases. In this and the following chapters we will begin to treat particular subject areas in which, on the one hand, there are many cases where the differences can be put down to *lexical variants*—that is, cases of each dialect using a different word for the exactly the same thing. But on the other hand, we will find ourselves much more in the domain of *functional equivalency*—where different terms denote things that are not exactly the same thing, but are at least comparable, and could be said to serve the same purpose in one country as they do in the other.

The attempt here is to present the main high-frequency terminology that readers and listeners are likely to encounter in various subject areas, giving exact equivalents in the other dialect where these exist, or explaining what the substitutes are where they do not. British and American readers will each find much here that they already know about their own countries, but it is hoped that this contextual presentation will make it easy to find and assimilate new terminology related to the various subject areas under discussion by hanging it on the hooks that already exist in your mind.

MONEY

Putting money first in this list before business and work may be putting the cart before the horse, but some would argue that the other two items exist merely for the sake of it, so here we begin.

Britain is flirting heavily at present with the idea of joining the Euro zone and abandoning its cherished currency, called *sterling*. Today it is a decimal system with the basic unit of the *pound* (symbol £), containing one hundred *pence* (symbol and abbreviation *p*). The two smallest coins have names, a *penny* and *tuppence* (though "two pence" is written on the coin). Other coins are referred to by their value: 5p, 20p, 50p (the abbreviation is usually pronounced as "pee"), one pound, and two pound. Denominations larger than this are paper and called *notes*. The older, non-decimal system, in use until 1971, was sometimes called the *lsd* system (sometimes written *£sd* but pronounced "el ess dee"), these being the letters that abbreviated the units of *pounds*, *shillings*, and *pence*, respectively. This currency system lives fondly in the memory of many Britons, and terms from it persist in speech, as well as in pre-1971 literature. This table sets out the values of coins used at various times under the old system.

OLD STERLING COIN VALUES

Coin	Value
crown	5 shillings
farthing	$1/4$ penny [withdrawn in 1961]
florin	2 shillings
half-crown, half a crown	2 shillings and sixpence
penny	$1/12$ of a shilling, $1/240$ of a pound
pound	20 shillings, 240 pence
shilling	$1/20$th of a pound, 12 pence
sixpence	$1/2$ shilling
threepence, thruppence	3 pennies, $1/4$ shilling

Readers of nineteenth-century literature may also encounter the *sovereign*, a gold coin worth a pound and out of circulation after 1914; it replaced the *guinea*, then worth 20 shillings (a pound). Today a guinea represents a value of £1.05 and is used in auctions, to set some professional fees, and in the world of horseracing, but it is not denominated in a coin or note.

Quid is the widely used slang term for *pound*; it is nearly always taken as plural, and in any case, there is no separate plural form except in the phrase *quids in*, for which the nearest American equivalent is "money ahead": *we'll still be quids in if we sell the boat now*. *Bob*, an old slang term (usually taken as plural) for shilling, persists in several expressions: *that'll cost you a few bob, earn a fair bob*, etc.

US currency is based on the *dollar* (symbol $); its widely used slang term, *buck*, has about the same register of informality as *quid* in British English and appears in many fixed expressions. *Fast buck* is a strongly established idiom for money made quickly and sometimes unethically; the attributive form *fast-buck* is increasingly common: *fast-buck lawyers/schemes/investments*. *Megabucks* (attributive form *megabuck*) and *big bucks* both have limited currency in British as well American English for large sums of money. *Make a buck* is the standard informal idiom for "earn money": *builders whose only interest is to make a buck*.

Dollar coins have been minted at various times in an attempt to displace the paper dollar, usually without success. The only enduring one is the *silver dollar*, which has not been minted for circulation since the 1930s but is still legal tender; they trade as collectors' items for amounts far above their face value. American English has names for all other coins that are used in preference to a value designation, except the *half dollar*, which in any case is hardly in circulation now. The dollar contains one hundred *cents* (symbol ¢). The coins currently in circulation are the *quarter* (25¢), *dime* (10¢), *nickel* (5¢), and *penny* (1¢). The denominations have not changed since their introduction; older coins are sometimes distinguished by the designs that were on them, such as the *wheat cent*, the *buffalo nickel*, the *liberty-head dime*. There are a handful of figurative expressions inspired by the names of the coins: the adjective *nickel-and-dime* means "trivial": *a nickel-and-dime offense*. *Nickel-and-dime* as a verb means to importune someone with constant demands for additional amounts of money. *Penny-ante* denotes low stakes, or a small amount of money: *a penny-ante investor/arms dealer*. Most other compounds and idioms with *penny* are common between the two dialects. The term *bit* persists in some older expressions though it is not used today. It represents a value of 12.5¢; thus a *two-bit piece* is a quarter.

The unit of US paper money is a *bill*, which is mostly used in combination: *a five-/ten-/twenty-dollar bill*. Curiously, all of these documents are identified on their face as *notes*, and Americans happily use *note* to describe the paper currency of other countries. The denominations of bills work as nouns for bill itself—*he gave me a five/ten/twenty/fifty*—*single* is the noun for a $1 bill: *50 singles.* British English has the same convention but uses *fiver* and *tenner* for five- and ten-pound notes, respectively.

Amounts of money considered so small as to be insulting in a given context are referred to by a strongly established idiom in British English: *derisory.* Thus, *a derisory fee/offer/pay rise.* American English has no strict equivalent but is fond of the slang term *chump change* to designate an amount of money that is trivial in its context: *a 10-grand fine that's chump change for a multimillionaire sports hero. Chicken feed* is used in both dialects.

Documents that may serve in place of money, such as those for the exchange of merchandise, are normally called *certificates* in American English, *tokens* or *vouchers* in British English. *Book tokens*, a popular item in the UK, are specifically for redemption at bookstores. The document issued by a retailer for returned goods that may be used toward purchasing more is usually a *credit note* in British English, a *credit slip* in American English. The exchanging of goods of nominally equal value is always *swapping* in British English, never *trading*, which has equal standing in American English; perhaps owing to the rather heavy burdens placed on the word *trade* in British English (see below).

Banking

Very similar banking systems exist in the US and the UK with slight differences reflected in terminology. Nearly every American of working age as a *checking account* on which *checks* can be written to make purchases and pay bills. The British equivalent is a *cheque account* or *current account*, on which *cheques* are written. A major difference between checks in the two countries is that a US check can be converted to cash by a bank or other institution (these days, at considerable trouble and sometimes expense); a British cheque is nearly always *crossed*, that is, it has two vertical bars through the line where the payee's name appears, indicating that it can only be deposited in the payee's account, and not converted to cash (for which American English uses the transitive verb *cash* and British English sometimes uses *encash*). British English has far more frequent use of the term *bank manager* with a particular meaning: the bank official who oversees one's personal bank accounts. Britons all seem to have personal and fraught relationships with theirs, a feature of life that is missing in the US where banking institutions are perceived as far more impersonal.

These banking terms are direct equivalents in the two dialects.

BANKING TERMS

American	British
teller	cashier
deposit slip	paying-in slip
savings account	deposit account
stub (of a check or slip)	counterfoil
certificate of deposit, CD	savings certificate
insufficient funds	RD (refer to drawer)

Automatic debiting and crediting of accounts is better established and more widespread in the UK than in the US; essentially the same facilities are found on both sides of the Atlantic but they go by different names. In Britain, an automatic payment in an unvarying amount that you authorize to leave your account on a regular basis is a *standing order*; an authority that you issue another institution to take money in variable amounts out of your account on a regular basis (for example, to pay a recurring bill) is a *direct debit*. The corresponding American terms are not rigidly fixed; *automatic payment* is often used for the former, *automatic draft* for the latter, but different institutions have different names for these. The system in the US that handles these transactions is called *ACH* (for *Automated Clearinghouse*); the equivalent UK organization in *BACS* (for *Bank Automated Clearing System*). The UK system in which banks cooperate with various private and government bodies for transfer of funds is denoted by *giro*; a *giro cheque* is one written to an individual receiving government benefits; *welfare check* is probably the nearest American equivalent.

Most people in the UK bank with a *high street bank*; one of the half-dozen largest banks in the UK that have branches everywhere, particularly on main shopping streets. Banking in the US is still considerably decentralized, despite the current atmosphere in which mergers and amalgamations are prevalent. There are very few banks that operate in every state, although *internet banks* that have no brick-and-mortar locations are gaining a share of the market.

OTHER BANKING INSTITUTIONS

In both countries there were formerly institutions offering many of the services of banks but different from them in being organized as cooperative savings and lending institutions rather than companies for profit. These were called *savings and loan associations* in the US and *building societies* in the UK. The latter still exist, though they are considerably reduced in number since the mid-1980s, when legislation enabled them to compete more effectively with banks and prompted many of them to convert to publicly held companies (called *demutualization*, since they were formerly organized as mutual societies), or to become takeover targets for already established banks. Savings and loan associations in the US still exist on paper but they have abandoned that designation following a damaging scandal in the 1980s growing out of deregulatory legislation from the Reagan era.

Banks that exist mainly for investments and transactions between other businesses are called *merchant banks* in the UK, *investment banks* in the US; both of these specialize in underwriting new stock issues. *Credit unions*, organized as cooperatives in which members use pooled deposits as the capitalization for banking activities, are an American invention and are well-established in the US, with a very limited presence in the UK.

The UK government operates an institution called *National Savings*, which is in essence a savings bank for the public. It offers a number of investment vehicles, including *premium bonds*, a sort of combination lottery ticket and certificate of deposit that pays fixed interest and is eligible for a monthly drawing in which winning bond numbers are awarded prizes. *ERNIE*, the computer that generates the winning numbers, is a national institution. The only common direct-to-the-public government investment in the US is the *US Savings Bond*, equivalent to the UK *savings certificate*.

NATIONAL BANKING

Institutions for the control of currency and tinkering with the economy are approximately analogous in the US and the UK. The *Bank of England* (sometimes quaintly referred to as *the Old Lady of Threadneedle Street*) issues currency[1] and sets benchmark interest rates in the UK; these functions are handled by the *Federal Reserve Bank* (popularly, *the Fed*) in the US. The *chairman* of the Federal Reserve Bank is roughly the counterpart of the *governor* of the Bank of England. Both are high-level appointees, though the Fed's chairman serves a far longer term (fourteen years) than the Bank of England's governor (five years). In both countries, these banks most frequently make the news when they alter interest rates that affect interbank lending; this is usually the *discount rate* in the US, a

1. For England and Wales only. Various Scottish banks issue their own banknotes that circulate in Scotland and are exchangeable for sterling.

term that is also used in British English along with *base rate* and *bank rate*. *Prime rate* has the same meaning in both dialects, the lowest rate available for commercial lending, but it is used far more often in American English; British English prefers *minimum lending rate*.

Investing

As with banking, investing by individuals and institutions follows very similar patterns in the US and the UK, with considerable difference in terminology. While designating exactly the same thing, Americans usually use *stock* and Britons *shares*. American English normally only gets into talk of *shares* when a quantity of units of a stock are under discussion. AmE *common stock* is BrE *ordinary shares*; AmE *preferred stock* is BrE *preference shares*. Owners of any of these are usually *stockholders* in the US, *shareholders* in the UK.

Investment in securities is seen in both countries as the primary means for security in old age, so it is appropriate to treat here as well the various terms relating to retirement savings. The term *pension* is used generally in British English for all forms of retirement income, whether as a benefit of former employment (an *occupational pension scheme*), from the government (the *state pension*), or from a privately-arranged fund (a *personal pension*). Likewise, the term *pensioner* is in common use for a person collecting a pension. This sometimes occurs as *OAP* (old-age pensioner) in headlines, derived from the now dated term *old age pension*. Such persons in the US are designated *senior citizens*, or *seniors*. Specifically in the context of those formerly working and now not, they are called *retirees*.

In American English, *pension* is associated mainly with employer-sponsored retirement benefits and may be called a *pension plan*, paid out of capital invested in a *pension fund*. A *retirement plan* may be the same thing as a pension plan, or it may be used to distinguish some arrangement for retirement income that is separate from an employment-related pension. Government benefits paid to senior citizens starting at age 65 or older, depending on one's date of birth, are called *social security*. Investments arranged by an individual generally go under the name of *IRA* (pronounced either as "eye-r-ay" or as a word), an abbreviation for *individual retirement account* (or *arrangement*). These come in a number of varieties governed by different rules about who may hold them and how they are taxed (e.g., *Roth IRA, Sep IRA*); the retronym *traditional IRA* applies to the original, no-frills variety.

The following table sets out terms that are widely used in the personal investing of one country but not the other; rough equivalents are indicated where they exist.

INVESTMENT TERMS

Name	Source	What is it?
401(k)	US	employer-sponsored, tax-deferred retirement plan that allows employees to contribute to a company investment account (usually into mutual funds)
AGM	UK	annual general meeting (AmE annual stockholders meeting)
AIM	UK	Alternative Investments Market; comparable to US NASDAQ
AVC	UK	additional voluntary contribution (to a company pension scheme)
bonus issue	UK	= AmE stock split
CFP	US	certified financial planner; = BrE IFA
Consols	UK	government securities without maturity date, paying fixed interest
DJIA	US	Dow Jones Industrial Average; the main stock index
FTSE	UK	Financial Times Stock Exchange index, called the footsie, the main UK share index
gilts	UK	HM treasury bonds; comparable to US T-Bills
IFA	UK	Independent Financial Advisor; = AmE CFP
ISA	UK	Individual Savings Account that is not taxed for interest income or capital gains; invested in cash or securities
Keogh plan	US	retirement plan for the self-employed and small businesses; like an IRA.
mutual fund	US	= BrE unit trust
NASDAQ	US	National Association of Securities Dealers Automated Quotations, a stock exchange for smaller companies and tech stocks; pronounced /nazdak/ or /nasdak/.
PPP	UK	personal pension plan
REIT	US	real estate investment trust, a real property investment vehicle
S&P	US	Standard & Poor, a securities rating agency; publishes the S&P 500, a mutual fund index
stakeholder pension	UK	low-cost private pension for people with no taxable income
stock split	US	= BrE bonus issue
T-Bill	US	US treasury bonds; comparable to UK gilts

Name	Source	What is it?
TEP	UK	traded investment policy; investment vehicle formed from repackaged participating insurance policies that are surrendered early
TESSA	UK	five-year tax-free savings plan, forerunner of the ISA and no longer available, but some are still maturing.
unit trust	UK	=American English mutual fund

Regulation of the securities industry in the US is handled by the *Securities and Exchange Commission*, or *SEC*, an independent federal agency. A comparable British government body is the *Financial Services Authority* or *FSA*, the statutory regulator responsible for deposit taking, insurance, and investment business. The UK government department that works with the criminal justice system to investigate serious or complex cases of fraud, which nearly always involve the financial and securities industries, is the *Serious Fraud Office*. In the US the SEC handles such investigations. Matters relating to monopolies and unfair competition are investigated and adjudicated by the *Competition Commission* in the UK, an independent body with connections to the Department of Trade and Industry. In the US this function is handled by the *Antitrust Division* of the Department of Justice.

BUSINESS

Before we go into the language likely to be encountered in various corners of the business world we look at two words that, as used in British English, can be considered true workhorses, plowing the fields tended by half a dozen different terms that American English uses in the same contexts. They appear in many business and other contexts and each deserves separate discussion because of the marked differences in usage between the two dialects.

Trade and *Goods*

The cabinet-level department in the UK concerned with trade is the *Department of Trade and Industry*; in the US it is the *Department of Commerce.*[1] A person doing business in the UK is typically called a *trader* or is *in*

---

1. There also exists the independent US government agency, the *Federal Trade Commission*.

trade; in the US, *businessperson, vendor, merchant*, and *retailer* are more likely terms. The UK *trade price* is the US *wholesale price*. A business that adopts a different name than its official one in the UK is said to be *trading as (t/a)* Acme Ltd; in the US it is *doing business as (dba)* Acme, Inc. A British company no longer in operation has *ceased trading*; An American company has *gone out of business*. American English is comfortable with *industry* to describe entire sectors of the economy that produce one thing or one kind of thing; British English uses *trade* in much the same way for industries that produce tangible products: *the motor trade, the tailoring trade*. Britain has *trade unions*; the US has *labor unions* (for more about these, see below). The main legislation governing fraud in retail in the UK is the *Trade Descriptions Act*; the nearest US equivalent to this is probably *consumer protection act*, a name that applies to various laws.[1] Laws established to maintain quality and safety standards in traded goods or services are classed as *trading standards* in British English, with no exact American equivalent.

While few of these usages would be misunderstood in the transatlantic country, they would all have a foreign sound and they require editing for presentation in the other dialect. The British editor's job is somewhat simpler, involving only the changing of various US terms to some form of trade. The Americanizing editor must make a selection from a number of different terms. A few other British English compounds using this general sense of trade are *off-trade* (the business of selling alcoholic beverages for consumption off the premises), *Sunday trading* (the practice of being open for business on Sunday), and *trading estate* (somewhere between an American English *industrial park* and a shopping center). Trade compounds that are common between the two dialects include *rag trade* (the garment industry), *trade edition, trade secret*, and the various terms from economics in which trade appears (*balance of trade, trade gap, free trade*, etc.). Ironically perhaps, two Americanisms using *trade* that became firmly established in British English are now found mainly in historical contexts: *trading stamp* and *trading post*.

Goods is the general purpose term in British English for (a) items offered for sale, and (b) items used in the manufacture of these. The word has been found so useful in these contexts that it has come to be used to mean any group of otherwise non-specified items. Consider these two definitions, one of *boot* and one of *trunk*, taken from a (1) British dictionary and a (2) American dictionary:

1. It is also the name of a particular 1987 UK act of Parliament that is mostly concerned with ensuring the safety of consumer products and the accuracy of warnings about risks associated with them.

1. a space at the back of a car for carrying luggage or other goods.
2. a large compartment in the rear of an automobile, in which luggage . . . and other articles may be kept.

The entire range of usage of *goods* is broader in British English than in American English, and Americanizing editors will find numerous opportunities to replace it with a different word, while Briticizing editors can plug *goods* into a spot occupied by several different American terms. Here we will look mostly at the usages having to do with business and commerce; other terms having to do with transportation can be found in chapter 8. American English divides up the main territory occupied by British English *goods* with a number of different terms. Items offered for sale at wholesale or retail are generally called *merchandise* in American English, or for individual or specific items, *products*; American English does however share many of the fixed compounds ending in *goods*: *baked goods, white goods, yard goods,* etc.

Items that are destined for further processing or manufacture are usually called *materials* or *raw materials* in American English, rather than *goods*. The door at which service people call and deliveries are made is the *goods entrance* in British English and may be labeled *goods in*; it is the *service entrance* in American English and may be labeled *deliveries*. Such items move vertically through a building in a *freight elevator* (AmE) or *goods lift*[1] (BrE). In legal contexts, British English sometimes uses *goods* where American English uses *personal property*. The use of *goods* in American English is mainly in economic contexts (*consumer goods*) in the fixed phrase *goods and services*, and in the various general categories of products used in statistical analysis: these terms are common to both dialects (*brown goods, white goods, durable goods*). British English *dry goods*[2] is more or less equivalent to US *commodities*.

Business Organization

The various forms of business organization in the US and the UK differ so little in particulars that they may be regarded as functional equivalents; most of the US institutions developed out of already established English models, the differences that have arisen are mainly ones of terminology. In

---

1. *Elevator* and *lift* are the standard separate terms for these in the two dialects, whether goods or people are moving.
2. For the AmE meaning of *dry goods*, see chapter 7.

the US, enterprises that are considered as separate legal entities are informally called *companies* in most cases, especially if they are large or produce a product. *Business* is a competing term, usually more general than company, not necessarily involving a product, and of any size. The legal and technical name for these is *corporation* in the US, abbreviated *Inc.* at the end of the company name. Corporations may be privately or publicly held; *Inc.* gives no indication as to which. Britons prefer *firm*, a term that gets preferential use in American English for businesses that employ professionals and provide a service (e.g., *a law/consulting/architectural/brokerage firm*). Companies in the UK that are publicly held and traded are designated by *plc* (or *Plc*) after the name, the abbreviation for *public limited company*. Companies with the abbreviation *Ltd* following the name are privately held, limited liability companies, the same as *LLC* in American English. Partnerships are similarly organized in the two countries. Many US states recognize the *limited liability partnership* (*LLP*), which protects a partner from personal liability from misdeeds of other partners or employees; it is usually restricted to professionals such as lawyers, accountants, architects, and physicians.

The document that sets out the rules governing a company is the *articles of association* in British English, the *bylaws* in American English. A British *sleeping partner* is an American *silent partner*.

Business Names and Venues

Many enterprises that do essentially the same thing sometimes go by different names in the US and the UK. Here is a list of the most common ones:

NAMES OF BUSINESSES

American	British
accounting firm	accountancy firm
car rental company	car hire firm
carrier, trucking company	haulier, haulage firm
chain store →	multiple shop, multiple store
drugstore	chemist
equipment rental	plant hire
funeral home, funeral parlor	funeral directors
hardware →	ironmonger
home improvement store	DIY centre [do-it-yourself]

NAMES OF BUSINESSES *(continued)*	
American	**British**
Laundromat®	launderette
liquor store[1]	off-licence
lumberyard	builder's merchant
moving company	(house) removals firm
newsstand	newsagent
slaughterhouse	abattoir
wrecking company	demolition contractor

[1] This is a very general term; laws governing sales of alcohol in sealed containers, and the terminology for where this happens, vary from state to state.

British English generally has the habit of using the possessive form of the agentive noun to refer to a small shop or business where that agent carries out work: thus the *butcher's*, the *hairdresser's*, the *estate agent's*. American English is more inclined to refer to these establishments by either (a) a name designating the business or office (*butcher shop, beauty salon, real estate office*), or (b) the name of the agent (*butcher, hairdresser, Realtor*).

The preference of Britons to say *shop* where Americans say *store* is widely known, though occasionally oversimplified. Both words are used in both dialects to designate retail establishments. Americans like *shop* for (1) small stores, (2) specialty stores, and (3) departments within larger stores that offer a particular line of merchandise. *Store* holds for just about everything else in American English. British English prefers shop for just about all retail establishments with a street address, except very large ones: *department store*, originally an Americanism, denotes the same thing in both dialects.

High-volume chain merchandising is differently organized and designated in the two countries. *Supermarket* is a more or less equivalent in the two dialects; the chain *discount stores* that are ubiquitous in the US (also called *super centers*, or *warehouse clubs* where a membership is required) are rare in the UK but have their closest equivalent in the *hypermarket*. This British term, derived from French *hypermarché*, nearly always designates a store that sells alcoholic beverages in addition to its many other offerings, and many of these are typically located at borders in other European countries.

The place where Britons go to look for a good many of the businesses listed above is *the high street*. This concept, owing to differences in urban geography and planning, doesn't really exist in the US. A limited comparison is possible with *Main Street*: the common elements are that (1) both in fact appear in the names of actual streets in many cities and towns in their respective countries, and (2) streets so referred to probably have a number of retail businesses on them; (3) both can be used, uncapitalized, to designate the principal business street in a village or small town. But there the comparison ends. The high street is the heart of UK retail trade, the place where both urban and village dwellers *go to the shops* (=AmE *go shopping*) for their routine needs. Outlying shopping areas offer some competition, but are a long way from killing off the high street, as the *mall* in the US is said to have done to Main Street. Aside from its literal denotation, *Main Street* in American English has quite a lot of figurative resonance, owing mainly to Upton Sinclair's 1920 novel by that name, a satirical portrait of small town life in the Midwest. It is used, both approvingly and disparagingly, to characterize traditional, usually conservative American values.

A scaled-down version of the high street is the *parade of shops*, a handful of retail outlets on a street that is not otherwise developed commercially. Its US functional equivalent is probably the *strip mall*—a row of single-story businesses with parking in front, on a street or highway—with the difference that you would be hard-pressed to find a parking space in front of a parade of shops. High street shops in the UK often observe a practice called *early closing*, in which they shut for one afternoon during the week.

Businesses that don't depend on walk-in customers, or whose products are not offered to the public, may be located on a *trading estate* in the UK, which is a mixed industrial and commercial area, or an *industrial estate*. The corresponding American terms are *business park* and *industrial park*, which are also used in British English. Businesses that require offices only are found in BrE *office blocks*, AmE *office buildings*.

In cities, such buildings are located in an area that American English dubs *downtown* and British English calls the *city centre*. Outside of large American cities, *downtown* also does some of the work of British *high street* in referring to the main commercial and retail area of a town: *She went downtown to do some shopping*. In New York City, specifically in Manhattan, *downtown* refers to the southern end of the island, where the financial district is located; the counterpart is *uptown*, the northern end of the island, with *midtown* occupying the space between.

Business Correspondence

There is little chance of a serious misunderstanding arising as a result of varying conventions in business correspondence in the US and the UK, but it is helpful to be aware of a few rules of thumb that operate especially in the UK. Business letters written to persons unknown by the sender, especially when that person is addressed only by title, are signed *Yours faithfully*. Those in which the addressee is known by the sender are signed *Yours sincerely*. Americans use this friendly closing or *Sincerely yours*, or simply *Sincerely* indiscriminately, regardless of the relationship between sender and addressee. The formula *To whom it may concern* is now considered too stuffy in American English for any kind of letter, though it may appear as part of a notice or testimonial; it has limited use in formal British English letters, without any intention to insult. Letter writers in both countries rely increasingly on software-supplied letter "wizards" in order to avoid responsibility for any choices in these matters.

The use of *Ms.* as a feminine courtesy title deliberately obscuring a woman's marital status has less currency in Britain than in the US, where it is often written, though less often pronounced, perhaps because its proper pronunciation is indistinguishable from some dialectal pronunciations of *Miss*, and thus defeats its own purpose. Britons, being far more advanced in the field of titles than Americans (see chapter 4), seem to reject this one for its purposeful vagueness. In American business correspondence, it is always proper to address a woman in the salutation as Ms. whether you know her marital status or not. In Britain, and indeed in many countries under the sway of British English, a convention exists whereby a woman may sign a business letter, for example, *Mildred Jones (Mrs)*, thereby tipping off her respondent as to the proper form for return correspondence.

Mailings in the UK that do not require a letter to accompany them and will suffice with a scrawled note or simply with the sender's identification use a handy device called the *compliments slip*, a small piece of paper on which a company's name, address, and logo are printed. An envelope in which a customer or consumer can write to a company without paying postage, because the postage is paid by the company, is a *business reply envelope* in American English. British English handles this convention under the term *Freepost*, the entire system of such envelopes and their users.

Business (and Personal) Failures

Businesses closed by their owners, possibly voluntarily, are *liquidated* in American English, *wound up* in British English. When the ending is not a voluntary choice, they are popularly said to *go bust* in American English, *go the wall* in British English, both standing for the more standard *go bankrupt.*

Some provisions of bankruptcy law in the US are known by the chapter of the statute in which they are enshrined, and are so reported in the media. These include

- *Chapter 11*, the commonest option, an arrangement under which an insolvent company (or once-wealthy individual) can reorganize and cooperate with creditors in order to avoid complete liquidation. This is usually reported in the media as *filing for Chapter 11 protection/reorganization/ bankruptcy.* Companies that *emerge from Chapter 11* have returned to successful operation.
- *Chapter 7*, also called *liquidation*, in which a court-appointed trustee liquidates the debtor's assets (if any) and distributes the proceeds among creditors who make a claim against them.
- *Chapter 13*, sometimes euphemistically called *debt consolidation*, in which a debtor with continuing income proposes a plan to repay creditors over a fixed period. At the end of the plan, remaining debts are discharged (but not debts for family support, fines, student loans, and drunk driving judgments).

The procedures for bankruptcy under English law that are commonly reported in the media are as follows, starting with the softest option:

- Under an *administration order*, a debtor makes regular payments to a court that distributes the money to creditors.
- A *creditors' voluntary liquidation* is initiated by a company's directors (or shareholders) but effectively controlled by creditors, who call all the shots regarding the disposal of assets and allocation of the proceeds therefrom.
- In *administrative receivership*, the assets of a company are put at the disposal of an official who liquidates them to pay creditors. This action is usually instigated by creditors. It is reported in the media as a company being *in receivership* or *in the hands of receivers.*
- *Compulsory liquidation*, also called a *bankruptcy order* (or informally, *winding-up*) is the closing of a business by court order, (usually initiated by a creditor) along with the appointment of an *official receiver* (a civil servant) who settles the company's debts.

The Business Alphabet

Both the US and the UK have a number of well-known companies and business organizations whose names (1) are reduced to initialisms in the press, or (2) consist only of an initialism, making what they do completely opaque to the uninitiated. Those already known internationally are omitted from the table.

BUSINESS ACRONYMS AND INITIALISMS

Name	Source	What is it?
ADM	US	Archer Daniels Midland; agribusiness conglomerate
BAA	UK	British Airports Authority; publicly traded company that owns major UK airports
BAT	UK	British American Tobacco
B&Q	UK	chain of home improvement stores
BP	UK	British Petroleum
BT	UK	British Telecom
CBI	UK	Confederation of British Industry [trade and influence group]
CSX	US	rail and transport conglomerate
CVS	US	drugstore chain
FT	UK	*The Financial Times*: daily financial newspaper
GE	US	General Electric [diversified conglomerate]
GM[1]	US	General Motors [makers of Chevrolet and many other cars]
HSBC	UK	a high street bank; formerly the Midland Bank
ICI	UK	chemical and manufacturing conglomerate
LSE	UK	London Stock Exchange
M&S	UK	Marks & Spencer, chain clothing retailer; affectionately called *Marks & Sparks*
MBNA	US	credit card issuer
MORI	UK	Market and Opinion Research International, the leading UK market research company
PG&E	US	Pacific Gas & Electric
3M	US	diversified manufacturing conglomerate
TIAA-CREF	US	financial services provider to professional educators
TRW	US	aerospace and defense giant
USS	US	US Steel
WSJ	US	*The Wall Street Journal*: daily financial newspaper

[1] This initialism in BrE is shorthand for *genetically modified*.

Woolies is the informal name in the UK for *Woolworth*, originally an American company that has now gone out of business in the US, though its former US stores were very much like the present-day Woolworth shops in the UK.

Business Products

A number of commercial products are so well known in their respective country that their trade name is used generically for all such products; some of these will be unfamiliar to the transatlantic reader or visitor. Products in the left-hand column of the table "Trademarked Products" are known in one country or another by a trademark name; the right-hand column identifies them for speakers of the other dialect. The list omits trademarks that are known in both countries (e.g., Frisbee, Spandex). Items in the right-hand column with an initial cap are also trademarks and can be considered equivalent or analogous products, unless indicated otherwise. Other chapters in the book have lists of trademarked, generically known food, household products, and clothing (chapter 7) and medicines (chapter 6).

TRADEMARKED PRODUCTS

Trademark	Source	What is it?
Anaglypta	UK	embossed wallpaper
AstroTurf	US	artificial grasslike playing surface
Autocue	UK	TelePromTer
Breathalyser	UK	a BrE spelling of Breathalyzer
Breathalyzer	US	Breathalyser
Bulldog clip	UK	sprung metal clip for holding papers; known in AmE but not noted as a trademark.
Calor gas	UK	liquid propane gas in portable tanks
Chubb lock	UK	deadbolt lock
Coleman lantern	US	portable gas light used by campers
Dumpster	US	skip
Elsan	UK	portable chemical toilet
Entryphone	UK	intercom between a building door and an apartment
Erector set	US	Meccano
Harlequin	US	publisher of women's romantic fiction; similar to BrE Mills & Boone
Identikit	UK	composite photograph [of a criminal suspect]
JCB	UK	backhoe
Mace	US	CS gas [not a trademark]

TRADEMARKED PRODUCTS *(continued)*

Trademark	Source	What is it?
Meccano	UK	Erector set
Mills & Boone	UK	publisher of women's romantic fiction; similar to AmE Harlequin
Naugahyde	US	Rexine
Orimulsion	UK	fuel consisting of bitumen emulsed in water
Perspex	UK	Plexiglas
Plexiglas	US	Perspex
Porta Potti	US	Portaloo
Portaloo	UK	Porta Potti
Primus stove	UK	portable cooking stove
Quonset hut	US	Nissen hut [not a trademark]
Rawlplug	UK	anchor bolt for drywall
Rexine	UK	Naugahyde
Rotavator	UK	a rototiller
Seeing Eye dog	US	guide dog for the blind
Sheetrock	US	plasterboard
Silly Putty	US	elastic claylike substance sold as a toy
Sterno	US	canned fuel used for cooking
Strimmer	UK	Weed-whacker
Styrofoam	US	polystyrene
Tannoy	UK	public address system
TelePrompTer	US	Autocue
Tilley lamp	UK	portable oil lamp
Tinkertoy	US	wooden toy
Tipp-Ex	UK	White Out
Weed-whacker	US	Strimmer
White Out	US	Tipp-Ex
Wiffle ball	US	perforated baseball-sized ball [a toy]
Winnebago	US	motorized caravan
Zippo	US	cigarette lighter with a hinged lid

Business Education

The term *business school* in American English is normally taken to mean a graduate institution with programs leading to an *MBA*. Admission to such programs normally requires a bachelor's degree, and scores from a battery of tests called the *GMAT*, for Graduate Management Admission

Test. In the UK, most business degrees are three- or four-year full time university courses leading to a BA, and requiring A-levels or GNVQs as part of the entry requirements. These terms are discussed in chapter 5. MBA courses in the UK are offered by some universities and tend to be modeled on the US variety with an emphasis on international business; some require GMAT scores for admission, as well as real-world work experience.

Insurance

Like many areas of business, the world of insurance operates in a similar fashion on both sides of the Anglophone Atlantic and differs mainly in terminology. The vocabulary of health and medical insurance is covered in chapter 6. The discussion below concerns all other kinds of insurance.

American English uses the word *insurance* for all particular types of insurance against loss or damage; British English does so as well except for *life insurance*, which is regarded as a general term for all forms of insurance against loss of life; *life assurance* is used specifically in British English for what American English deems *ordinary life* (or *whole-life*) *insurance*, as distinct from *term life insurance*. The part of loss payable by the insured before benefits begin is called the *deductible* in American English, the *excess* in British English.

British English has a few terms common in insurance that have no direct equivalents in American English; these include:

contents insurance. Insurance for the contents of one's house or flat, as distinct from insurance on the buildings. In the US these are usually combined into what is called a *homeowner's policy*, or for tenants who only need to insure contents, it is called *renter's insurance*.

fidelity insurance. Employer's insurance against losses due to dishonesty by employees.

with-profits. A policy that returns a portion of the profits of the insurance company to those insured by it. This is more or less the same thing as an AmE *participating policy*.

Likewise in American English there are a handful of commonly encountered terms that don't have a direct British English analog:

assigned risk. A risk, typically a driver, whose coverage is assigned by law to an agreed pool of insurers because no one would take the risk voluntarily, owing to a bad history.

convertible insurance. Insurance with a provision that entitles the policyholder to change it to a different form of insurance.

double indemnity. Payment of twice the stated benefit in the event of loss (usually death) resulting from specified causes or circumstances.[1]
first dollar coverage. A policy with no excess (deductible).

WORK

Employment

There is little difference in practice, but much difference in terminology between the US and the UK in matters of employment. Jobseekers in the US who prepare a written summary of their experience for presentation to prospective employers are likely to call it a *résumé*; the word is often written *resume*, without the accents, because context always makes clear that the verb *resume* is not meant. In the UK this same document is called a *CV* for *curriculum vitae*; in American English, the use of this term is limited to certain professions, such as medicine and academia, where it is presented in a different format and is considerably more detailed than a résumé.

A successful jobseeker is *hired* in the US, *taken on* in the UK. At this point he or she becomes an *employee* in the US. In British English, *employee* is usually used for nonexecutive workers, and is more or less synonymous with *member of staff*. Those at higher levels would more likely be called *(members of) management*. Workers found to perform satisfactorily may eventually be given a *raise* (AmE), or a *rise* (BrE), which is delivered, in the case of Britons, in their *pay packet*. This term should not be mistaken as an equivalent of American English *pay package*, which means the complete set of pay and benefits that come with a job. *Pay packet* in British English normally means the envelope in which pay is delivered to the employee, though it gets a fair amount of figurative use. Amounts of money that disappear from one's pay before it is seen (for taxes and the like, explained in the next chapter) are called *deductions* in American English, *stoppages* in British English.

When an employer wishes to terminate someone's employment for a specific reason she *fires* him in American English. The usual British English verb is *sack* or put differently, *give* someone *the sack*. Both terms have limited currency in the other dialect. Getting rid of a worker by assigning

---

1. This is the source (and title) of the 1944 noir film classic in which Barbara Stanwyck plots with an insurance salesman to benefit from an unexpected death.

him to duties he will probably find unacceptable is called *constructive dismissal* in British English, a term with no direct equivalent in American English. *Downsize*, an Americanism that now has universal English currency, started out being applied to companies but it is now conventional in American English to downsize individuals, that is, end their employment as part of a payroll-reducing exercise. The older and still current way of saying this is *make layoffs* or *lay off* workers in American English, and *make redundancies* in British English. A Briton so treated is said to be *redundant*.[1]

The American worker in such circumstances applies for *unemployment*, in full *unemployment compensation* or *unemployment insurance*; the Briton *signs on* or goes *on the dole*, the commoner terms for applying for *unemployment benefit*. It should be noted that *dole* is a general term in British English for any sort of benefit paid by the government that takes the place of wages; there are many, and their proper names change on a regular basis as different governments overhaul the benefits system. *Unemployment* in American English means only the benefit that partly replaces wages for a recently unemployed person, and is usually not available for more than six months. *Welfare* is the term, almost always used disparagingly in American English, for government support of the chronically unemployed and unemployable, though it is not the official name of any US government benefit.

JOBS AND PROFESSIONS

Professions that are more or less equivalent go by different names in Britain and the US.

JOBS AND PROFESSIONS

American	British
advice columnist	agony aunt/uncle
bar owner	publican
bartender	barman, barmaid
bellhop	bellboy →
carpenter	joiner[1]
certified public account (CPA)	chartered accountant
custom tailor	bespoke tailor

1. In BrE these terms apply by analogy to equipment, buildings, and other abstract objects that are not needed or not used: *a redundant warehouse/copy of a newspaper*. These usages do not exist in AmE, where *redundant*, apart from some technical usages, is more or less confined to (1) "repeated unnecessarily" and (2) "existing in excess."

JOBS AND PROFESSIONS *(continued)*	
American	**British**
flight attendant	air hostess/host
janitor	caretaker
longshoreman	docker
magician	conjuror
mover	removals man
pharmacist	chemist
(switchboard) operator	telephonist
traveling salesperson	commercial traveller
truck farmer	market gardener
floorwalker	shopwalker

[1] Both *carpenter* and *joiner* are used in both dialects, though *joiner* has negligible currency in AmE, while being the preferred BrE term for one who does fine or permanent woodwork.

Labor Disputes

An institution with very high visibility in the UK and no obvious US counterpart is the *employment tribunal*, a tribunal empowered to hear and adjudicate disputes between employees (individuals or small groups) and employers about such matters as redundancy, unfair dismissal, harassment, and the like. Such matters in the US are normally handled by private litigation and the courts. Major confrontations between management and unions are often mediated by the *NLRB* (National Labor Relations Board) in the US; a comparable body in the UK is *ACAS*, the taxpayer-funded Advisory, Conciliation, and Arbitration Service.

Unions

Besides the already noted distinction between American English *labor union* and British English *trade union*, a few other terms associated with organized labor deserve mentioning. Owing to the historically greater power that unions held in the UK there is more general terminology current in nontechnical British English that has its origins in labor than can be found in American English. Examples include *work to rule*, that is, to closely follow official working rules and hours in order to decrease production as a form of industrial action, and *down tools* as a way of saying *stop work*. Both of these enjoy some figurative use. British union members pay *subscriptions*, usually called *subs*, American members pay *dues*.

Acronyms and other terms associated with unionism that often appear unglossed in the press include the following:

UNION NAMES AND ACRONYMS

Term	Source	What is it?
AFL-CIO	US	umbrella organization for US unions
AFSCME	US	union representing state, county, and municipal government workers
AEEU	UK	Amalgamated Engineering and Electrical Union; see Amicus
AFTRA	US	American Federation of Television and Radio Artists
Amicus	UK	Union formed in 2002, merging the AEEU and MSF
ASLEF	UK	Train Drivers Union
BIFU	UK	Banking, Insurance, and Finance Union
CWU	UK	Communication Workers Union [includes post office staff]
IBT	US	International Brotherhood of Teamsters [more usually called the *Teamsters' Union*]
ILGWU	US	International Ladies' Garment Workers Union; forerunner of UNITE
ILWU	US	International Longshore and Warehouse Union
MSF	UK	broadly-based union representing skilled and professional workers in manufacturing, science, and finance [see Amicus]
NEA	US	National Education Association, a union of primary and secondary school teachers
NFU	UK	National Farmers' Union
NUJ	UK	National Union of Journalists
NUM	UK	National Union of Miners
NUT	UK	National Union of Teachers
RMT	UK	National Union of Rail, Maritime, and Transport Workers
SAG	US	Screen Actors Guild
TGWU	UK	Transport and General Workers' Union
TUC	UK	Trades Union Congress, an umbrella organization for unions
TWU	US	Transport Workers Union of America
UAW	US	United Auto Workers

UNION NAMES AND ACRONYMS *(continued)*

Term	Source	What is it?
UFW	US	United Farm Workers, a union that includes many low-paid migrant workers
UNISON	UK	broadly-based union representing workers in the health service and public sector
UNITE	US	Union of Needletrades, Industrial, and Textile Employees

CHAPTER FOUR

The Government and the Law

Most would agree that the collective will of the people is effected in roughly equal degrees in Britain and the United States, although the way this is achieved differs considerably in its general design and in all its particulars. The results of these differences on English is twofold: on the one hand, there are sets of terms relating to the workings of law and government that are very common in one country and unfamiliar in the other; on the other hand, there are identical terms that have quite different connotation or denotation in the two countries. This chapter focuses on the language relating to law and government that is likely to be encountered in general reading and in broadcast media whose meaning may not be readily apparent to the foreign reader or listener.

GOVERNMENT

Before we take a top-down look at the systems of government and the democratic process in each country it is worthwhile to examine the use of the most general term under consideration, namely, *government*. This word should be flagged by listeners, readers, or editors from both countries unfamiliar with its usage in the other. Without further qualifying context, *government* in the UK often means the political party currently in power, including the prime minister and all other ministers; it is they who form *the government*. The closest American English equivalent is *administration*, although an administration does not have control over a legislative program in the way that a government (in the British sense) does. The use of *government* or *federal government* in American English normally refers to the Congress and to the standing federal bureaucracy in Washington that exists, to some degree, independently of the current administration (which is chiefly identified with the president) and that has statutory authority to implement or enforce various laws and policies. An analogous British English term for this phenomenon—the unchanging part of national government—is *Whitehall*, but it is not an equivalent and interchangeable term for American *government*, as the following overviews should make clear.

The American System of Government

The US Constitution, ratified in 1788, defines the form of government in the United States. The Constitution provides a method for its own amendment (in Article 5) and this method was exploited almost immediately in the fledgling nation, resulting in ten amendments, ratified in 1791, that are popularly known as the *Bill of Rights*.[1] They guarantee various rights and freedoms to Americans and it is generally in reference to these that laws stand or fall; a law, ruling, or judgment that is found to breach an article or amendment of the constitution is deemed *unconstitutional* and is rescinded, voided, or withdrawn on that account.

The federal government is designed to have an in-built system of *checks and balances*, whereby any one of the three branches is prevented from seizing too much power. The court system (discussed below) is the judicial branch of federal government; the executive branch is represented by the president and vice-president, along with *executive agencies*; the legislative branch is made up of the *Congress*, which consists of the *Senate* and the *House of Representatives*. Members of the former are *senators*, of the latter *representatives*, though they are also called *congressmen, congresswomen*, or in cases of extreme correctness, *congresspersons*. The Senate consists of 100 members, 2 from each of the 50 states. The *House* consists of 435 members, each of whom represents a *congressional district*. All such districts (the same thing as a *constituency*, though that term

---

1. It was modeled on the English *Bill of Rights* (1688–89) in spirit, but is quite different in content. There are, however, many phrases from the English Bill of Rights that made their way intact into the American one and are now enshrined there, such as *cruel and unusual punishment*. The English Bill of Rights, along with the *Act of Settlement* (1700) were the main statutory instruments reducing the power of the sovereign in what became the UK.

is little used in American English in this sense[1]) are roughly equal in population, resulting in the most populous states having large numbers of representatives, and the smallest states having as few as 1. District boundaries are redrawn periodically as a result of population changes reflected in census figures; this process, almost always highly charged with politics, is called *redistricting*.

The leader of each of the two political parties in both houses of Congress is called the *floor leader*.[2] These are sometimes expanded to *Senate majority leader*, *House minority leader*, etc. The House majority leader is more typically called the *Speaker of the House*.

Legislation may be introduced in either house of Congress, but does not become law until passed by both houses and signed by the president. Bills are introduced by individual members of Congress via a convention called the *first reading*, in which the general purpose of the bill is made known. The bill is then referred to a *committee* whose business is to scrutinize its particulars, sometimes holding public *hearings* in which experts and others can make their views known. A committee may also decide to *table* a bill, that is, kill it altogether. The bill modified by committee returns to the house that originated it for the sentence-by-sentence *second reading*, which initiates a period of debate and amendments. In the House, debate is limited by a convention called the rule of *cloture*. No such rule exists in the Senate, where senators may effectively stop serious debate on a bill by means of a *filibuster*, in which a senator rattles on about nothing but refuses to yield the floor, thus effectively stopping debate. A bill that passes its second reading returns for a *third reading*, merely a formality that precedes a vote. If the bill passes, it goes to the other house, where it can be defeated, or passed, with or without (further) amendments. If passed with amendments, a *joint committee* is set up, comprising members from both houses, to reconcile the differences. A bill in this period is often referred to as being *in conference*, and it is a time-honored place for legislation to meet an untimely end. When this happens, it is reported that a bill *died in conference*. After final passage by both houses, the bill is sent to the president to sign or *veto*. The president effects a *pocket veto* by refusing to sign a bill within ten days sent to him by Con-

---

1. *Constituency* in American English is not used of Congressional districts, but may be used of the people inhabiting one; its more usual use is to denote a body of supporters or advocates of something: *baseball's constituency, the constituency supporting reparations for slavery*.

2. This term has made its way into basketball figuratively to denote the team captain or leading player of a team.

gress at the end of their session, before they adjourn. The proceedings of Congress are recorded in an official publication called the *Congressional Record*.

The president is aided and advised by his *cabinet*, a group of fourteen heads of the main government departments whom the president appoints, but who are subject to approval by the Senate. Members of the cabinet, called *secretaries*, (except for the *attorney general*, the chief law enforcement officer) are not members of Congress but are nearly always of the same political party and philosophy as the president and are typically chosen from the Congress, private industry, and from state government. They have limited executive powers and they are not meant to be, nor are they perceived as, the spokespeople and proponents of government policy that British cabinet members are. Some other officials attend cabinet meetings and are for all practical purposes members of it, including the vice president, the president's *chief of staff* (in effect, his office manager and spokesman), and the heads of the Environmental Protection Agency, the Office of Homeland Security, and the Office of Management and Budget.

The British System of Government

Though often called a constitutional monarchy, Britain in fact has no constitution and its status as a democracy rests on the sovereignty of the democratically elected constituent of its *parliament*, which is the *House of Commons*. The history of British politics can be seen as the gradual separation of church, state, and *Crown*, which is the power or authority residing in the monarchy. These three coexist with each other comfortably today in large part by not overstepping the limits of their authority, which in the case of the Crown and the Church is very limited. The Crown and the Church (the officially established *Church of England*) have largely ceremonial functions and considerable influence behind the scenes, but no vested legislative or executive powers. The parliament consists of two houses, the *House of Commons* and the *House of Lords*. (Technically the monarch is the third component of parliament but is probably least in people's minds when they use the term.) The *Commons* is popularly elected, with each of 659 *constituencies* (political divisions, similar to US districts) of the country electing 1 member of parliament, or *MP*. The House of Lords, formerly populated mostly by members of the hereditary aristocracy, now is made up largely of *life peers* (see below, under "Royalty and Aristocracy"). *The Lords*, as they are popularly called, cannot initiate legislation but they can significantly alter legislation that originates in *the Commons*. The makeup of the Lords is in transition at present as it moves from the historical body composed of hereditary peers to a more representative one made up of elected or appointed members.

The political party that wins the greatest number of seats in a *general election* (see below, under "Political Parties and Elections"), forms a *government*, which consists of the *prime minister* (leader of the winning political party) and the *cabinet*. The cabinet consists of about two dozen officials, called *secretaries of state*, who are also MPs from the ruling political party and who are appointed to their posts by the prime minister. Their qualifications for such posts are not usually called into question, and in any case they change jobs with some regularity, when the prime minister does a *cabinet reshuffle*. These cabinet members head various departments, offices, and ministries. In all the prime minister chooses over one hundred officials from among his MPs to fill top government posts. These officials are mostly called *ministers*, although only one top level department is still called a *ministry*, the Ministry of Defence; the modernizing trend has been to change the names of ministries to *departments*. Cabinet members whose job is not necessarily obvious from their title include:

- The *Chancellor of the Exchequer*, who is the finance minister. His role is analogous to that of the US *Secretary of the Treasury*, except that he is vested with more authority and is a much more high-profile public figure.
- The *Lord Chancellor*, who presides in the House of Lords and is the chief law officer; to some degree comparable to the US *Attorney General*.
- The *Secretary of State for Foreign and Commonwealth Affairs*, or *Foreign Secretary* for short (like the US *Secretary of State*).
- The *Secretary of State for the Home Department* or *Home Secretary* for short, who heads the *Home Office*.

The *Home Office* deals with domestic affairs including law and order (police departments ultimately report to it), immigration and passports, and broadcasting. There is no equivalent US department, these functions being divided up by different departments and agencies of the US government. The newly created *Office of Homeland Security* in the US may prove to be a functional equivalent of the UK Home Office. Comparison is sometimes made with the US *Department of the Interior*, which is not a close analogy: *Interior* deals mainly with federally owned lands, the geological survey, national parks, and Indian affairs.

Among the first duties of a newly elected British government is to propose a program of legislation. It is advocacy of this program that, in principle, led to their election, and since they have a majority in parliament, carrying out the program successfully would seem to be a mere formality. The program of legislation is laid out in the *Queen's speech*, delivered to the assembled parliament by the monarch soon after the new government is in place. The legislative program is introduced to parliament in the form of *government bills* introduced in the House of Commons. The *first reading* of a bill is a formal announcement before it is printed and published. On its *second reading*, the bill is explained to the House by the minister responsible for it, so that it can be debated. If the bill passes its second reading, it is then considered clause by clause in *Committee*, which may amend it. If this happens it is reported back to the House, where it is further considered. MPs may *table* amendments, that is, bring them forward for discussion; thus *table* means nearly the opposite in British English political contexts to what it is in American English. The next stage is the *third reading*, which if successful causes the bill to pass to the House of Lords, where a similar process takes place. When all differences are reconciled, the reigning monarch gives perfunctory approval, called the *Royal Assent*, and the bill becomes an *Act of Parliament*.

Discussion of a bill may sometimes be brought to a rapid close by a *guillotine motion*, sometimes just called a *guillotine*, which sets a specific time for a vote on part or all of a bill. Legislation may also be introduced by individual MPs in the form of *private member's bills*. These rarely become law and are introduced mainly as a way of calling attention to a particular matter. Another device frequently used and reported in the media is the *early day motion*, which can be introduced by a member without the expectation that it will be debated but with the intention of drawing attention to an issue, and to elicit support for it by inviting other members to sign on to it. The proceedings of Parliament are recorded in an official publication called *Hansard*.

The business of Parliament is conducted for the most part in a gentlemanly way that camouflages to some degree the dualistic antagonism that is inherent in it. MPs sit facing each other on long rows called *benches* in the House of Commons, with ruling members on one side and opposition members on the other. The prime minister and the cabinet, composed of senior members or technically, secretaries of state, sit on the *front bench* on their side of the house. Other MPs who hold no ministerial positions sit behind them, and are thus called *backbenchers*.

The main opposition party forms a *shadow government*[1] that mirrors all the positions in the real government; thus the shadow home secretary is the opposition party MP who would be appointed home secretary if that party were in power, and so forth. The media sometimes does not bestow such makeshift titles on these "shadow" figures and may identify them as, for example, the "shadow spokeswoman for education" instead of the "shadow education minister."[2] The leader of the main opposition party is simply called the *leader of the opposition*, not the shadow prime minister. All of these, the would-be government if the election had gone the other way, sit on the front bench of the opposition side. The British media does not permit a single word or deed of a government minister to pass without eliciting a (usually disparaging) comment about it from that minister's shadow figure in the opposition.

On Wednesday afternoons when Parliament is in session, there is half an hour for *prime minister's question time* (occasionally reduced to *PMQ* in the press), in which the prime minister and leaders of the other parties have an opportunity to air their views on important questions. The occasion is usually viewed as a performance gauge of opposition party leaders, as well as of the prime minister.

The political parties in the legislatures of both countries have members who are called *whips*. Their job is roughly the same, to inform and organize the members of their parties and to ensure their presence at important votes. Congressional whips are elected by their parties; parliamentary whips are appointed by their leaders. Whips of the ruling party in the UK are called *government whips*. In British English the term *whip* also applies to the weekly circular that parliamentary members receive notifying them of upcoming business. The degree of importance ascribed to each item in the circular is indicated by the number of times that it is underlined; a *three-line whip* is a matter of great urgency for which attendance is mandatory.

ROYALTY AND ARISTOCRACY

A matter of opacity for foreigners except those who take a studied interest in it, Britain's aristocracy and its relationship to royalty and to the

---

1. This term has an altogether different meaning in American English, where it is been recently resuscitated from a twentieth-century wartime use: that of having a functional skeleton government in hiding at a secret location that would wield the levers of power in the event of an attack on the actual seat of government. British English has dubbed this *parallel government* to prevent confusion with its established use of the term.

2. The compound *opposite number* is also used in British English in this context and many others, for which the nearest American English equivalent is *counterpart: her opposite number on the government bench; a senior diplomat meeting with his opposite number in Cyprus.*

government via Parliament is a cornerstone of British society and a pivotal component in its politics, so it is appropriate to treat it here. The aristocracy is the bedrock on which the British class system rests, quite heavily in the minds of many, and it is the institution that mainly perpetuates the class system. The titles associated with it are taken very seriously by Britons; the media takes them up for newly-made aristocrats the moment they are announced. Titles are always used in address and with reference to those who hold them in all formal and non-intimate contexts. Here is a primer.

The five ranks of *peerage* are graded, in order of seniority from the top: *duke, marquess, earl, viscount*, and *baron*. These are all titles for men. The title or position of a *duke* (*dukedom*) is hereditary and associated with a holding of land. The eldest son of a duke is a *marquess* who will eventually succeed to the dukedom. The eldest son of a marquess is a *viscount*, who will succeed his father in turn. The title of *earl* was traditionally associated with appointed government officials and is regarded as the equivalent of the continental title of *count*, which does not exist in the British aristocracy. A marquess, an earl, and a viscount are referred to by their titles and addressed as *lord*. A baron is addressed and referred to as *Lord*. Below all of these titles is the hereditary *baronet*, who is considered a commoner but addressable as *sir*. Baronets collectively make up the *baronetage*.

Women normally accede to titles by marriage; those who hold titles in their own right are not styled differently than the wives or widows of titleholders. Women who hold titles as widows have *dowager* prefixed to the title name. The corresponding feminine titles for the five ranks noted above are *duchess, marchioness, countess, viscountess*, and *baroness*. The last four are addressed and referred to as *lady*.

In addition to the hereditarily titled persons, the government creates a few new title holders by recognizing individuals twice yearly for their outstanding achievement in various fields. These *honours* have the whiff of the aristocracy about them; they are chiefly a vehicle for democratizing the hereditary aristocracy, supplying titular distinction to those who didn't get it by accident of birth. *Birthday Honours* are announced in June, coinciding with the queen's birthday; *New Year's Honours* are published at the new year. Recipients (about fifteen hundred each round) receive *investiture* from the queen or a lesser royal in a ceremony around those times.

The vast majority of people receiving government *honours* do not receive titles but instead are nominated to membership of various orders. Most are admitted to the grand-sounding *Order of the British Empire* (created when there still was an empire). This order is divided into five classes, each with military and civilian divisions, ranked as follows from the top. The initialisms are sufficient to identify the divisions to most Britons, and they follow the name of those on whom the honor is conferred.

ORDERS OF THE BRITISH EMPIRE

Initialism	Expansion
GBE	Knight or Dame Grand Cross
KBE/DBE	Knight or Dame Commander
CBE	Commander
OBE	Officer
MBE	Member

The two highest classes entail the awarding of a knighthood and the title of *knight* for men and *dame* for women, which entitle the bearer to be styled *sir* or *dame*, a convention that is immediately and strictly observed by the media. Wives of knights are styled as *lady*. Their children become *honourable*, though usually only in written address (with the abbreviation *Hon* preceding their names).

Life Peerages are also awarded by the government as part of the honours system; these carry the title of *baron* or *baroness* and give the holder the right to be called *sir* or *lady*, but the title is not heritable. Bearers are also entitled to sit in the House of Lords. All members of the House of Lords carry either a hereditary title or a title arising out of a life peerage. Together they comprise the *Lords Temporal*. (For clerics in the House of Lords, see under "Religion" in chapter 11). The Lords was formerly made up mostly of hereditary peers; they were removed by legislation at the end of the twentieth century and promulgated early in the twenty first, but they retain their titles. The Lords now consists mainly of members with life peerages, that is, barons and baronesses.

The monarch is the *head of state*; besides reading the annual speech to Parliament (noted above), she and her family have many official functions to perform. They act as *patrons* to many charitable and nonprofit institutions, thus lending them legitimacy and aiding in their fundraising efforts. The monarch is also the *Head of the Commonwealth* and the head of state many Commonwealth countries. Official expenses for the monarchy are provided for by the *Civil List*, a multimillion-pound sum provided annually by Parliament to meet her official expenses, which consist largely of paying her staff. In addition, *Grants-in-Aid* from Parliament provide upkeep of the royal palaces and for royal travel. The *Privy Purse* is income for the

Sovereign's public and private use; its main source is income earned by the *Duchy of Lancaster*, a landed estate owned by the crown since the late middle ages and administered by a cabinet minister. The royal family owns many other properties throughout the UK, some of which have multiple accommodation units on them which are let free, often to retired royal servants. These are referred to by the term *grace and favour*: *a grace and favour cottage/house/apartment.*

Political Parties and Elections

The US Constitution provides for presidential elections to be held every four years; this happens in years that are evenly divisible by four. Voting takes place on *election day*, the first Tuesday in November. In anticipation of this, aspirants to national office attempt to win *primary elections* (*caucuses* in some states serve a similar function) in which voters in each political party nominate their candidates for national office. The presidential and vice-presidential candidates for each party are chosen at large and noisy conventions during the summer preceding the election; together, these two constitute the *ticket* for that party. It is at the conventions that the party *platform* (BrE *manifesto*) is finalized and presented; it consists of various *planks* (individual items in the platform addressing various issues). Politicians campaigning for office are said to be *on the stump* and they make *stump speeches*.

Only two political parties have any significance in American politics, the *Democratic* party, and the *Republican* party, which is also called the *GOP* (for Grand Old Party). The press identifies legislators with an agreed shorthand that indicates which house of congress they belong to and which political party they represent: *Rep. Roscoe Bartlett R Maryland* says that he is a *Republican* congressman from Maryland; *Sen. Hilary Clinton D New York* says that she is a *Democratic* senator from New York.

A UK *general election* (one in which every seat in the House of Commons is up for grabs) must be held at least every five years. In practice they are held about every four years, on a date chosen by the prime minister; this is when he decides to *go to the country*, as the pundits have it. When the date (*polling day*) is fixed, the prime minister introduces a bill that brings about the *dissolution of parliament*, and the entire country is then subjected to a brief but extremely intense period of campaigning, sometimes called the *hustings* or the *run-up to the election*, during which the main political parties set out their *manifestos*, that is, their beliefs as

expressed through specific legislative proposals. MPs, both sitting and as-
piring, are said to *stand for election* (AmE *run for office*). An MP who
chooses to retire rather than stand for election again is said to *stand down*.
Candidates for the various constituencies are chosen by the political parties and are not required to have been a resident of that constituency, as
they are in the US. The main political parties are the *Conservative* party,
also called *Tories*, and the *Labour* party. There are several smaller and
generally insignificant parties. One, the *Liberal Democrats*, generally wins
enough seats to be considered a strategic instrument by the other two parties. The press has two standard formulas for associating MPs with their
party and constituencies: the long form is, *Diane Abbott, the Labour MP
for Hackney North*; the short form is *Diane Abbott* (*Lab, Hackney North*).
Abbreviations for the other main parties used in the short form are: *C*
(Conservative), and *LD* (Liberal Democrats). A handful of small parties
who together hold just over two dozen seats in the commons are the *SNP*
(Scottish National Party), *PC* (Plaid Cymru, the Welsh national party),
DUP (Democratic Unionist Party), *SDLP* (Social Democratic & Labour
Party), *SF* (Sinn Fein), and *UUP* (Ulster Unionist Party). The last four are
confined to Northern Ireland.

As the votes are counted and the winner is determined in the wee
hours following polling day, the *seat* is *declared* for a particular party. Political parties that feel assured of a victory in a particular constituency call it a
safe seat and assign a candidate to it whose presence in the Commons is
considered essential. The party winning the most seats in an election is the
winner, and forms a government. This is called the *first past the post* system, and is often contrasted with *proportional representation*, a system
whereby seats are assigned to parties on the basis of the percentage of votes
cast for that party or for candidates for that party. If there is no clear majority in the voting, a *hung parliament* results. If an MP dies or resigns in
office, a special election, called a *by-election*, is held to fill the seat.

There is a difference in usage of the term *majority* when reporting
election results between American English and British English. An American English *majority* is the number of votes by which the greater number
surpasses the remainder of votes and must exceed 50 percent of the total
number; a British English *majority* is the number of votes by which the
greater number surpasses those cast for the next party in rank. This would
be called a *plurality* in American English, or a case of *no clear majority*.
British English uses *absolute majority* in the American sense, i.e., more
than half of votes cast.

Government Alphabet Soup

The following two tables set out alphabetically the acronyms for government departments, agencies, and organizations that are typically encountered unglossed in journalism, particularly in headlines. Also included are organizations that are not strictly a part of the government but have governmental links. An explanation is provided for those entities whose name is not transparent. In the UK more than in the US there is a tendency for the national government to reorganize itself regularly, throwing out rafts of initials as it does so; for that reason, the ones associated with the UK tend to date or become obsolete more quickly.

US GOVERNMENT ACRONYMS

Acronym	What is it?
ATF	Bureau of Alcohol, Tobacco, and Firearms [investigates crimes involving these]
BIA	Bureau of Indian Affairs [part of DOI]
BLM	Bureau of Land Management [part of DOI]
CAA	Civil Aeronautics Administration[1]
CDC	Centers for Disease Control, public health branch of HHS
CIA	Central Intelligence Agency
DOC	Department of Commerce
DOD	Department of Defense
DOI	Department of the Interior
DOT	Department of Transportation
EEOC	Equal Employment Opportunities Commission
EPA	Environmental Protection Agency
FBI	Federal Bureau of Investigation
FCC	Federal Communications Commission [regulates broadcasting and telecommunications]
FDA	Food and Drug Administration
FDIC	Federal Deposit Insurance Corporation [insures bank deposits]
FEMA	Federal Emergency Management Agency
FTC	Federal Trade Commission [consumer protection and education; antitrust enforcement]
GAO	Government Accounting Office [audits use of public resources within the government; the investigative arm of Congress]

US GOVERNMENT ACRONYMS   *(continued)*

Acronym	What is it?
GPO	Government Printing Office [see "Government Publications," below]
GSA	General Services Administration [manages federal property, records, etc.]
HHS	Department of Health and Human Services [administers most benefit programs]
HUD	Department of Housing and Urban Development [administers public housing and home ownership programs]
IRS	Internal Revenue Service [see "Taxation," below]
NASA	National Aeronautics and Space Administration
NEA	National Endowment of the Arts
NEH	National Endowment for the Humanities
NG	National Guard [like the TA in the UK]
NIH	National Institutes of Health, research arm of HHS
NLRB	National Labor Relations Board [like ACAS in UK]
NOAA	National Oceanic and Atmospheric Administration
NRC	Nuclear Regulatory Commission
NSA	National Security Agency [intelligence gathering, decoding, and security]
NSC	National Security Council [standing committee chaired by the president and including top military officers and advisors]
NSF	National Science Foundation [oversees funding for scientific research]
OMB	Office of Management and Budget
OPM	Office of Personnel Management
OSHA	Occupational Safety and Health Administration [like HSE in UK]
SBA	Small Business Administration [aid programs for small businesses]
SEC	Securities and Exchange Commission [like FSA in UK]
USDA	US Department of Agriculture
USGS	US Geological Survey [publishes maps and other geological information]
USPS	US Postal Service [the post office]
VA	Department of Veterans' Affairs [administers all benefit programs for former armed forces members]

[1] See identical initialism in the UK table.

UK GOVERNMENT ACRONYMS

Acronym	What is it?
ACAS	Advisory, Conciliation, and Arbitration Service [mediates labor disputes; like NLRB in US]
CAA	Civil Aviation Authority
CID	Criminal Investigation Department [of the police]
CPS	Crown Prosecution Service [see under "Law," below]
Defra	Department for Environment, Food, and Rural Affairs
DfES	Department for Education and Skills
DfID	Department for International Development
DoE	Department of the Environment
DoH	Department of Health
DPP	Director of Public Prosecutions [see under "Law," below]
DSS	Department of Social Services [administered benefits; now defunct, partly replaced by DWP, but the name persists in popular usage]
DTI	Department of Trade and Industry
DTLR	Department for Transport, Local Government, and the Regions
DVLA	Driver and Vehicle Licensing Agency
DWP	Department for Work and Pensions [administers pensions, benefits, and employers' services]
EOC	Equal Opportunities Commission
FCO	Foreign and Commonwealth Office [responsible for overseas relations and foreign affairs; analogous to US State Department]
FSA	Financial Services Authority [like SEC in US]
GCHQ	Government Communications Headquarters [where intelligence is gathered and analyzed]
HMSO	Her Majesty's Stationery Office [see "Government Publications," below]
HSE	Health and Safety Executive [like OSHA in US]
IMRO	Investment Management Regulatory Organization [now defunct; predecessor to FSA]
IR	Inland Revenue [see "Taxation," below]
MAFF	Ministry of Agriculture, Fisheries, and Food [now defunct; replaced by Defra in 2001]
MI5	secretive national security service
MI6	international intelligence service
MOD	Ministry of Defence

UK GOVERNMENT ACRONYMS   *(continued)*

Acronym	What is it?
MOT	Ministry of Transport [defunct, but the name persists; see chapter 8]
NDPD	see "Quangos," below
NHS	National Health Service
NRA[1]	National Rivers Authority
OFT	Office of Fair Trading [consumer protection]
PCC	Press Complaints Commission [independent print media watchdog]
RDA	Regional Development Agency
RUC	Royal Ulster Constabulary [N Ireland police]
TA	Territorial Army [like the NG in the US]
VOA	Valuation Office Agency [evaluates properties for tax purposes]

[1] This initialism in the US is overwhelmingly associated with the *National Rifle Association*, a private organization that opposes legislation to control gun ownership.

A number of industry watchdog organizations in the UK under the OFT have a common naming scheme; these are OFGEM (gas & electric markets), OFSTED (education), OFTEL (telecommunications), and OFWAT (water services).

Quangos and Their Kin

The UK has a class of organizations that go by the name of *quango*, an acronym for *quasi-autonomous national governmental organization*. In the past the workings of these were cloaked in secrecy and they were popularly believed to consist entirely of mutually admiring establishment figures, thus constituting a closed old-boy network, which led to a negative perception of them by the public and the media. They are now called *NDPDs* by the government—an initialism for *non-departmental public body*—though *quango* persists in popular usage. There is no exact equivalent in the US, though many of the *independent agencies* and *independent commissions* of the federal government (i.e., ones that do not answer to a particular government department) might be seen as functional equivalents, such as the Environmental Protection Agency, the National Endowment for the Arts, or the US Information Agency. The unifying idea of all these organizations is that they are supposed to act independently of politics and the influence of vested interests, and this is of course the substance of the main charges usually leveled against them.

Government Publications

As would be expected in two advanced democracies, the governments in the UK and the US publish a bewildering variety of documents, in many cases as a necessary step in complying with law. The government bodies overseeing official publications are *Her Majesty's Stationary Office* (*HMSO*) in the UK and the *Government Printing Office* (*GPO*) in the US. Access to US government information is provided for in the *Freedom of Information Act* (*FOIA*), a very wide-ranging piece of Federal legislation (1966) that sets out rules for disclosure from federal agencies. It is sometimes compared, as a contrast in approach, with the UK *Official Secrets Act*, a 1989 Act of Parliament that was passed with the intention of saving governments from the embarrassment of disclosures from former spies.

Besides the above-mentioned *Hansard* and *Congressional Record*, the two most important government publications are the *London Gazette* in the UK, the official newspaper of the Crown which has been published regularly since the seventeenth century, and the *Federal Register*, a daily publication of the US government. They are roughly functional equivalents. The *London Gazette* publishes a wide range of official notices, corporate and personal insolvency notices, lists of those receiving honors and awards (see "Royalty and Aristocracy," above), and armed forces promotions and regradings. The *Federal Register* publishes rules, proposed rules, and notices of federal agencies and organizations, as well as executive orders and other presidential documents. Both are accessible on the Internet: the *London Gazette* at www.london-gazette.co.uk, and the *Federal Register* via the GPO website, www.gpo.gov.

Subnational Political Geography

There is considerable overlap in the terminology of political and administrative divisions below the national level in the US and the UK; identical terms sometimes do, and sometimes don't represent the same thing. The UK as a whole, and the individual states of the US, are divided into *counties*. The exceptions are the state of Louisiana, where the equivalent unit is the *parish*, and the state of Alaska, where the unit is the *borough*. Counties in the two countries should not be considered comparable units, however, because of vast disparities in population and the very different scales they represent on the whole: some US states have more counties than the whole of the UK has, while some UK counties have a population greater than that of entire US states. The North Slope borough of Alaska is roughly the same size as the island of Great Britain.

In the UK, counties are sometimes called *shires* and many of their names end with this word; but *shires* also has the connotation of a rural place that upholds traditional values, and thus may be used in contrast to urban areas and values. The counties that form a ring around London are called the *home counties*. The town serving as the administrative center of a county is called a *county town* in British English, a *county seat* in American English.

It is usual in the US to have a single popularly elected official at the head of every political subdivision, more or less mirroring the federal system of having an executive office separate from the legislature. Typical names for such officials are as follows:

LOCAL US ELECTED OFFICIALS

Political Division	Title
state	governor
city	mayor[1]
county	commissioner

[1] *Mayor* also exists as a title for a local official in the UK. Their functions are often ceremonial and they typically do not have the executive powers that US mayors enjoy, except for the newly created office of the mayor for London, which is distinct from the *Lord Mayor*, who is a ceremonial figure.

Administrative divisions below the county level in the UK may go by the name of *city*, *town*, *parish* (England only), *community* (Wales only), *district* (often mainly rural), or *borough* (nearly always urban). Each of these units has an elected governing council that is referred to merely as *the council*, where it means roughly, the authority that is responsible for whatever thing is under discussion. A *unitary authority* is one that has supplanted authorities that formerly overlapped or were in a hierarchy. Councils are typically under the control of a single political party, typically the one whose philosophy prevails in the area. A council with no clear majority is a *hung council*. Laws at the local level are usually called *bylaws* in British English and may be called *ordinances* in American English.

London is separate from the county system and is divided into boroughs, which belong either to *Inner London* or *Outer London*. At the center of these is the *City of London*, or just *the City*, which is in effect the financial district of London.[1] *Greater London* (comprising all of the foregoing) is governed by an entity called the *Greater London Authority* (*GLA*).

The six counties of Northern Ireland are collectively called *Ulster*.

US states devise their own governments, which vary considerably in their organization and terminology; some have a bicameral legislature that mirrors the federal government; others have a single elected house. The place where this legislature meets is typically called the *statehouse*. Within US states, it is the business of the state government to devise divisions smaller than the county, and they vary considerably. East of the Mississippi, and in the Northeast especially, the *township* (*Twp.*) is a common sub-county division. Some less populous western states have no administrative divisions below the county level except cities and towns. Typically these are governed by popularly elected *councils*. The term *village* is little used in American English for settlements within the contemporary US; *small town* takes its place. *Village* in American English is more typically associated with Old World or Third World locales. Divisions within US cities are typically called *wards*, *precincts*, or *boroughs*.

Taxation

Methods whereby all of the foregoing is prevented from collapsing in a heap, generally called taxation, are similar in their effects in both countries and differ mainly in terminology. The chief UK taxing authority is the *Inland Revenue* (*IR*), which answers to Treasury ministers. The US counterpart is the *Internal Revenue Service* (*IRS*), a division of the US Treasury. Citizens of both countries pay income tax. The UK system is relatively simple and straightforward; many individuals in regular employment do not file a return at all and simply assume that the IR will figure their taxes correctly, deducting what is owed them from employment pay and returning any excess to the taxpayer in a yearly reckoning. The US system is astonishingly byzantine; an entire industry peopled by lawyers, accountants, tax return preparers, and software vendors assists individuals in preparing their annual income tax returns, which are too complicated and time-consuming

1. The UK media uses *the City* in about the same way that the US media uses *Wall Street*.

for the average taxpayer to prepare alone. As a result, the vocabulary of taxation in American English is more detailed and more widely circulated than its equivalent in British English.

The main tax form that Americans fill out is called the *1040* (pronounced "ten-forty"). Hundreds of other forms are available by means of which the taxpayer tries to find relief. The most popular is *Schedule A*, the form on which *itemized deductions* are listed; British English would probably phrase this as "claims against tax." The amount of tax-free income allowed is called *exemption* in American English, *personal allowance* in British English. In addition to federal income tax, many US citizens also pay state and sometimes local income taxes as well, and submit forms to their state governments for these.

TAXES ON GOODS AND SERVICES

VAT (Value Added Tax) is a UK (and European Union) tax on nearly all goods and services (exceptions: most food, books, newspapers, and young children's clothing) at the point of consumption, and is administered by *HM Customs and Excise*, a government department that exists mainly for this purpose. The billions of pounds of revenue that VAT generates yearly is used mainly to fund spending by the European Union. VAT may be compared to US state or city *sales tax*, with these differences: (1) VAT is a whopping 17.5 percent, higher than any US body would dare to charge for fear of inciting revolution; (2) VAT is usually already included in quoted prices at the retail level, even though this may not be specifically stated. A price quoted as *exclusive of VAT* will be 17.5 percent higher when you hand over the money. US *sales tax*, on the other hand, is added at the point of sale, and thus occasionally presents an unpleasant surprise for visiting British shoppers. The rate is set by individual states and municipalities; some places have none whatever, and it rarely exceeds 10 percent in the most heavily taxed areas, usually big cities. States also differ in which items are exempt from sales tax.

TAXES FOR PUBLIC SERVICES

Most Americans who are homeowners pay *property tax*, a tax usually administered at the state or local level and based on a percentage of the property's assessed value, which is periodically reevaluated. Amounts vary widely even from one community to another, and in very affluent communities may reach several hundred dollars a month; the tax is typically paid monthly into an escrow account by adding an additional amount to mortgage payments. The functional equivalent of this in the UK is the *council tax*, the contemporary term for a charge to all adults that pays for government services, mostly local ones. Starting in the 1980s, when it replaced the time-honored *rates*, it has been through several modifications under different governments and variously called the *community charge*, or pejoratively, the *poll tax*. The amount payable by each adult is set by local authorities and varies according to the value of property, set out in *council tax property bands* (currently there are eight); properties are valuated by a central government authority, the *Valuation Office Agency* (*VOA*). Relief is available to unemployed and low-income people. Businesses still pay *rates*, based on the size of their premises and its location.

EMPLOYMENT TAXES

Money is taken out of employment pay by various authorities for similar purposes in the US and the UK, but goes by different names. The largest chunk in each country goes for income taxes; after this comes what the US government calls *social security* and what HM government calls *national insurance*. True to the terminology, every working American has a *social security number* (*SSN*) and every working Briton has a *national insurance number* (*NINO*). The funds fed by these income streams support retired people and disabled people. *FICA* (for Federal Insurance Contributions Act) is the recurring initialism for Social Security deductions in the US; in the UK, there are three buzzwords: *PAYE* (for pay as you earn, designating deductions for tax); *Serps* (for State Earnings-Related Pension Scheme); and *Nics* (National Insurance contributions). A major difference between the two systems is that Britons can opt out of Serps, but Americans at present cannot opt out of FICA deductions. Serps was replaced in 2002 by a new initialism, *SSP*, for State Second Pension, but the old acronym remains popular.

Other Government Bodies and Institutions

Two confusingly similar terms in British English are *the Met* and *the Met Office*. Both are popular short forms, the first for the *Metropolitan Police*, the force that patrols London, and the second for the *Meteorological Office*, which is the UK equivalent of the US *National Weather Service*.[1]
The system whereby a government body may seize privately owned

1. In American English, by contrast, *the Met* denotes either the Metropolitan Opera House, or the Metropolitan Museum of Art, both in New York.

real property when it is in the public interest is accomplished by means of a *compulsory purchase order* in the UK. In the US, the property is first *condemned*, which in law has the special meaning of declaring it unfit for any other purpose. It can then be acquired by the competent authority under the right of *eminent domain*.

LAW

Criminal Justice, Courts, and Police

Both countries have an adversarial justice system and many elements of the early American system were modeled on the English ones. They have evolved independently over time to become separate systems entirely with unique terminology and a few identical terms that do not designate the same thing. We will look at the legal systems of each country in turn, highlighting terms likely to be encountered in literature and the news media that need explanation for speakers of the other dialect.

THE PROSECUTION OF CRIME

The trail from crime to punishment follows similar pathways in the US and the UK, what mainly differs is the names of the players. Criminal prosecution in the UK is handled by the *Crown Prosecution Service* (*CPS*), a government department under the Home Office. It is staffed by civil servants and is independent of the police but works closely with them. Police hand over the results of their investigations to a *crown prosecutor*, who decides whether there is sufficient evidence to prosecute and whether it is in the public interest to do so. Cases deemed worthy of prosecution are presented in a *Magistrates' Court*, the courts of general jurisdiction; the defendant in such cases is said to be *bailed to* the court, from the police. The most famous of these courts is probably *Bow Street* Magistrates' Court in London, which is frequently mentioned in the media.[1] Magistrates' Courts are presided over by three *magistrates*, who are lay justices; in official language they are *justices of the peace* or *JPs*.[2] A few busy magistrates' courts have full-time, paid justices who were until recently called *stipendiary*

---

1. The *Bow Street Runners*, occasionally referred to in historical fiction, were predecessors of the police force in London.

2. In the US, a *justice of the peace* is a local law official, typically in a rural area, who can make judgments in minor matters, solemnize oaths, and perform marriages.

magistrates, and now are called *district judges* of the magistrates' court. The handling of minor crimes (called *summary offences*) begins and ends here, in what is called a *summary trial*: the magistrates hear the case and make their decision. More serious crimes (*indictable-only offences*) are referred immediately to the *Crown Court*. The best known venue for the Crown Court is the one in London technically known as the Central Criminal Court, but popularly known as the *Old Bailey*. A small number of offences are *either-way offences*, in which the defendant has the right to elect trial by jury or by the magistrates; there is an attempt to introduce legislation that would give magistrates the power to decide this.

The first appearance in the Crown Court is a *plea and directions hearing (PDH)*, where the *indictment* is read and the defendant may enter a plea. If the plea is "not guilty," a date for a *trial by jury* is set. At this stage, the case for the Crown is handled by a *barrister* (lawyer trained to act in court), who is *instructed* by the CPS. The defendant will have a *solicitor* (see below, "The Practice of Law"), who will instruct another barrister to represent the defence case. Those unable to pay for these services are awarded *legal aid* in some cases; there is also an *official solicitor* who can be appointed by the Lord Chancellor to represent people who are incapable of sorting out their own affairs, such as minors or persons suffering from mental illness. While waiting for trial the accused may be freed on bail, or held, in which case he is called a *remand* prisoner.

In some cases a court may choose as punishment to *bind over* a criminal, which is effectively a form of probation in lieu of actual punishment. The usual form of words is that someone is e.g., "bound over for the sum of £1,000 to keep the peace and be of good behaviour for the next 12 months."

In the US, any of various law enforcement agencies, including the police, refer cases that they deem worthy of prosecution to the office of the *District Attorney (DA)*, an elected official at the county or state level. Cases deemed worthy of prosecution by the DA's office are presented in that state's or county's court of general jurisdiction (see below for more details on the court system). If the suspect is not already in custody, the court may issue a *warrant* for his arrest. The first court appearance is called an *arraignment*, in which charges are read and the defendant enters an initial plea. The defendant is represented by counsel of his own choosing, or if he cannot afford one, by a court-appointed *public defender*. For serious crimes the next court appearance is likely to be a *preliminary hearing*, in which the evidence against the defendant is considered. If the judge deems it worthy, the defendant is ordered to *stand trial*. An alternative to this method, less often used, is that of a *grand jury*, a body comprised of citizens convened by a court and empowered to investigate allegations of a felony. If the grand jury finds sufficient evidence to support criminal charges it issues an *indictment*, which lists the charges against a defendant. In the time leading up to the trial, the prosecution or the defense may file *motions*, which are formal requests for the judge to hear and decide a particular disputed issue. While waiting for trial the accused may be freed on bail, or held, which is called *pretrial detention* (BrE *remand*).

System of Courts

The size of the US and the constitutionally enshrined federal philosophy mean that there is no uniform national system of courts, but the court systems of each state are coordinated with the federal courts, for the cases that occasionally move between them. The federal court system is a three-tiered hierarchy. At the top is the *Supreme Court*, consisting of nine *justices*, one of whom is the *chief justice*, and all of whom are appointed by the president to life terms, subject to Senate approval. As the court of highest appeal in the US, the Supreme Court ultimately hears cases involving only the *constitutionality* of a law or of a lower court's decision, or in some cases it resolves disputes between *states' rights* and federal power.

The ninety-four *US District Courts* are at the bottom of the hierarchy. They are courts of general jurisdiction and they hear civil and criminal cases that involve a *federal offense*. There is at least one district in each state, with the largest and most heavily populated states having multiple districts. In between the District Courts and the Supreme Courts is the *US Courts of Appeals*, often referred to as the *Circuit Courts* because judges travel among them to preside over trials. There are eleven numbered circuits, each covering at least three states, and a twelfth circuit for the District of Columbia. The federal system also has trial courts of special jurisdiction that deal with matters such as copyright, taxes, the military, and veterans' affairs.

Most states have a three-tiered judicial system that mirrors the federal one; a few states have a two-tiered system. State trial courts are variously styled (*superior courts*, *district courts*, or *circuit courts*, to which the name of the state is always prefixed to distinguish it from a federal court). The intermediate appellate court is often called the *court of appeals*, and the court of last resort is usually called the *supreme court* with the name of the state or simply the word *state* prefixed to distinguish it from the US Supreme Court. Individual states also have any number of different courts that deal with particular matters (divorce, motor vehicle violations, and the like); these go by different names in different states.

The UK court system is uniform throughout England and Wales; a top-down view is the best way to take it all in. Though it is principally in business as a legislative body, the *House of Lords* is the court of highest appeal in the UK, occasionally taking cases referred from the Court of Appeal and the High Court (described below). The *Lord Chancellor* is the highest law officer of the Crown; he presides in the House of Lords and in some other courts. Other members of the Lords who perform its judiciary functions are called *Law Lords*. The next step down is the *Court of Appeal*; it has two divisions, civil and criminal, and hears only cases that arrive at it from lower courts. Below this level there is a fairly clear division between civil and criminal matters. The setup for criminal matters is described in outline above in the discussion of the *Magistrates' Courts* and the *Crown Court*. Civil matters may also begin litigation in a Magistrates' Court, or in a regional court called a *county court*.

More important civil cases are tried in the *High Court*, which has three divisions: the *Queen's Bench (QB)*, the *Family Division*, and the *Chancery Division*. These branches of the High Court, especially in press law reports, are identified as *Divisional Courts*. As well as being the court of first instance for important civil cases, the *High Court* also hears cases on appeal from lower courts. The *Queen's Bench* division hears criminal appeals, as well as being the first court for contracts and torts and other commercial matters. In addition the Queen's Bench division takes the majority of *judicial review* cases, in which the decisions of various nonjudicial government bodies are subject to scrutiny. The *Family Division* deals with divorce, matrimonial proceedings, and child custody proceedings, either originally or on appeal from the county and magistrates' courts. The *Chancery Division* deals with equities and trusts, contentious probate, tax matters, bankruptcy, patents, and some other commercial areas, as well as appeals from the County Courts dealing with bankruptcy and land.

Aside from these courts are various *tribunals* which hear appeals from decisions of government bodies on immigration, social security, child support, pensions, tax, and real property; cases from the tribunals are appealed directly to the Court of Appeal.

A few terms require particular discussion, being associated with the court proceedings in both countries, but with different meanings:

bailiff. In the US court system a bailiff is a court official, nearly always present in a courtroom, who carries out various minor duties, such as escorting witnesses and maintaining order. A bailiff in the UK is empowered to execute court orders, particularly ones concerning repossession of property and eviction, and it is usually in this connection that the term is used in British English. Saying that bailiffs come, or are brought in, is often shorthand for referring to a repossession order.

brief. In American English, a written argument submitted to a court; in British English, the instructions given to a barrister about a case by a solicitor or Crown prosecutor. A barrister may also have a *watching brief*, a brief to follow a case on behalf of a client who is not directly involved; this has made its way into general usage to denote an interest in a matter in which one is not directly concerned now, but which could develop in a way that would concern one: *We're keeping a watching brief on the negotiations.*

circuit judge. In the US, a judge in a circuit court. In the UK, a judge in a county or crown court.

ouster. In British English, an eviction order. It has this narrow meaning in American English as well but has far more currency in the meaning of "removal of a person from a position," a meaning not much used in British English.

It might be argued that there are no exact equivalents in legal terminology between the two dialects because the exact definitions of each differ, and in any case, such a thing wouldn't want to be argued with a lawyer. With that caveat, the following table lays out, in layman's terms, the names of some crimes and related legal jargon in the two dialects:

CRIME AND LEGAL TERMS

American	British
annulment	nullity (suit)
by reason of insanity	on the grounds of diminished responsibility
(child) support order	affiliation order
drunk driving	drink driving
felony	indictable offence, arrestable offence
jury duty	jury service

CRIME AND LEGAL TERMS *(continued)*

American	British
larceny	theft
minor →	infant
misdemeanor	non-indictable offence
pandering	procurement
restraining order	exclusion order
sexual assault	indecent assault
state's evidence	Queen's/King's evidence
witness stand	witness box

The British English term *housebreaking* is officially replaced by *burglary* but the older term is still widely found. British English uses *maintenance* as a term that includes American English *alimony* (ongoing payments for one divorced spouse from the other) and *child support* (ongoing payments for the support of children by the noncustodial parent).

A few other legal terms occur frequently in media reporting about litigation that do not have exact equivalents. These include:

LEGAL TERMS IN THE MEDIA

Term	Source	What is it?
class action	US	litigation undertaken by an individual representing a class of like-affected people, usually against a corporation
decree nisi	UK	court decree stating when a marriage will officially end, associated with divorce proceedings. The final act is the *decree absolute*
deed-poll	UK	document by which an individual legally changes his or her name
disorderly house	UK	a house of prostitution; usually in the phrase *keeping a disorderly house*
no contest	US	technical name *nolo contendere*; a plea in a criminal case in which the accused does not admit guilt but accepts the punishment that a guilty plea would bring
scofflaw	US	one who flouts minor laws in the hope of escaping detection or punishment

The British phrase *loitering with intent* no longer has legal status but lives on as a useful idiom; it was formerly short for "loitering with intent to commit a crime," and similar to American *vagrancy*. It is now used to characterize someone whose presence and intentions are both suspect.

Prisons

The word *prison* has all but disappeared from official nomenclature in the US, perhaps as part of a general cosmetic operation to disguise the high proportion (relative to other countries) of Americans who spend much of their lives behind bars. The contemporary preferred terms are *correctional institution* and *correctional facility* for the names of institutions, though *prison* is still the conversational word for them. A few older US institutions still have *penitentiary* as part of their name. In the UK, all such institutions are still generally called prisons. For incarcerated juveniles the UK has the *young offender institution*; various names appear in the US, more or less along the same lines: *youth correction facility, youthful offender facility*. These terms in both countries replaced the older institutions called *borstals* in the UK and *reform schools* or *reformatories* in the US.

Prisons in the UK are administered by *HM Prison Service*, under the Home Office. A separate body, *HM Inspectorate of Prisons*, acts as a prison watchdog. The US Federal system of prisons is administered by the *Federal Bureau of Prisons* under the Department of Justice. Each state also has an extensive system of prisons organized under a department that is typically called the *Department of Corrections*.

The name or location of a few prisons in each country has come to stand for the prison itself and thus may constitute an opaque reference for the transatlantic English reader or visitor. The best known ones are:

PRISONS

Prison	Where?	What is it?
Dartmoor	Devon	remote moorland area with a prison that once housed the criminally insane
Holloway	N. London	women's prison
Leavenworth	Kansas	site of a Federal prison
Pentonville	N. London	HM Prison
Rikers Island	New York City	an island in the East River that houses ten prison facilities for New York City
San Quentin	California	a California state prison; oldest in the state, built in the Gold Rush days
Sing Sing	New York State	maximum security Correctional Facility in Ossining
Wormwood Scrubs	W. London	HM Prison

The head of a prison in the US is a *warden*, in the UK a *governor*.

The Practice of Law

Qualification to practice law in the US is conferred by the *Bar Association* of the state in which a lawyer wishes to be licensed, on passing the *bar exam* of that particular state. This is called *admission to the bar*. Candidates normally sit for this exam after attending *law school*, a post-graduate institution that may be independent or affiliated with a university. The degree typically conferred is a *J.D.* (doctor of jurisprudence). Those seeking admission to law school normally take a standardized set of tests, the *LSAT* (Law School Admission Test), the results of which weigh heavily in the decision to admit or reject a student. College students wishing to prepare for a career in law, or for law school, may follow a course of study designated as *pre-law*.

Educational programs also exist for the position of *paralegal*, a lawyer's assistant who performs routine work in a law practice. The qualification for this can be completed in two years or less. A *legal secretary* performs some of the same functions or lowlier ones and may have a qualification, or only on-the-job training.

The legal profession in the UK is divided between two kinds of practitioners, *solicitors* and *barristers*. Solicitors deal with *conveyancing* (settling real estate contracts), the drawing up of wills, and some other legal matters, but they don't normally represent their clients in courts. *Barristers*, acting under the instruction of solicitors, act as advocates in most courts. Would-be barristers and solicitors attend post-secondary courses offered at various institutions leading to a *CPE* (Common Professional Examination) degree. Those going on to become solicitors then obtain a *LPC* (Legal Practice Course) degree that will lead to qualification to obtain a training contract with a firm of solicitors. During this time they complete the *PSC* (Professional Skills Course), on successful completion of which they are *admitted to the rolls*. The *Law Society* is the representative and regulatory body for solicitors in England and Wales, which issues and renews their licenses.

The profession of barristers collectively (not including solicitors) is called *the bar*. Qualifying barristers are *called to the bar*. The *Bar Council* is the representative and regulatory body for barristers in England and Wales, which overviews their education and qualifications, and handles complaints against them. The vast majority of barristers are *junior barristers*, that is, not entitled to have the initials *QC* (for Queen's Counsel) after their names. Those on whom this honor is conferred are said to *take silk* (because they are entitled to wear gowns of silk when in court). Barristers' offices are called *chambers*, which are also associations of barristers who work together and share some common resources. In London, most barristers' chambers are located in one of the four *Inns of Court*.

Those wishing to be barristers join one of the Inns of Court after their CPE in order to use its facilities for the rest of their education. They then take the *Bar Vocational Course* (*BVC*) in one of the Inns (or in another institution) in order to qualify for a *pupillages* (a form of apprenticeship under a qualified barrister). Those succeeding in their pupillage may obtain a *tenancy* in a chambers, or go on to work outside the chambers system. There is a winnowing process at each stage where many are eliminated, giving the profession its prestigious reputation.

The Police

Since policing is overwhelmingly a responsibility of state and local government in the US, there are a wide variety of systems in place for which no uniform description is possible. Terminology that applies generally is given here, with the proviso that no particular state or municipality will necessarily conform exactly to the described pattern. Nearly all political subdivisions in the US (state, county, township, borough, city, etc.) that have the authority to tax also have the authority to police, so there are police of various descriptions with overlapping jurisdiction. Police employed by a state are typically called *troopers* or *state troopers* and are familiar to most people from their preoccupation with traffic and other vehicle violations. *County police* exist in many nonurban areas, with responsibility for unincorporated areas. Police associated with cities and towns are what most people have in mind when they use the word *police*, or informally, *cop*. The chief police officer in a city is usually called the *chief of police*. Where a police force is organized as a part of local government it is often referred to as the *police department*, a designation that typically becomes initialized: *LAPD, NYPD*. Cities are typically divided into *precincts* for policing, with each precinct having a headquarters called a *precinct house*, or *police station*. Police officers of smaller jurisdictions are often called *sheriffs*, who are especially associated with county police, or *marshals*, as they were in the Old West.

British police forces are regional or metropolitan and are administered uniformly throughout England and Wales. Each force has a name that usually includes some reference to its geographic area followed by *constabulary* or *police*: *Durham Constabulary, Merseyside Police*. The police force governing Greater London is called the *Metropolitan Police*; its headquarters is *New Scotland Yard*, though *Scotland Yard* is used metonymically in the media to represent this police force. The head of a force is the *chief constable*. Police officers are called *constables*, popularly abbreviated *PC*. A female police constable is a *WPC*, though this designation is considered sexist by many and is slowly disappearing from the mainstream media. Additional, nongeographic police forces include the *British Transport Police* and the *National Crime Squad*, which combats national and transnational serious and organized crime.

The *Special Branch* of the British police service deals with terrorism, threats to public order by extremist and subversive groups, and serious crime. It has a slightly secretive air about it and is probably best compared to the American *FBI* or *ATF*.

The small number of policing terms that are lexical variants between American and British English are

POLICING TERMS

American	British
auxiliary policeman	special constable
(Denver) boot	wheel clamp
desk sergeant	station sergeant
drunk driving, DUI, DWI	drink driving, drunk in charge
lineup	identity parade
nightstick, billy club	truncheon, baton
patrol wagon, paddy wagon [slang]	police van
stool pigeon, stoolie, stool [slang]	grass [slang]

A few other terms from policing unique to each country are widely found in the media or have figurative uses. These include

POLICING TERMS UNIQUE TO ONE DIALECT

Term	Source	What is it?
APB	US	all-points bulletin: broadcast message with instructions to arrest a particular suspect or suspects. Used figuratively when someone is needed but not to be found: *Put out an APB on her.*
canteen culture	UK	conservative and racist attitudes said to exist within various police forces
charge sheet	UK	a written record of the charges against an arrested person

Mighty Fine Words and Smashing Expressions

POLICING TERMS UNIQUE TO ONE DIALECT *(continued)*

Term	Source	What is it?
CID	UK	Criminal Investigation Department, the detective branch of the police force
cop shop, nick	UK	slang: police station
flying squad	UK/US	squad dispatched to a crime in progress; BrE use is mostly literal, AmE is figurative: *a flying squad of anthropologists examining newly uncovered ruins*
fraud squad	UK	squad investigating company fraud
GBH	UK	grievous bodily harm
incident room	UK	notional room established in a police station for the investigation of a single crime
K-9	US	designates the use of dogs in police work, a play on *canine*: *a K-9 unit/patrol*
Miranda Rights	US	constitutionally guaranteed rights that an arrested person must be informed of at the time of the arrest
police blotter	US	ledger in which police arrests are recorded, or a newspaper column reporting the contents of this
rap sheet	US	informal: a written record of a criminal's past charges and convictions

The terms *patrol car* and *squad car* are common in both dialects. British English also has *panda car* for a police vehicle traditionally painted back and white; American English has *cruiser*. Many slang and informal terms designate police in both dialects. British English has *the Bill* or *Old Bill* to designate the police generally. The term *bobby* is dated in British English and has more circulation among American tourists than anyone else. American English has *Smokey* for a state trooper, since their hats in many states resemble those worn by *Smokey the Bear*, the Forest Service's mascot for fire prevention. The UK profession of *traffic warden* has no direct American counterpart. They earn their living by observing illegally parked cars and issuing tickets, a function performed mainly by police in the US. The profession is much derided and the subject of jokes.[1]

British English has the euphemism "helping (or assisting) the police with their enquiries" to denote a person who is detained as a suspect in a crime.

---

1. The American professions occupying the same niche in terms of low prestige and minimal qualifications are *flipping burgers* and *greeter at Wal-Mart*.

CHAPTER FIVE

Education

Aside from the common medium of the English language it is probably safe to say that the educational systems in Britain and the United States differ as much as those between any other two Western industrialized countries. Despite some inevitable borrowing of terminology early on in American history, the two systems of education have evolved independently to serve specific ends, with the result that each country now has its own brand of educationese, and some identical terms carry different meanings or connotations on different sides of the Atlantic. We start with an overview of the systems of compulsory education in each country, with important terminology highlighted. Elective education of all kinds is treated separately afterwards.

The American Education System

Although primary and secondary education in the United States is under the control of state governments, considerable autonomy is granted to individual *school districts*, which are areas containing more than one school under a single governing body. This body is usually called a *school board* or *board of education*; whose members may be appointed but are more often popularly elected at the local level. The chief executive of a district is typically the *superintendent of schools*. Individual schools are managed by an administrator called a *principal*. Despite this systematic decentralization, the style of education in *public schools* (those supported by taxpayers via government departments) is remarkably uniform through-out the United States, although the quality varies considerably from state to state and even from district to district. The uniformity in style is in part due to the influence of the federal government on education, through acts of Congress that provide funding for specific programs via state government and through the *Department of Education* with its cabinet-level head, the *Secretary of Education*.

Compulsory and free education was formerly for all children from age six, but in practice children usually begin their formal education with *kindergarten* at age five, and several states now make this compulsory. Thereafter children progress through *grades* one through twelve, at which point successful students *graduate* with a *high school diploma*[1] at about age seventeen. Children in grades one through eight are typically called *first-graders*, *second-graders*, etc. Students in grades nine through twelve are called *freshmen*, *sophomores*, *juniors*, and *seniors*, respectively.

Elementary school (also called *grade school* or *primary school*) is for children in grades one through grade five or six, in some places through grade eight; such schools usually contain a kindergarten as well. *Middle school* is for children in grades five or six up to grade eight or nine. In some states these are called *junior high schools*. The last part of secondary education, up to grade twelve, takes places in *high school*, occasionally called *senior high school*. The term *K-12 education* refers to this entire system, from kindergarten through the twelfth grade; qualified teachers are typically licensed to teach either the elementary (up to eighth) or the secondary grades, but in general they are designated *K-12 teachers*. Recently children younger than five have attracted the adjective *pre-K* in educational contexts.

Most children attend the school closest to them that is suitable for their grade, but larger school districts may also have *magnet schools*, which may have a curriculum centered on a specific theme, such as math and science, fine arts, or languages, or which attempt to achieve a racial and ethnic balance that would not be achieved by accepting only local students. Parents wishing to send their child to a school other than the local one may make various arrangements with their school district.

A high school diploma is the minimum requirement for entry into higher education, further vocational education, and most jobs. Those success-

---

1. *Diploma* is so overwhelmingly associated with high school in the US that it tends not to be used as much for other qualifications, lest it be tainted with this plebeian status. In British English it is associated with many different professional qualifications and courses, for which American English would more likely use *certificate*.

fully obtaining one are called *high school graduates*. This is an important rite of passage for American children and is marked with a solemn ceremony called *high school graduation* or *commencement*. Young people who fail to complete secondary education are called *high school dropouts*, and are assumed to be a present or future burden on society. A system exists for such people to get a certification equivalent to a high school diploma, called a *GED* for *general equivalency diploma*. Obtaining a GED can also be a means for students to get on with the rest of their education or career earlier than they otherwise would, and the test for it is sometimes taken by students in home schooling (discussed below) in order to obtain a recognized qualification.

High school students in larger and better-funded school districts who are bound for higher education may have an opportunity to take *AP* courses (for *Advanced Placement*). These enable them to meet some requirements of higher education without further study. For purposes of comparison, the content of these courses is about the same as UK A levels. Also gaining ground is the *IB* (*International Baccalaureate*) curriculum.

Until recently a standard system was used for assessing and reporting on students' work through a system of *grades* using the letters A through D and F. A is for exceptional or outstanding work; B is for satisfactory work, that is, above average; C is for average work; D is for unsatisfactory work; and F is for failing work. These letters can be further modified with a + or −, e.g., B+, C−. The grades have equivalent numbers, with A=4, B=3, C=2, D=1, and F=0. Converting the grades to numbers and then averaging them results in the *GPA* or *grade point average*, a handy reference for a student's general ability, and the number used to determine a student's rank among peers. The same system is also used in higher education. In fact, students in higher education are obsessed with this figure and seem to view the maintaining of it at a high level as the key to all future success. Several times during the school year school children are given *grade reports*, showing their grades in all subjects. This system is now falling from fashion to some degree but was once the standard for all schools, when the reports were called *report cards*, and many figurative uses have arisen from these terms: *give someone a bad report card, get an A+/a failing grade*.

OUTSIDE THE MAINSTREAM PUBLIC SYSTEM

While the vast majority of American children attend *public schools* (those supported by tax revenues and whose highest-level administration is often popularly elected), there is a wide range of educational alternatives, with its attendant terminology. American cities are particularly well-supplied with *parochial schools*, which are normally assumed to be associated with a Roman Catholic parish or religious order. This term may be applied loosely to more recently established private schools with a non-Catholic, Christian-based curriculum, though these are more likely to be called *Christian schools* or *Christian academies*. Where there are sufficient numbers to support them, private schools are run by other religious denominations; they tend to choose the designation *academy* rather than school, except for *friends schools*, run by the Quakers. Other private schools include *boarding schools*, *day schools*, and *military academies* (which prepare boys—some accept girls—for a military career, or impose discipline on those whom the public school system failed). All these sorts of schools require parents to pay tuition fees; attempts by some legislators to introduce *school vouchers*, a sort of tax-credit applicable to private education, have failed so far, but they are hotly debated in many locales and it is likely that they will succeed in some form before very long.

Intermediate between the public and private system is the *charter school*, which is usually funded by the school district where it is located, but not administered by it, having instead a very local administration in which parents and teachers are closely involved.

The British Education System

Compulsory education throughout the England and Wales[1] is administered and funded by *local education authorities*, or *LEAs*. These are in turn funded by and very strongly under the influence of the *Department for Education and Skills* and its cabinet-level head, the *Secretary of State for Education*, popularly the *Education Secretary*. This department administers the statutory framework that governs the education system, and works with schools to implement the *National Curriculum*, which is universally taught and tested for at specific points throughout a child's education. Schools directly under the control of an LEA are popularly called *state schools*; their technical designation is *county school*, a term that appears in the names of many of them. Schools not directly under the control of an LEA but funded by central government were until recently called *grant-maintained schools*. This term is out of use now, under a reorganization that created

1. Education in Scotland and Northern Ireland is independent. Their systems have functional equivalency with the system in England and Wales at all levels, but terminology differs in several areas.

community schools (managed by a *head teacher*[1] and a board of *governors*), *voluntary schools* (those owned by and with links to a religious denomination, and so also called *denominational schools*), and *foundation schools* (those formerly entirely independent of an LEA but now maintained, though not governed by it). Most of these schools chose to *opt out* of control by the LEA, in the interest of their own improvement; under the reorganization they are still funded by it. Particularly successful schools are called *beacon schools*, a distinction conferred by the government in their attempts to improve education standards. The term *charter school* as developed in the US is gaining currency as a designation of schools that have opted out of local authority control but are still funded by it. In an effort to goad improvement at underperforming schools, the government publishes performance records of all schools, allowing parents to compare them; these have become popularly known as *league tables*.

There are twelve years of compulsory education, beginning with the first year (*reception class*), followed by eleven termed *Year 1, Year 2*, etc. Reception class is for children who are five or will turn five during the academic year; they are called *rising fives*. A range of terms describes different schools depending on the ages of children (normally called *pupils* rather than students) taught there.

BRITISH STATE SCHOOLS

Age Range	Name of School
4 to 7	infant school
4 to 9	first school
4 to 11	primary school
7 to 11	junior school
9 to 13	middle school
11 to 16	secondary school

A secondary school that takes all local children (those in its *catchment area*) is called a *comprehensive school*; *secondary modern* also designates this kind of school. A secondary school that implements admissions testing and minimum standards is a *grammar school*. A *city technology college* is a comprehensive school funded by the state but with ties to urban business and industry to train students in particular needed skills.

School-leaving age is sixteen, when students normally have completed

---

1. This term, or simply *head*, is winning out over the now old-fashioned sounding *headmaster* and *headmistress*. The position of being a head teacher is called *headship*.

their compulsory education. Those who do so are called *school-leavers*,[1] and they take with them a *GCSE* (*General Certificate in Secondary Education*) in any number of individual subjects, upon satisfactory completion of exams administered in these. This is the equivalent of what used to be called *O levels*, now only a historical or nostalgic term. Pupils with a more practical than an academic bent may leave school with a *GNVQ* (*General National Vocational Qualification*), tests for which are administered in a number of subjects and are the qualification for entry into various skilled trades and professions.

The time in school before the GCSE or GNVQ is divided into four stages, called *Key Stages 1 through 4*, each of which has specific educational goals that are coordinated with the National Curriculum. These are tested for by tests called *SATs* (*Standard Assessment Tasks*).[2]

A number of different systems for *marks* (AmE *grades*) exist at different UK educational institutions and these have evolved or been replaced wholesale by various reforms at different times, with the result that there is no system that is considered standard or is found in figurative use, such as the American lettered system. Currently students are awarded *points* for successful completion of various subjects tested for in the key stages. Idioms containing the phrase *high marks* seem to be as common in American English as in British English, though to give someone *full marks* (high praise) for something is confined to British English.

Outside the State-Supported System

Private day and boarding schools in the UK are often called *public schools* (for pupils eleven to eighteen), or generally, *independent schools*, and are thus distinguished from *state-supported schools* and the other sorts of schools mentioned above that are funded by an LEA. Education in these schools must be paid for by parents, and plans for the introduction of *school vouchers* have failed in the UK as they have in the US, although the issue is far from dead in both countries. The UK has an *assisted-place scheme* that provides financial aid for students accepted to private schools that their parents cannot afford to send them to. Private scholarships fulfill this function in the US.

---

1. Though not standard in American English, most American speakers would take this term to be synonymous with *high-school dropout*, when in fact it designates a student who has successfully completed school.

2. Note the identical American initialism from *Scholastic Aptitude Test*, discussed below.

Both the US and the UK allow *homeschooling* and use the same general term for it, though British English hasn't settled on whether this should be an open, closed, or hyphenated compound. Its British English technical designation is *elective home education*. Both countries also employ the practice of separating students according to ability within the same level of education: this is usually called *tracking* in American English, (with students in different tracks), and *streaming* in British English (with students in different streams). There are a small number of other terms from education that are equivalents:

MISCELLANEOUS EDUCATION TERMS

American	British
field day	sports day
proctor	invigilator
substitute teacher	supply teacher

Elective education

Post-secondary education is used in both American and British English to designate institutional education after the completion of compulsory education, while the term *higher education* is also used in both countries to designate education that leads to the conferment of degrees or professional qualifications. American English prefers *vocational education* (*Voc. Ed.*) for schooling that leads to qualification in crafts and trades; British English usually calls this *vocational training*. For all of these paths, American students generally pay *tuition* (in American English, the cost of education charged by various institutions), while British students receive *tuition* (in British English, the learning and instruction itself). British English uses *tuition fees* or *school fees* to denote payment made in exchange for education. Herewith, overviews of the systems of elective education in the US and the UK.

AMERICAN HIGHER EDUCATION

A high school diploma or equivalent GED is the minimum qualification for entry to US higher education. Most prospective students also take standardized tests called *SATs* (originally an abbreviation of Scholastic Aptitude Test), the scores of which help to establish a student's general ranking and desirability as a student. These tests are also called *college boards* because they are a product of a body called the College Entrance Examination

Board. An alternative or complement to these is the *ACTs* (American College Testing). These tests are usually taken, for a fee, during the junior or senior year of high school and can be retaken in order to attempt to get higher scores. Armed with these, high school graduates then begin applying directly to colleges of their choice, usually at considerable expense to their parents. They may be accepted or rejected; the best schools are highly competitive and reject far more students than they accept.

Higher education takes place initially in a *college*, which can be of several kinds. A *junior* or *community college* normally offers qualifications and degrees that can be completed in two years or less of study. The highest such degree is called an *associate's degree* (*AA* or *AS*) and is usually a stepping-stone to a more advanced degree, or a certification for competence in a semiprofessional trade. Many students attend low-cost junior colleges as a way of fulfilling general education requirements before moving on to a four-year institution. The more usual understanding of *college* is a four-year college, which may or may not be part of a *university*. The difference is normally that colleges only offer a four-year *bachelor's degree* (a *bachelor of arts*, *BA*, or *bachelor of science*, *BS*) while a university also has programs leading to advanced degrees such as *masters* (*MA* or *MS*), a *doctorate* (*PhD*), and other advanced professional degrees.

By the third year of college a student has chosen a *major*, or main field of study. A student may also have a *minor*, or secondary field of study, or even a *double major*, two main fields of study. Colleges prescribe the number and type of courses that must be completed to satisfy the major; courses taken outside the major field of study are called *electives*.

The cost of education (tuition) is usually borne by students themselves, their parents, or both. *Financial aid* is available for a majority of students through *scholarships* (outright gifts based on merit or need) and *student loans* (loans from commercial banks at a low rate of interest with payment deferred until after graduation, subsidized by the government). Tuition costs are lowest at non-competitive *state colleges* and *state universities*, which are partly funded from tax revenues and are cheaper for residents of their respective states. *Private colleges* and *universities* set their fees on the basis of their standing in the academic community, their popularity, and their relative attractiveness to prospective students. The most prestigious of these are the *Ivy League*, normally taken to mean Yale, Harvard, Princeton, Columbia, Dartmouth, Cornell, and Brown Universities, and the University of Pennsylvania. They are all in states on the eastern seaboard of the

US and were established well over a hundred years ago. The short-hand designation for these is the *Ivies*. There are also many very competitive colleges and universities that are not part of the Ivy League, and *Ivies* is increasingly used to designate top-ranking schools: *new/second-tier Ivies*.

Students who have completed a bachelor's degree are called *college graduates*. Those continuing their study for higher degrees are called *graduate students*. Unlike British institutions, which distinguish minutely among the qualities of degrees (see below), degrees from US schools are generally equal in principle. Some colleges may designate certain degrees with the ascending three-stage scale of *cum laude*, *summa cum laude*, and *magna cum laude*; but these distinctions do not hold much sway in the marketplace. Instead it is the reputation of the school that enhances the status of the degree holder. Universities with high reputations are simply called *good schools* or prestigious schools; one designated a *party school* or *diploma mill* is assumed to be willing to confer an unimpressive degree on anyone.

Requirements for admission to graduate programs of study are highly variable but usually include lesser degrees, in addition to the results of a series of tests called the *GRE*, for *Graduate Record Examination*. Students applying specifically for admission to law school, medical school, or business school take other tests that are mentioned in other chapters of this book.

Administration. Colleges and universities differ in their terminology for senior administration, but nearly all have a chief executive, who may be the *president*, the *provost*, or the *chancellor* (a term that is used especially in *state university* systems, that is, public universities supported by state tax revenues). Various *deans* or *vice-chancellors* are in charge of different aspects of college or university life. All of these may teach on a limited basis in addition to their administrative duties. The rest of the teaching hierarchy, starting from the top, is the *(full) professor*, who has *academic tenure*, that is, not subject to dismissal by the institution except in extreme cases, such as criminal behavior. Below this is the *associate professor*, followed by the *assistant professor*. Some institutions may have lesser beings than these, called *instructors* or *lecturers*. An *adjunct* faculty member is employed on contract and has no standing within the university hierarchy. Other university officials include the *bursar* (in charge of financial affairs) and the *ombudsman* (who fields and resolves student complaints), and the *registrar* (in charge of registering students).

BRITISH HIGHER EDUCATION

School-leavers with a GCSE wishing to obtain a *university degree* normally go from secondary school to a *sixth-form college*[1] where they study for *A levels*. Both of these names persist from earlier systems of education whose associated elements are obsolete. A levels are subject-specific courses of study, normally lasting one year, that become the necessary qualification for entry to a university degree program, and in some cases, to other courses of professional study that do not lead to a university degree but instead to some other qualification. *Sixth-formers* typically study from one to five A levels simultaneously, depending on their aspirations. A college providing both sixth-form classes and further education classes for sixteen- to nineteen-year-olds may also be called a *tertiary college*. Some British *public schools* (expensive private ones) incorporate a sixth-form college.

On completion of their A levels, students may take a *gap year*, that is, a year away from studies when they travel or pursue some other interest, such as volunteer activity or work; a small industry is growing up around accommodating students who make this choice. The alternative is to apply for a *degree program* or *course*[2] at a university for which they have the necessary prerequisite qualifications. This system requires students to specialize quite early in their academic careers, a point that is often criticized. Students are said to *read* rather than study, at university, when working towards a degree: *reading maths at Oxford.*

British higher education is designed around the idea of *places* to a degree that will seem rather bizarre to the transatlantic student. Each course or program has a fixed number of places in it for which students apply, and when the program is filled, excess applicants are turned away. The act of applying for admission to a university is sometimes called "applying for a place." An institution called *UCAS*, the Universities and Colleges Admissions Service, exists to match up students and vacant places.

There is a strong emphasis in the UK on making higher education available to people who did not come up through the British education system. Supporting this are a number of institutions offering *access courses* (also

1. The other forms leading up to the sixth have disappeared from British state-funded education, but are still used in some British private schools, and also in some of the long-established private schools in the eastern US.
2. Note that *course* in British English often denotes the entire program of study leading to a degree; in American English it generally denotes a single subject studied over a fixed academic period; thus an American college student is normally *taking* four or five courses at a time, while a British student is *enrolled on* a single course.

foundation courses), year-long courses that prepare a non-traditional or non-British student for entry into the university system. The *Open University (OU)*, which offers courses mainly through correspondence, television programs, and other media, best exemplifies this tradition.

The names and hierarchy of degrees offered by UK universities are generally the same as in American universities, but with many more distinctions among them. Courses of study may be further distinguished by being an *honours course* leading to an *honours degree* (one with more prestige, higher entry qualifications, and more demanding work). Students completing these are called *honours graduates*. Degrees are also graded as *first-class*, *second-class*, and so forth; the degrees, or the persons obtaining them, are sometimes called *firsts*, *seconds*, etc. Sometimes even finer distinctions are noted (an *upper second-class degree*). This is a means of attaching an enduring judgment on the degree holder's general ranking within the program of study; thus the emergence of short-hand designations such as a *good degree* or a *mediocre degree*; these distinctions are more enduring than those attached to American degrees are and may even figure into graduates' ability to find work. (See also "Degrees", below.) Students who have completed a bachelor's degree are called *graduates*. Those continuing their study for higher degrees are called *postgraduates*; thus UK *postgraduate students* or *courses* are the equivalent of US *graduate students* or *courses*.

Until fairly recently education in the UK was said to be "free to the first degree," that is, until the student has obtained a degree from a post-secondary institution. Today this system is slowly eroding and cost of higher education is increasingly borne by students and their parents. At the undergraduate level some help is available in the form of *maintenance support* (this replaced *maintenance grants*), a government benefit that is administered by LEAs. *Student loans* are also becoming more common and are administered by a government-owned company called the *Student Loan Company*. One well-established way of avoiding student poverty is the *sandwich course*, a course that combines full-time higher education with full-time work. It typically focuses on mastery of a particular profession, in which the student works full-time in between years of study. Grant money for undergraduate or graduate study at a university awarded privately is sometimes called a *bursary*, a *studentship*, or a *scholarship*. Only the last of these three terms is used in American English.

Costs of education vary depending on the prestige of the school or of the particular degree course enrolled in. The bottom of the hierarchy are the universities formerly called *polytechnics*, many of which still offer qualifications in various trades in addition to degrees. Next up are the traditional *red brick universities*, mostly founded in the nineteenth and early twentieth centuries, that form the backbone of UK higher education and are located throughout the country. Top of the table is *Oxbridge*, that is, *Oxford University* or *Cambridge University*, each of which comprises several colleges.

Administration. Colleges and universities vary considerably in the hierarchy of their administration and teachers, many adopting terminology that is not widely used. A typical constellation has a university headed by a *vice-chancellor*, assisted by a *deputy vice-chancellor*, with a titular and mainly honorary *chancellor*, often a royal or other aristocrat, lurking in the background as a patron. There is usually a governing body called a *senate, court*, or *council* to whom the administrators answer. Various *provosts* and *deans* are in charge of different aspects of college or university life, or of different academic divisions. Particularly at Oxford and Cambridge Universities, the senior faculty within particular colleges are called *dons*. Teachers with the title of *professor* are at the top of the teaching hierarchy. Next in line are *senior lecturers* (also called *readers* in some universities) and *lecturers*, who may hold full-time positions with the hope of attaining professorship. *Fellows* are senior members of some colleges who may also teach, along with *research fellows*—postgraduates on a stipend who do research and may also teach. The latter term parallels the use of *fellow* in American universities.

Degrees

Academic degrees and the abbreviations for them are shared by both dialects for the most commonly conferred ones: BA, BS, MA, MS, and PhD. Beyond these, American institutions generally do not draw as many distinctions as British ones do, and educated Americans generally do not attach a string of abbreviations representing their accomplishments onto the end of their names except in contexts where their qualifications are of particular interest: doing so otherwise (on a business card, for example) would be perceived as needlessly ostentatious. A code of sorts exists in British English for abbreviations of the many degrees awarded. The first letter (usually *B* for *Bachelor*, *M* for *Master*, and *D* for *Doctor*) represents the level of the degree, and the remaining letters represent the field. These are conventionally abbreviated as follows:

BRITISH DEGREE DESIGNATIONS

Abbreviation	What is it?
A	Arts [bachelors and masters only]
Eng	Engineering
Litt	Letters
Mus	Music
Phil	Philosophy
Sc	Science

The names of the universities in which these distinctions were achieved is parenthetically noted after the degree abbreviation in the most full blown form; these are mostly obvious, except for *Oxon* (=Oxford) and *Cantab* (=Cambridge). Example: *Harold Mytum MA(Cantab), DPhil(Oxon)*.

Degrees of the kind noted are always obtained at universities in the UK; in the US, degrees up to the level of Bachelor's, and sometimes Master's, may be obtained at a college or a university. These two are combined informally as *school*, so to an American, *Where did you go to school?* means "where did you attend college or university?" In British English, *school* refers to only primary and secondary school, *college* is used for a sixth-form or technical college, and *university* is used for degree-granting institutions.

Classes for Adults

American English generally uses *continuing education* and British English uses *adult education* (which is also used in American English) to describe classes, sometimes leading to degrees, for adults who are past the usual age or need for the mainstream education system. *Life-long learning* is now gaining ground as the general term for this phenomenon in American English. The institutional setting for it in both countries has considerable overlap with the mainstream system; in the US it typically takes place in *community colleges*, which are described above; in the UK, popular designations are *adult education centre* or *adult education institute*, many of which exist in buildings used for other educational purposes.

The Division of Knowledge

There is considerable overlap in the names of the subjects studied at the primary, secondary, and tertiary levels in both countries. The following differences and unique designations are worth noting:

- *Civics* is an Americanism and usually designates (obligatory) classes or lessons about the privileges and obligations of citizens; it has little currency in British English; the nearest equivalent in the National Curriculum is *Citizenship Education*.
- *Creation Science* is a term coined by US Christian fundamentalist educators in an attempt to lend scientific credibility to the Biblical doctrine of creation. It is only taught in private Christian schools.
- *Greats* is the designation for a course of study at Oxford that combines classics, philosophy, and ancient history.
- *ICT* is the UK National Curriculum shorthand for Information and Communications Technology.
- *Mathematics* has the short form *math* in American English, *maths* in British English, treated as a singular noun in both cases.
- *MFL* is the UK National Curriculum shorthand for Modern Foreign Languages.
- *Modern Greats* is the designation for a course of study at Oxford that combines philosophy, political economy, and history.
- *RE* is short for *religious education* in British English; it exists as an institution, if not an industry, because there is an established church. Lately it has more emphasis on inculcating ethical values independent of Christian theology.
- *Social Studies* in American English is a subject in primary and secondary education that combines aspects of history, politics, economics, and geography. In British English it is a university-level educational discipline that undertakes the study of various branches of human society.

The Division of the Time

Term is preferred in British English at all levels of education for the continuous period when instruction is given at a school. The time when this is not happening is called *vacation* (or informally *vac*), or *school holidays*. A shorter break in the middle of the term is called *half-term*. American colleges and universities are mostly on a *semester* system, in which study is continuous for periods of fifteen to eighteen weeks, with breaks (usually *winter break* and *spring break*) in between. Some universities use *quarters* corresponding to the seasons, in which the summer quarter is least attended. In either case, a break in the middle of these periods is called *midterm break*, and tests administered about in the middle of them are called *midterms*. Primary and secondary schools mostly use a semester system, but vary considerably in the terminology for it. *Marking period* is becoming increasingly common in K–12 education, indicating a period at the end of which students grades are reported. A rest or play period between lessons in primary school is called *break* in British English, *recess* in American English; neither noun takes an article.

The Division of Domains

Knowing the differences between Internet addresses for educational institutions in the US and the UK may help the surfer locate resources more easily. Institutions of higher learning in the US have the terminal domain *.edu*. Those in the UK mostly have the terminal domains *.ac.uk*. Public primary and secondary schools in the US with websites have the terminal domain *.k12.xx.us* where *xx* is the official two-letter state abbreviation where the school is located (see chapter 7). Primary and secondary schools in the UK have the terminal domains *.sch.uk*, unless they have been able to secure a more prestigious .org or .ac domain.

Preschool Education and Childcare

The UK has a government-subsidized program of universal preschool education called the *nursery class*, which is in effect an introduction to primary education, for four- and sometimes three-year-olds. Like all other educational institutions in the UK it starts out with the idea of places, then finds the bodies to fill them. The only government-sponsored system in the US for preschool is *Head Start* (often written as one word), a child development program that serves low-income children up to kindergarten age. There are however numerous private *preschools* for children usually of age three to four, with properly qualified teachers.

CHILDCARE

American English *babysitter* is a dependable substitute in nearly all contexts for British English *childminder*, designating either a person who takes care of others' children in her home, or in the children's home. The verb *babysit* and noun *babysitter* are used in both dialects for the carer (or as American English would have it, the *caregiver*) who works in the child's home. British English uses *crèche*[1] for a childcare facility within some other institution for children of the parents visiting or using that institution:

---

1. The main American English meaning of *crèche* is a model depiction of Jesus's nativity, and it is not even a first-choice word for this (*nativity* is).

a church, festival, or company, for example. The closest American English equivalent is *daycare center*, often abbreviated simply to *daycare*. This term is also used in both dialects (British English *daycare centre*) for a commercial enterprise in which children, sometimes less than a year old, are cared for while their parents work. All must be licensed in the UK by the Local Education Authority.

CHAPTER SIX

Sickness and Health

The very different systems of healthcare in the US and the UK are at the heart of the widely differing vocabularies that have developed to talk about essentially the same phenomena: human sickness and health. We start with overviews of the healthcare systems in both countries, which in many cases inform the language that surrounds sickness and health.

HEALTHCARE

Healthcare systems in the US and the UK presumably begin with the same objective, that is, to keep the greatest number of people as well as possible. They are popularly perceived to fall short of the ideal in this for different reasons: in the US, because the *healthcare industry* operates as a gigantic and extremely influential profit-making enterprise that often seems to put the needs of patients last in its list of priorities; and in the UK, because the *National Health Service* alternates as the show pony, guinea pig, and whipping boy of transient government ideologies. As a fairly telling indication of the differences in the two cultures, each country has produced documents in recent years intended to redirect their healthcare systems. The American *Patients' Bill of Rights*, passed by the US Senate in 2001, is mostly about how, who, and when you can sue for inadequate healthcare provision. The British *NHS Plan* outlines a framework to provide more power to patients, more hospitals, doctors, and nurses, and much shorter waiting times for hospital and doctor appointments. Each system is comprehensible mainly through its attendant terminology and jargon, highlighted in the following profiles.

The American Healthcare System

ORGANIZATION AND ADMINISTRATION

With the exception of *Medicaid* (government-paid healthcare for the poor) and *Medicare* (government-subsidized healthcare for the elderly), the US healthcare industry is privately run, by hospitals, doctors, insurance companies, and *HMOs*, all of which operate as private enterprises with the exception of a few hospitals. HMO is shorthand for *health maintenance organization*, a private membership organization that, in exchange for a fixed monthly fee, covers the cost of all healthcare for its members that it deems necessary. Decisions about what measures are actually necessary are taken under the rubric of what is called *managed care*, a set of protocols based on cost-benefit analysis. Patients who are treated under managed care tend to think of it as a system that enables healthcare providers to completely abnegate their responsibilities, and use of the term is often emotionally or politically charged; for this reason, it is likely to be replaced soon by a new term that carries less baggage. Some HMOs employ a system called *capitation*, under which doctors get a fixed yearly fee per member patient and have to keep all the costs of treatment and tests for patients, and their own income, within that budget.

Provision for healthcare is typically provided as part of an employee's benefit package, either free (rare these days) or partly subsidized by the employee. In addition to HMOs, people may choose a form of *indemnity health insurance*, which defrays the cost of healthcare in exchange for monthly or quarterly premiums. Such policies are also characterized as *group insurance* since those insured are required to belong to a definable group, which in most cases is all the employees of a company. Most such schemes are coordinated with a *PPO, a preferred provider organization*, wherein the insured receives preferential rates by using particular doctors, hospitals, and laboratories for testing. Most insurance packages come with a *deductible* (BrE *excess*), an amount of money that must be paid out of pocket by the insured before the insurance benefit becomes effective. Some plans work on a system of *copayment*, wherein the insured pays a token amount or small percentage of incurred healthcare costs and the insurance company pays the rest. In every state there is a insurance company popularly called *Blue Cross* that insures in total about 25 percent of Americans. Most of these operate on a not-for-profit basis, although some are now privatizing. Individuals who lose their insurance as the result of leaving a job are usually covered at their own expense for a limited period under a plan referred to as *COBRA*, an acronym for the legislation the provides for this.

Individuals who do not have insurance coverage as a part of their employment may apply to insurance companies or HMOs for health coverage, which is at the option of the company or the HMO, although both of these are normally required by law to have a period of *open enrollment* each year, at which time they are compelled to insure anyone who applies to them, usually at inflated premiums or membership fees. This is an option that is sometimes exercised by self-employed people, or those whose work does not provide insurance benefits. Some people also qualify for a *medical savings account (MSA)*, an arrangement with certain tax benefits in which money can be set aside for and used to pay for medical expenses.

Delivery

The patient's point of contact with the healthcare system is a *primary care physician (PCP)* who is typically a *family practitioner*[1] (a designation for a doctor whose specialty is *family practice*), or a specialist in *internal medicine* (sometimes called an *internist*). A woman may have an *ob/gyn* (specialist in obstetrics and gynecology) as her PCP, and a pediatrician may be the PCP for the children in a family. These doctors operate out of private offices simply called a *doctor's office*, if they are not employed by an HMO, a hospital, or the government. Typically doctors with different specialties or interests coordinate their services under one roof, called a *group practice*. They either treat the condition presented or refer the patient to a specialist. All doctors have agreements with nearby hospitals where they have *admitting privileges*, that is, the right to hospitalize a patient.

Britain's National Health Service

Organization and Administration

The *National Health Service (NHS)* is funded through government revenues, including income tax. It is organized under the cabinet-level

---

1. The term *general practitioner* doesn't have contemporary official use in American English; it may be used loosely as a synonym for family practitioner, or it may designate a physician who went into practice after only a year of postgraduate experience, without graduating from a residency program (see below under "Medical Education in the US").

Department of Health and administered through *health authorities*, headed by a *medical officer*. They are bodies that manage all the hospitals, doctors, and other health services within a geographical area. The health
authorities in turn manage various *NHS trusts*, which actually employ
most of the NHS workforce. Patients affiliate with the system through a
registration process that assigns them an *NHS number*. This number follows the patient through all NHS services provided. Within the NHS an
internal market operates, in which various entities such as hospitals and
departments purchase each other's services contractually.

There are two organizations that, while independent of the NHS, have
complicated interrelationships with it: one is the *General Medical Council*
(*GMC*), a nonprofit quango, which maintains the register of doctors in
good standing practicing in the UK and also brings disciplinary actions
against malpracticing doctors. It is also the competent authority overseeing
UK medical education, and in general represents the interests of patients.
The *British Medical Association* is a professional organization representing
doctors; it is the UK functional equivalent of the AMA (see below under
"Medical Education in the US").

DELIVERY

Local *GPs* (*general practitioners*) are the point of contact for patients
with the health service. They provide primary care and make all referrals to
specialists. A GP's local office is usually called a *surgery*, and this term may
also denote the specific times when a GP has hours to see patients. Different surgeries may have *clinics*, where specialist advice or treatment is
given. The word *clinic*[1] may likewise refer to the hours when such treatment is available.

Alongside the NHS system is a smaller private system that works much
like the system of private insurance described for the United States. Patients who do not wish to deal with the bureaucracy, minimalist facilities,
or sometimes excessive delays of NHS care may *go private*. The main
provider of private health insurance is a company called *BUPA*. In between these, patients may upgrade to an *amenity bed* in an NHS hospital
(one in a private room) for a fee—most beds in NHS hospitals are in

---

1. The American English medical use of *clinic* is narrower and typically denotes a specialist medical facility, sometimes associated with a hospital. In urban settings it is often used of free, general medical facilities.

wards holding multiple patients, an arrangement that hardly exists in US hospitals except for the indigent.[1] Foreign patients who use the NHS are put in *pay beds*.

MEDICINE

The content of the field of medicine is nearly identical in the US and the UK; there are however many terminological differences, and the systems under which people receive medical education are also quite different. There is also considerable disparity between the content of the generally known medical vocabulary in the two countries because of the differences in healthcare delivery. Nearly all doctors and nurses in the UK work for the NHS (technically, they work for NHS trusts) and so there is much greater uniformity of terminology in hospital organization and hierarchies than in the US. Since everyone uses the NHS, much of this terminology is fairly standard and has wide currency in British English. Equivalent or analogous terms in American English are not even standardized, much less generally known.

The Medical Lexicon

Though we might properly have treated this area exhaustively in chapter 1, since the differences between several predictable classes of words are in spelling only, the specialized nature of the vocabulary makes it sensible to point out the general patterns here. Nearly all words in the following classes entered English from Latin and Greek, occasionally via French, and nearly all were subject to Webster's nineteenth-century spelling reforms in American English only. Words introduced to medicine since that time continue to conform to the patterns set in each country. If an international standard does eventually emerge it is likely to be the American one and there is some pressure to do this within the scientific community, but for the present, the British spellings noted are still considered the only correct ones in the UK. The spellings containing diphthongs occur in American English but are generally not preferred.

1. US hospitals do, however, use *ward* to describe different areas of a hospital: *a cancer/jail/maternity ward*.

SPELLING DIFFERENCES IN MEDICAL TERMINOLOGY

Word pattern	AmE example	BrE example
words ending with *-rrhea* (AmE) and *-rrhoea* (BrE)	diarrhea, gonorrhea, menorrhea	diarrhoea, gonorrhoea, menorrhoea
words ending with *-emia* (AmE) and *-aemia* (BrE)	anemia, septicemia	anaemia, septicaemia
words ending with -ena (AmE) and -aena (BrE)	melena, phlyctena	melaena, phlyctaena
words beginning *hem(at)*- (AmE) and *haem(at)*- (BrE)	hemorrhage, hematocyst, hemmorhoid	haemorrhage, haematocyst, haemmorhoid
words derived from *esthesia*- (AmE) and *aesthesia*- (BrE)	anesthesiology, synesthesia	anaesthesiology, synaesthesia
words derived from *ameba* (AmE) and *amoeba* (BrE)	amebiasis, amebocyte	amoebiasis, amoebocyte
words derived from *estrus* (AmE) and *oestrus* (BrE)	estrogen, stilbestrol	oestrogen, stilboestrol
words derived from *ped*- (AmE) and *paed*- (BrE)[1]	pediatrician, orthopedics	paediatrician, orthopaedics

[1] Where the Greek root is *paidos*, "child." Words formed from the Latin *ped*-, "foot," are spelled *ped*-in both dialects, e.g., *pedometer*.

Other common words, most easily represented by their main representative pairs but showing the same spelling differences in all their derivatives, include AmE *apnea* and BrE *apnoea*; AmE *edema* and BrE *oedema*; AmE *esophagus* and BrE *oesophagus*[1]; AmE *feces* and *fecal*, BrE *faeces* and *faecal*; AmE *gynecology*, BrE *gynaecology*; AmE *leukemia,* BrE *leukaemia*. AmE uses *Cesarean* for the invasive method of childbirth intervention, and *Caesarean* when referring to the Caesars of the Roman Empire; British English uses *Caesarean* for both of these. Complicating matters further, British and American English prefer *homeopathy* (and derivatives) but British English sometimes shows *homoeopathy*.

Editors and writers requiring more particular detail than is provided here can invest in a medical spell checker, which may contain thousands of terms with the variants proper to each dialect.

DIVIDING UP MEDICINE

Spelling differences aside, a number of areas in medicine go by slightly different names in the two dialects, and the specialists associated with

1. British English uses *gullet* as a synonym for the human esophagus far more commonly than American English does, which tends to associate *gullet* with animals.

them may have different titles. These terms would generally be classed as medical *specialties* in American English; the terms *speciality* and *specialism* are used in British English.

MEDICAL SPECIALTIES

American term	British term
internal medicine	general medicine
anesthesiologist	anaesthetist
physical medicine, rehab medicine	rehabilitation
internist	internal medicine specialist
emergency medicine	A&E [accident and emergency] medicine

An *osteopath* in the UK is a complementary practitioner who delivers treatment through manipulation of the spine and musculature; this is more or less equivalent to what is called a *chiropractor* in the US, though without the nearly exclusive focus on the spinal column that characterizes chiropractic medicine. In the US, an *osteopath* is a medical doctor with credentials that are functionally equivalent to an M.D., and with additional training in skeletal manipulation. Such doctors are identified by *D.O.* rather than M.D., after their names.

American English uses *pathologist* in its broadest sense, i.e., a specialist in the origin, nature, and course of diseases. In British English a pathologist is more often one whose job is to determine the cause in an unnatural death. For this meaning American English uses *medical examiner*.

Medical Education in the US

The areas of overlap in medical education terminology between the two dialects is probably greater than the differences, even though the actual implementation of the education is under different systems entirely. To begin with, overviews of both.

Would-be doctors in the US attend *medical schools*, which are typically associated with universities that have on-site research hospitals. Competition for admission is fierce and preparation for it usually begins during undergraduate years by concentration in programs that are informally called *pre-med*: a college major with the majority of courses in the physical and biological sciences. A standardized test called the *MCAT* (Medical College Admission Test) gives applicants to medical schools a ranking that is highly influential in their admission. Those unsuccessful in gaining admission to US medical schools sometimes apply to *offshore medical schools*, mostly located in Caribbean nations. Once the program of instruction in medical school (lasting four years) is completed, graduates are awarded the degree of *M.D.* or *D.O.* (if their medical school was a college of osteopathy). At this point they typically apply for a *residency program* (lasting three to seven years) in a hospital in which they work various *rotations* that enable them to gain experience in various fields of medicine, under the supervision of fully qualified physicians. This system is referred to as *graduate medical education*. It has gradually replaced the more informal system of medical *interns* and *internships*, though these terms persist in popular usage to describe the same phenomena, especially the first year of postgraduate work. The length of a residency depends on the specialty chosen.

Before being licensed as physicians, doctors must pass tests administered by the various state *medical boards*. The test itself is sometimes referred to by this term. Doctors are typically licensed to practice medicine in one state only. Most doctors also choose to become *board certified*, that is, shown competent by examination in any of dozens of specialties or subspecialties, requiring periodic renewal by further examinations, informally called *medical boards*. Most doctors also become members of the *American Medical Association* (*AMA*), the professional organization that represents their interests to Congress and in other areas of public life.

Medical Education in the UK

There is a functional distinction between UK doctors who see patients in a practice—usually called *GPs*—and *hospital doctors*, who specialize in particular areas of medicine. The education starts at the undergraduate level with *medical school*.[1] These have programs generally lasting five years, divided into the *preclinical* (theory) and *clinical* (working under doctors' supervision) phases. Each medical school sets its own entry criteria; most require multiple good science A levels. These schools are applied to through UCAS (see previous chapter), like all UK undergraduate programs. On successful completion of medical school, doctors are awarded any of various degrees with unpronounceable and opaque abbreviations, such as *BMBS*, *MBChB*, or *BMedSc*. Education received after this time is referred to as *PGME*, post-graduate medical education. Typically, newly

---

1. Note that US *medical schools* are graduate schools, entered only after obtaining an undergraduate degree.

qualified doctors begin to work for the NHS as a *house officer*[1] for one year. Then they apply to the General Medical Council to become a fully registered doctor. From this point it takes at least three more years of further education to become a GP or at least seven years to become a hospital *consultant*, which is the highest grade of hospital doctor. Consultants typically have salaried work under the NHS and also accept private, paying patients to supplement their income. There are two grades of doctor on the way to becoming a consultant, *registrar* and *senior registrar*.

Because the overwhelming number of UK residents use the NHS, uses of the word *private* and its derivatives, when used in relation to medicine, have particular meanings that may not be obvious to non-British English speakers. A doctor who sees patients *privately* is not merely closing the door while they talk; she is consulting with a patient who is paying for the service, rather than getting it through the NHS. Such patients are the doctor's *private patients*. A doctor in *private practice* is one who works outside the NHS. *Private wards* and *beds* are those in NHS hospitals that require the patient to pay, used by foreigners or Britons wanting upgraded service.

Nursing and Midwifery

The public perception of nurses in the US and the UK is remarkably similar; they are regarded as overworked, underpaid, underappreciated, and in demand in both countries. The terms used in these accounts vary considerably. First, the British hierarchy, starting at the top: a *senior nursing officer* is in charge of nursing in a hospital; the former, and still informal designation for this person is *matron*. A *charge nurse* is a nurse in charge of a ward or department in a hospital, and is the technical equivalent of the more popularly used *sister*[2]. Junior to her is the *staff nurse*.

Also working within the NHS but generally outside of hospitals are the *district nurse*, who undertakes various public health responsibilities; the *health visitor*, employed by a local health authority to make home visits; and the *nursery nurse*, who takes care of the medical needs of young children and babies in a nursery or crèche. The UK also has a fully qualified network of *midwives* who work mostly within the NHS, assisting with births in and out of the hospital and with postnatal and *antenatal* (AmE *prenatal*) care.

1. This term is displacing *houseman*, with its obvious gender limitations.
2. *Sister* is used of nurses in American English only in Catholic hospitals for nurses who are also nuns.

Both nursing and *midwifery* have career tracks in the UK that begin with GCSEs or A levels; schools are associated with universities, hospitals, or both.

American nurses graduate from similarly designed programs, typically emerging with an associates degree in nursing or a *BSN*, bachelor of science in nursing. Those wishing to be certified as fully qualified nurses must pass a standardized examination. These are usually called *RN*s, for *registered nurse*; this is the qualification required for most hospital nurses. Those in charge of a department or unit in a hospital usually have the title *head nurse*, the functional equivalent of British *charge nurse*. Doing similar but less detailed and responsible work is the *LPN* or *licensed practical nurse*, a qualification that can be earned in a one-year program of study. In some states these are called *LVN*s or *licensed vocational nurses*. The job of a *visiting nurse* is similar to that of a British *health visitor*, except that the visiting nurse may be employed privately. More typically she works through a Visiting Nurse Agency, whose services are contracted for directly or via physician referral.

Within American nursing a number of specialties have arisen, mostly in response to market demand. These include *certified nurse midwife* (*CNM*), *nurse anesthetist*, *nurse practitioner* (a qualified nurse who assists in a medical practice, doing routine consultations), and *forensic nurse*, a specialty mostly devoted to working in medical-legal contexts, acting as expert witnesses in the vast medical malpractice industry in the US. A *physician's assistant* (*PA*), does about the same work as a nurse practitioner. A low-paid hospital worker with no training other than that provided on the job is a *nurse's aide*; one who does this on a voluntary basis, typically a high-school girl, is a *candystriper* (name derived from their traditional red-and-white striped uniforms).

Both dialects have the term *home help* referring to a person employed in the home of an invalid to help with routine tasks. In the UK these are often supplied as a health benefit under the NHS and are widely established; in the US they are paid for by insurance or by the household receiving the services. Home health care is now developing as an industry in the US because of the desire of hospitals to minimize in-patient stays. In the UK it seems to fall between the gap of the NHS and other government benefit programs. One symptom of this is *bed-blocking*, wherein NHS beds are alleged to be unavailable because they are occupied by patients too ill to be released under their own care and having no one who is able to take care of them.

Tools of the Trade

The following table shows differences in terminology between common implements and procedures of medical practice; those that are trademarks are presented after these.

MEDICAL PROCEDURES, SUPPLIES, AND EQUIPMENT

American	British
absorbent cotton	cotton wool
adhesive tape	surgical tape
EKG[1]	ECG
gurney, stretcher	(wheeled) stretcher
I.V. [an intravenous drip]	drip
lidocaine	lignocaine →
mouth-to-mouth resuscitation	kiss of life
operating room	(operating) theatre[2]
rubbing alcohol	surgical spirit
shot [informal, for injection]	jab
sponge bath	bed bath, blanket bath
tongue depressor	doctor's spatula

[1] American English spells the full form as *electrocardiogram* and also uses *ECG*.
[2] American English uses *operating theater* only where the operating room is equipped with tiers of seats around it for spectators in an educational setting.

MEDICAL TRADEMARKS

This table sets out trademarks for medicines and other products associated with healthcare that have succeeded in displacing a generic term in popular usage, or of getting there before the generic term was known. Items in the right-hand column with an initial cap are also trademarks unless indicated otherwise.

MEDICAL TRADEMARKS

Trademark	Source	What is it?
Accutane	US	isotretinoin [prescription drug for acute acne]
Ace bandage	US	beige-colored stretch bandage
Advil	US	ibuprofen; BrE Nurofen
Band-Aid	US	sticking plaster; BrE Elastoplast
ChapStick	US	lip salve
Dilantin	US	phenytoin

MEDICAL TRADEMARKS *(continued)*

Trademark	Source	What is it?
Dramamine	US	seasickness remedy
Elastoplast	UK	Band-Aid
Excedrin	US	headache formula: aspirin, acetaminophen, caffeine
Geritol	US	iron-rich vitamin supplement for older people [often used figuratively and humorously]
Halcion	US	benzodiazepine; BrE Mogadon
Kaopectate	US	antidiarrheal medicine
Largactil	UK	chlorpromazine; AmE Thorazine
Levonelle	UK	morning-after pill (Levonorgestrel)
Mifeprex	US	misoprostol; BrE RU486
Mogadon	UK	benzodiazepine; AmE Halcion
Nembutol	US	pentobarbitone
Nurofen	UK	ibuprofen; AmE Advil
Panadol	UK	acetaminophen; AmE Tylenol
Q-Tip	US	cotton bud
RU486	UK	misoprostol; AmE Mifeprex
Thorazine	US	chlorpromazine; BrE Largactil
Tylenol	US	acetaminophen; BrE Panadol
Zimmer frame	UK	walker

An American would look for all of these items in a *drug store*, which is normally assumed to contain a *pharmacy*, the only place that can dispense prescription drugs. The major chains of drug stores have now abandoned that name but it persists in usage. British English uses *chemist's* in about the same sense that Americans use *drug store*. One chain so dominates this trade in Britain, *Boots*, that its name is used generically to indicate the type.

ILLNESS

Terms for various ailments, treatments, devices, and procedures differ between the two dialects and are most easily presented as strict equivalents:

MEDICAL CONDITIONS AND REMEDIES

American	British
appendectomy	appendicectomy
Aztec two-step [informal]	gippy tummy [informal]

MEDICAL CONDITIONS AND REMEDIES *(continued)*

American	British
crib death	cot death[1]
goiter	goitre
mononucleosis, mono [informal]	glandular fever
prefrontal lobotomy	leucotomy
sleeping sickness	sleepy sickness

[1] Both dialects use *SIDS*, sudden infant death syndrome, as the technical name for this phenomenon.

AIDS is now the standard presentation for *acquired immune deficiency syndrome* in both dialects, although a few British publications, notably the *Guardian,* use *Aids*. Two other diseases have achieved initialism status in British English because of their frequent mention in the media that may need unpacking for American readers; these are *BSE* for *bovine spongiform encephalopathy*, the technical name for *mad cow disease*; and *CJD* for *Creutzfeldt–Jakob disease*, a human form of BSE believed to be contracted by eating meat from animals infected with BSE.

There is a noteworthy difference in the two dialects' use of the word *sick*. In American English it is a synonym for *ill*, and the only one used in many compounds and phrases, such as *sick pay, call in sick,* and *sick day*. In British English, *sick* also has the more particular meaning of *nauseated* or *vomiting*, which is apparent in such constructions as *be sick* (vomit), *sick-making* (nauseating), and *sick sth up* (vomit it). British English is more inclined to use *ill* for the meaning *unwell*, though many of the same compounds with *sick* exist in British as in American English. *Sick pay* in particular goes by the initialism *SSP* (statutory sick pay) in the UK.

The Language of Mental Health

A large number of voluntary self-help programs exist in the US based on the *AA* (Alcoholics Anonymous) model, which consists mostly of talk therapy combined with spirituality as a means of undoing an addiction. They are often called *twelve-step programs* because they require participants to work through that number of successive steps in coming to terms with their problem. These programs exist in the UK as well but have not penetrated the culture to the same degree as in the US, perhaps because their methods are essentially homegrown American in nature and their style is sometimes off-putting to the average Briton. A considerable amount of terminology from these programs has drifted into American

English generally and occurs frequently in speech, sometimes with over-tones of irony, though this is slowly disappearing as the terms become standardized and new users of them are unaware of their origins. The chief examples are

higher power. A notion of a Godlike entity that avoids any of the historical or established religious baggage accompanying God.

codependency. The notion that it takes two people to sustain a really successful addiction, one to practice it and the other to form an unhealthy dependence on the continuation of the addiction.

in recovery. Code phrase that refers to the status of participants in these programs. Recovery has come to mean the flipside, and happy alternative to, addiction.

boundaries. The limits of acceptable behavior toward oneself or others that people with addictions have difficulty distinguishing or maintaining.

CHAPTER SEVEN

Food, Clothing, and Shelter

We examine in this chapter differences between British and American English that are largely differences in vocabulary, although along the way we will encounter different styles, treatments, and forms in the objects of everyday life that give rise to these differences.

FOOD

The following five tables set out the terms likely to cause confusion to the transatlantic reader or listener. All are foods that are identical for practical purposes but go by different names, divided by category.

FRUITS, VEGETABLES, AND OTHER UNPROCESSED FOODS

American	British
arugula	rocket
beet	beetroot
blueberry	bilberry
bok choi	chinese leaves, pak choi
chicory	endive
cilantro	coriander →
corn	maize

FRUITS, VEGETABLES, AND OTHER UNPROCESSED FOODS (*continued*)

American	British
daikon	white radish
eggplant	aubergine
endive	chicory
fava bean	broad bean →
filbert →	hazel nut →, cob nut
garbanzo	chick pea →
golden raisins	sultanas
jícama	yam bean
legumes [beans]	pulses
lima bean	butter bean
okra →	ladies fingers
patty pan squash	custard marrow
persimmon	sharon fruit
romaine [lettuce]	cos
rutabaga	swede
scallion, green onion, shallot	spring onion
snow peas	mangetout
summer squash	(vegetable) marrow[1]
sweetsop, cherimoya	custard apple
tangerine	clementine →
winter squash	pumpkin
zucchini	courgette

[1] What are sold as *vegetable marrows* in the UK look, to an American eye, like any sort of summer squash that was left on the vine too long and allowed to grow too large.

American English uses *sweet potato* and *yam* interchangeably and imprecisely; British English, and precise Americans, use the first to designate the edible, tuberous root of the plant of *Ipomoea batatas*, of the morning glory family, and the latter to designate roots of the tropical genus *Dioscorea*. A vegetable sold in the UK under the name *greens* is a non-heading form of cabbage. Vegetables sold as *greens* in the US without more specific labeling are likely to be collard greens, mustard greens, or kale.

FISH AND MEAT PRODUCTS AND BYPRODUCTS

American	British
beef bouillon	beef tea
blood sausage	black pudding

FISH AND MEAT PRODUCTS AND BYPRODUCTS *(continued)*

American	British
chop [of lamb or pork]	cutlet
corned beef	salt beef
crown rump roast	silverside
double sirloin	baron of beef
fishstick	fish finger
ground beef, hamburger	mince
headcheese	brawn
link sausage	banger [*informal*]
liverwurst, Braunschweiger	liver sausage →
pig's feet	trotters →
pork rinds	pork scratchings
roast	joint
rump roast	topside
shrimp	prawn
tenderloin	fillet (steak), undercut
trout [some varieties]	char
variety meats	offal

British English classes several pork products under *bacon* that American English treats separately or doesn't know about. In the US, bacon is what Britons would call smoked, streaky *rashers* (that is, thin slices). The default sort of bacon in British English, the kind that comes with a cooked breakfast, is leaner than American bacon and not always smoked. American English *Canadian bacon* is similar to UK *back bacon*. Several varieties of smoked pork are sold as *gammon* in the UK; most of these would be called *ham* in the US.

SWEET FOODS

American	British
candied fruit	crystallized fruit
candy	sweets
candy apple	toffee apple
candy bar	chocolate bar[1]
conserve	preserves
cookie	biscuit [sweetened]
cotton candy	candy floss
doughnut, donut	ring doughnut

SWEET FOODS *(continued)*

American	British
hard candy	boiled sweet
jawbreaker	gobstopper
jelly doughnut	doughnut
jelly roll	Swiss roll
nonpareils	hundreds and thousands
sourball	acid drop

[1] *Chocolate bar* is used in American English only for bars that consist entirely or almost entirely of chocolate.

American English normally uses *dessert* for the sweet course following a meal. British English more commonly uses *sweet* or *pudding*. In American English, *pudding* is a particular kind of dessert of a smooth, gloppy consistency that resembles British English *blancmange*, with the difference that it is creamier and that any number of flavors can be added to it (chocolate, lemon, butterscotch, etc.).

Custard in American English is normally understood to be an old-fashioned boiled or baked dessert made from eggs, milk, and sugar. In British English it is more often a sauce, made by mixing milk with a store-bought powder, and poured over desserts.

PROCESSED FOODS AND FOODSTUFFS

American	British
canola oil	rapeseed oil
cornmeal	maize meal
cornstarch	corn flour
granulated sugar	caster sugar, castor sugar[1]
molasses	treacle, golden syrup[2]
pasta flour	semolina →
peanut oil	groundnut oil
powdered sugar, confectioner's sugar	icing sugar
quick oats	porridge oats
self-rising flour	self-raising flour
wholewheat flour	wholemeal flour

[1] Caster sugar is in fact more finely granulated than American granulated sugar, but each is substitutable for the other in cooking. *Superfine sugar* is a more exact American English equivalent.

[2] *Golden syrup* is a pale cane sugar syrup that is a standard ingredient in English cooking. American *light corn syrup* can substitute.

Although they are identified on the package as *rolled oats*, most Americans use *oatmeal* to describe both the raw and cooked version of this food. The cooked version is *porridge* in British English. UK supermarkets sell two forms of sugar not found in the US; *demerara* (for which US *turbinado* or *light brown sugar* can substitute) and *muscovado* (for which *dark brown sugar* can substitute).

MANUFACTURED FOODS AND PREPARED DISHES

American	British
baked potato	jacket potato
cracker →	biscuit [savory]
french fries	chips
gyro	doner kebab
potato chips	crisps
saltine	salted cracker

Pickle requires separate treatment because of its variable use. As a verb it has the same meaning in both dialects (preserve food in a salt or acid solution). Without further qualification, *pickle* in American English is a count noun meaning a cucumber pickle; these are subdivided into *dill pickles* (sour and flavored with dill) and *sweet pickles* (preserved in a sweet, spicy solution). A product very like an American sweet pickle sold in the UK is labeled as *gherkin*. Without qualification, *pickle* in British English is a mass noun to denote a condiment of any pickled vegetable. The pickle on a cheese and pickle sandwich is usually a commercial preparation called *Branston pickle*. There are a few other differences in the treatment of names of foods in terms of countability; these were treated in chapter 2.

Bread

Forms in which bread is sold in the two countries show fewer equivalents. American English *bun* is usually a good substitute for British English *roll* when it is part of a sandwich; thus (AmE) *hamburger buns,* (BrE) *hamburger rolls.* British English has a large, round form of bread that to Americans looks like an oversize hamburger bun; it's called a *bap.* The breakfast food that American English terms *English muffin* is what you might hope in British English, that is, just *muffin.* But the food that American English designates *muffin,* that is, a small, unfrosted, dome-top, usually sweetened cake, when seen in Britain, is also called a *muffin,* because it is an American import. What Americans term a *biscuit* is more or less identical to the British *scone*, except that scones are sometimes sweetened or contain raisins, features that don't often appear in American biscuits.

Other forms of bread possibly unfamiliar transatlantically and having no near equivalent term are

BREAD

Name	Source	What is it?
bannock	UK	round, flat, often fried bread from Scotland
bialy	US	flat, baked roll topped with onions
bloomer	UK	large loaf of white bread with diagonal slashes on the top
cornbread, cornpone	US	bread made from maize meal
crumpet[1]	UK	about halfway between an English muffin and a pancake
digestive biscuit	UK	bland cookie made with wholewheat flour
hush puppy	US	deep-fried cornbread
kaiser roll	US	roll with a cross pattern formed by folding the corners of the dough to the top
sopaipilla	US	deep-fried bread dough that forms a pocket
zwieback	US	rusk in very thin slices

[1] *Crumpet* is also a popular slang term for a sexually attractive woman or man.

The sandwich on a long bun with various fillings that American English calls a *sub* or a *hoagie* has no distinct name in British English, and the bread on which it is served would probably be called a *roll* in Britain; *sub* is likely to make headway in British English in the wake of the American fast food chain Subway, which now has outlets in the UK.

The modifier *salad* tacked onto the name of a sandwich filling in American English means a usually homogenous filling consisting of chopped ingredients, held together by mayonnaise: *ham salad.* In British English, *salad* means "with lettuce, tomato, and cucumber added." Thus a *cheese salad sandwich,* which would seem incomprehensible to American ears. Unless requested without it, a British sandwich always has butter (or substitute thereof) spread on the bread; an American one doesn't.

CAKES

As antidotes to human suffering, cakes occupy a cherished place in the lexicons of all English speakers. Here are the ones that may be unfamiliar to the nonnative of one country or the other.

CAKES

Name	Source	Equivalent or Explanation
angel cake	UK	angel food cake
angel food cake	US	angel cake
Banbury cake	UK	round or oval pastry filled with candied fruit
black forest cake	US	black forest gateau
Boston cream pie	US	chocolate-iced yellow cake enclosing a layer of custard
buckwheat cake	US	usually yeast-raised pancake made with buckwheat flour
Bundt cake	US	ring-shaped cake made in a pan with fluted edges
Christmas cake	UK	rich fruit cake topped with marzipan and white icing
cupcake	US	fairycake
devils food cake	US	a rich chocolate cake with chocolate icing
Dundee cake	UK	fruit cake decorated with almonds
Eccles cake	UK	small round flat cake with currants
fairy cake	UK	cupcake
funnel cake	US	batter extruded from a pipe into hot fat and dusted with sugar; sold at fairs
hotcake	US	pancake
Jaffa cake	UK	cookie with a layer of orange jam topped with chocolate
johnnycake	US	cornbread, often sweetened
Kendal mint cake	UK	peppermint candy sold in rectangular blocks, popular with hikers
Madeira cake	UK	dense, rich sponge cake
oatcake	UK	thin, flat cracker made from oatmeal
rock cake	UK	large, crude biscuit with currants baked in it
Simnel cake	UK	fruit cake covered with marzipan
strawberry shortcake	US	a scone split and topped with strawberries and whipped cream

A *flapjack* in British English is a dense cake made from compressed oats, held together by sugar and butter and cut in squares. In American English, *flapjack* is a synonym for pancake.

FROM THE DAIRY

Both countries have taken to removing the fat from milk to produce a dizzying variety of products. Equivalents are roughly as shown.

DAIRY PRODUCTS

American	British
whole milk	full cream milk
2% or reduced fat milk	semiskimmed milk
lowfat milk (1% milkfat)	—
nonfat milk, skim(med) milk	skimmed milk

At the other end of the scale, cream of various concentrations goes by different names, and here there are not always equivalents, just approximations. They are listed here by their fat content:

FORMS OF CREAM

Type	Fat Content
Clotted (or Devonshire) Cream (UK)	55%
Double Cream (UK)	48%
Heavy Cream (US)	36%
Whipping Cream (both countries)	33%
Single Cream (UK) or Light Cream (US)	18%
Half Cream (UK) or Half and Half (US)	12%

US *sour cream* is a thicker and richer product than UK *soured cream*. For cooking, the UK product called *crème fraiche* is a suitable substitute for US sour cream. *Cream cheese* in both countries has about the same taste but a much thinner consistency in the UK, except Philadelphia brand, which is the same in both countries. *Fromage fraise* is a UK product, sometimes seen in the US, with the consistency of yogurt, eaten plain or used in cooking like yogurt. All of these products are sold in versions with less fat, usually called *reduced fat* in American English, *half fat* in British English.

All the foregoing are found in a part of the supermarket that American English dubs the *dairy case* for historical reasons that are now obscured.

Indigenous Foods

A proper treatment of the many foods that are the particular genius of each country could fill a whole book; this table presents those that are probably familiar to every native, but possibly not known to the transatlantic visitor. Many in the UK are of French origin; many in the US are of Mexican or German origin.

INDIGENOUS FOODS

Food	Source	What is it?
Bakewell tart	UK	pie filled with red jam and almond spongecake
BLT	US	bacon, lettuce, and tomato sandwich
bubble & squeak	UK	fried cabbage and potatoes
Buffalo wings	US	spicy chicken wings
chicken-fried steak	US	inferior beef steak, battered and fried
chip butty	UK	french fry sandwich
cobbler	US	dessert with fruit on the bottom, sweet cake on the top
corn dog	US	deep-fried, batter-dipped frankfurter on a stick
fajitas	US	strips of marinated and grilled meat, served with tortillas and condiments, of Tex-Mex origin
gumbo	US	stew served with rice, containing okra
haggis	UK	a sheep's stomach stuffed with oats, suet, and organ meats; from Scotland
hash browns	US	shredded or cut fried potatoes
lemon curd	UK	spreadable sweetened lemon conserve
pease pudding	UK	split peas boiled with onions and carrots and mashed
pie & mash	UK	steak and kidney pie with mashed potatoes
Reuben cheese	US	a sandwich of corned beef, sauerkraut, and swiss on rye bread
Rocky Mountain oyster	US	calf testicle; also called *prairie oyster*
Salisbury steak	US	inferior beef steak cooked in gravy
sauerbraten	US	beef marinated in pickling solution before roasting
saveloy	UK	dried and smoked pork sausage
spotted dick	UK	suet pudding with currants
succotash	US	maize and lima beans cooked together
taramasalata	UK	cod-roe based spread of Greek origin
toad-in-the-hole	UK	sausage baked in batter

Trademarks

Certain brands of foods, and some other household products, are known primarily by their trademarked name, either because of being unique, or because of being so successful as to attract imitators. Those that have achieved international acclaim in the Anglophone world (Nescafé, Spam, etc.) are not listed here because they are already familiar in both countries. The table identifies the product for the group of speakers who may not know what it is, or in some cases gives the name of a product that occupies a similar niche in the other country. Items in the right-hand column with an initial cap are also trademarks unless indicated otherwise.

FOOD TRADEMARKS

Trademark	Source	What is it?
A-1 Sauce	US	like HP Sauce
Bisquick	US	powdered mixture requiring only water (and eggs) to make scones (and pancakes)
Bisto	UK	gravy mix
Bovril	UK	concentrated beef broth
Britvic	UK	citrus-flavored soft drink
Cambazola	UK	camembert cheese with gorgonzola mold
Certo	UK	fruit pectin
Chiclets	US	pelletized chewing gum
Cracker Jack	US	candy-coated popcorn
Cream of Wheat	US	farina-based hot breakfast cereal
Crisco	US	solid vegetable fat used in baking
Eskimo Pie	US	chocolate-coated ice cream on a stick
Fig Newtons	US	biscuit wrapped around fig filling
Fritos	US	maize chips
Fudgsicle	US	frozen chocolate confection on a stick
Gentlemen's Relish	UK	salty anchovy paste for spreading
Granary bread	UK	bread with softened whole wheatberries baked in
Hob-Nobs	UK	oat cookies
Horlicks	UK	powdered sweetened malt for mixing with milk; similar to Ovaltine
Hovis	UK	white bread
HP sauce	UK	like A-1 Sauce
Iron Bru	UK	high-caffeine soft drink
Jell-O	US	sweetened gelatin dessert; BrE jelly
Kool-Aid	US	flavored, colored sugar-water drink
Lucozade	UK	soft drink with glucose
M&M's	US	like Smarties
Marmite	UK	salty, dark brown yeast extract for spreading on toast and sandwiches

FOOD TRADEMARKS *(continued)*

Trademark	Source	What is it?
Miracle Whip	US	salad cream with the consistency of mayonnaise
Mountain Dew	US	high-caffeine soft drink
Ovaltine	US	powdered sweetened malt for mixing with milk; similar to Horlicks
Pablum[1]	US	bland cereal baby food
Pam	US	aerosol cooking oil
PG Tips	UK	leading brand of tea bags
Popsicle	US	ice lolly
Ribena	UK	blackcurrant juice
Smarties	UK	like M&M's
Twinkie	US	yellow serving-sized sponge cake filled with sugary white foam
Vegeburger	UK	soy protein sold in patty form
Wheaties	US	breakfast cereal featuring famous athletes on the box; reputedly the "breakfast of champions"

[1] *Pablum* is also used figuratively to disparage overly simplified argument or explanation.

Drinks

Beverage is the standard technical and trade term for *drink* in both dialects, though it has more currency in American English than in British English, where it has an old-fashioned ring and collocates mainly with *alcoholic*. The names designating all the most popular beverages are the same in both dialects, with these exceptions:

- **beer.** Without further qualification, Americans mean *lager* when they say *beer*, that is, a bottom-fermented, aged, somewhat fizzy, and usually light-colored beer. Britons normally mean *ale* when they say beer, that is, a top-fermented, minimally aged, not very fizzy, slightly darker beer; though they may call this *ale* as well. When Britons mean lager beer, they say *lager*. *Stout* is also drunk in both countries, but is considered a slightly exotic import in the US. *Porter* (ale from roasted barley) and *bitter* (ale with lots of hops) are not much known in the US. *Malt liquor* is an ale/beer hybrid with high alcoholic content sold in the US, mostly drunk by those interested in its effect rather than its taste.
- **cider.** Without qualification, Britons mean fermented *cider*, i.e., cider with alcoholic content. For Americans, cider is just freshly pressed apple juice, and *hard cider* is the one with alcoholic content. The

distilled version of this is in American English is *applejack*, not much
known in the UK.

- **cordial.** In British English, a concentrate of fruit juice mixed with
  water; in American English, an alcoholic liqueur.
- **lemonade.** In British English this is a lemon or lemon-lime flavored
  carbonated drink, like Sprite® or Seven-Up®. Lemonade in the US is
  made from lemons, sugar, and water (or more often, from a frozen concentrate of this). This is designated in the UK as *fresh lemonade*.
  Shandy is a UK concoction of lemonade (British-style) and beer.
- **whisky/whiskey.** See chapter 1, where this is treated under spelling.

British English uses the handy designations *fizzy* and *still* to distinguish
what American English more awkwardly calls *carbonated* and *noncarbon-
ated*; all of these are especially used to label mineral waters. British English
fizzy water is an informal designation for beverages variously called *club
soda*, *seltzer*, and *mineral water* in the US. British English uses *fizzy drinks*
for what American English formally calls *carbonated beverages*, and more
informally calls *pop*, *soda pop*, or *soda*. A product common in the UK but
not sold in the US is called *squash*, which is concentrated, sweetened fruit
juice, diluted to make a drink. Juice concentrates are mainly sold frozen in
the US.

Mealtimes

The three main meal terms, *breakfast*, *lunch*, and *dinner*, are similarly
used in both dialects, with *dinner* usually denoting

- the main meal of the day, whenever served
- a formal meal
- the evening meal when eaten somewhere other than at home

Supper usually denotes a lighter and later meal in British English than in
American English, because British English has *tea* to designate a meal that
most Americans would call dinner or supper, that is, a cooked meal eaten
after work, in the early evening. *Tea*, along with *high tea*, can also designate
a late afternoon meal consisting of tea and small sandwiches or pastries.[1]
British English also has *elevenses*, a snack eaten around eleven in the morning, for which the nearest American English equivalent is *mid-morning
snack*.

1. *High tea* is increasingly being usurped by expensive hotels as the designation for a fancy afternoon service mainly for tourists who want to experience something quaintly British.

Cooking and Kitchen Terms

The art of *cooking* (as American English has it) or *cookery* (as British English has it) shares a large vocabulary in the two dialects that includes most of its activities and implements. Here are some variations.

COOKING AND KITCHEN TERMS

American	British
breadbox	bread bin
broil, broiler	grill *n,v*
can	tin
cookbook	cookery book
cookie sheet	baking tray, baking sheet →
cooktop	hob
dish towel	tea towel →
double boiler	bain-marie, double saucepan
faucet	tap →
flatware, silverware	cutlery
french press pot	cafétière
napkin →	serviette
package [as a food container]	packet
paper towels	kitchen roll
pitcher	jug
pour [from a bowl to a pan]	tip
punch down [bread dough]	knock down, knock back
range, stove	cooker
salt shaker	salt cellar
set the table	lay the table
slotted spatula	fish slice
tableware, dishes	crockery
tube pan	angel cake tin

Some older British recipes and ovens have numbered temperature settings prefixed with *gas mark*. Equivalents are shown in the table with Fahrenheit and Celsius.

COOKING TEMPERATURE EQUIVALENTS

Celsius	Fahrenheit	Gas Mark
130	250	1
150	300	2
170	325	3
180	350	4
190	375	5
200	400	6
220	425	7
240	475	8
250	500	9

The following table contains trademarked household items that, if not used in cooking, are mainly used in the kitchen and are familiarly known by the trademark. In many cases the trademark name is used to denote similar products. Items in the right-hand column with an initial cap are also trademarks unless indicated otherwise.

TRADEMARK HOUSEHOLD ITEMS

Trademark	Source	What is it?
Aga	UK	heavy cooking stove that also provides heat
Baggie	US	sandwich-sized plastic bag
Brillo pad	US	soap-impregnated steel wool blob
Clorox	US	household bleach
Crockpot	US	slow electric cooker made of crockery
Dettol	UK	disinfectant household cleaner
Dixie cup	US	disposable paper cup
Drano	US	corrosive liquid for unblocking drains
Fairy liquid	UK	dishwashing detergent
Frigidaire	US	fridge [becoming *dated*]
Handi-wipe	US	J-cloth
J-cloth	UK	Handi-wipe
Kilner jar	UK	Mason jar [not a trademark]
Mr. Clean	US	household cleaner
Pinesol	US	household cleaner, supposed to smell of pines
Saran wrap	US	cling film
Teasmade	UK	automatic tea maker

Cooking Personalities

Both the US and the UK have names that are inseparable from cookery and food products. These are sometimes used to characterize a style of food, or of cooking. Here's the Who's Who:

COOKING AND FOOD PERSONALITIES

Name	Source	Who is it?
Aunt Jemima	US	fictitious emblem associated with pancake mixes and syrups; a trademark owned by Quaker Oats. Formerly depicted as an African-American "mammy," which has resulted in the name meaning a subservient black. Her image today is considerably modernized.
Betty Crocker	US	fictitious author of cookbooks and a brand name of several processed foods; a trademark owned by General Mills. The true daughter of cuisine and capitalism.
Delia Smith	UK	doyenne of modern mainstream British cooking; familiarly known simply as Delia
Julia Child	US	chef largely credited with bringing French cuisine to the US through books and television programs; now retired
Mrs Beeton	UK	author of a still-respected nineteenth-century book on cooking and housekeeping; represents the order of the past

Restaurant Notes

Entrée usually means "main course" in American English and it is gaining ground with this meaning in British English, but at a formal British dinner the entrée is served before the main course. Anything so designated on an American menu is a main course. British English *takeaway*, used as a noun and attributively, is sometimes heard in American English, although *carryout* and *takeout* are commoner. Americans usually *reserve* a table; Britons *book* one. American English has adopted the nonsexist terms *server* (singular) and *waitstaff* (plural) to include waiters and waitresses together; both terms are gaining currency in British English. Americans ask for the *check* at the end of the meal, Britons for the *bill*.

A handful of restaurant types exist mainly in one country as an institution and in the other, if at all, as an exotic imitation.

RESTAURANTS

restaurant	Source	What is it?
caf, café	UK	simple restaurant serving fried food for breakfast and sandwiches at lunch; often closed in the afternoon
chippy	UK	a takeaway restaurant serving mainly fish and chips
deli	US	mainly urban establishment specializing in sandwiches with quality ingredients
diner	US	originally a long, narrow restaurant clad in chrome, now a larger roadside restaurant, still clad in chrome and serving mainstream American food
lunch counter	US	a corner in a retail business where sandwiches are prepared; fast becoming obsolete
ockabasi	UK	Turkish restaurant featuring a charcoal grill; ubiquitous in London and spreading

Café in American English doesn't denote a type of restaurant but is used in the names of particular restaurants from greasy spoons up to haute cuisine establishments. Informally in British English, *Indian* and *Chinese* are used as nouns to indicate restaurants featuring those cuisines, or food from them: *dinner at the local Indian, she doesn't like Chinese.* In American English the food is designated this way, but not the restaurant.

Food Additives

The names of food additives do not differ much between American and British English but their designation on packaging does, since Britain conforms to the rest of the European Union in identifying food additives by *E numbers*, perhaps to spare the consumer the direct knowledge of what is really added to food!

E Numbers 100–199 are approved food colorings and includes many about which health concerns have been raised in the US and elsewhere; E950–957 are sweeteners, including *E951 aspartame, E952 cyclamates,* and *E954 saccharin.* Here is a table of the most common ones, with their chemical name or occasionally, their more common American English name:

E NUMBERS

E200	Sorbic acid	E410	Locust bean gum
E202	Potassium sorbate	E412	Guar gum
E203	Calcium sorbate	E413	Tragacanth
E210	Benzoic acid	E414	gum arabic
E211	Sodium benzoate	E415	Xanthan gum
E212	Potassium benzoate	E420	Sorbitol
E213	Calcium benzoate	E432	polysorbate 20
E220	Sulphur dioxide	E433	polysorbate 80
E221	Sodium sulphite	E434	polysorbate 40
E226	Calcium sulphite	E435	polysorbate 60
E249	Potassium nitrite	E436	polysorbate 65
E250	Sodium nitrite	E440	Pectins
E251	Sodium nitrate	E450	Diphosphates
E252	Potassium nitrate	E451	Triphosphates
E260	Acetic acid	E460	Cellulose
E270	Lactic acid	E500	Sodium carbonates
E281	Sodium propionate	E501	Potassium carbonates
E282	Calcium propionate	E503	Ammonium carbonates
E283	Potassium propionate	E504	Magnesium carbonates
E284	Boric acid	E507	Hydrochloric acid
E285	borax	E508	Potassium chloride
E290	Carbon dioxide	E509	Calcium chloride
E296	Malic acid	E511	Magnesium chloride
E297	Fumaric acid	E512	Stannous chloride
E300	Ascorbic acid	E513	Sulphuric acid
E301	Sodium ascorbate	E514	Sodium sulphates
E302	Calcium ascorbate	E515	Potassium sulphates
E322	Lecithins	E516	Calcium sulphate
E325	Sodium lactate	E517	Ammonium sulphate
E326	Potassium lactate	E520	Aluminium sulphate
E327	Calcium lactate	E524	Sodium hydroxide
E330	Citric acid	E525	Potassium hydroxide
E331	Sodium citrates	E526	Calcium hydroxide
E332	Potassium citrates	E527	Ammonium hydroxide
E333	Calcium citrates	E528	Magnesium hydroxide
E334	Tartaric acid	E529	Calcium oxide
E338	Phosphoric acid	E530	Magnesium oxide
E339	Sodium phosphates	E553	Magnesium silicates
E340	Potassium phosphates	E553	Talc
E341	Calcium phosphates	E576	Sodium gluconate
E343	Magnesium phosphates	E577	Potassium gluconate
E406	Agar	E578	Calcium gluconate
E407	Carrageenan	E579	Ferrous gluconate

E NUMBERS *(continued)*			
E585	Ferrous lactate	E904	Shellac
E620	Glutamic acid	E905	Microcrystalline wax
E621	Monosodium glutamate	E920	L-Cysteine
E901	Bees wax		

A useful and annotated complete list can be found at http://www.bryngollie.freeserve.co.uk/Enumbers.htm.

Some notes on the terminology of cooking measures can be found in Appendix 3.

SHELTER

The built landscapes in the US and the UK developed independently and organically out of their own locations and therefore differ a great deal in both appearance and description; we will start at the top and work our way down to the smallest particulars, noting differences along the way.

Types and Organization of Communities

From the level of city down to the level of neighborhood there is substantial overlap in the terminology that denotes settled areas in the US and the UK.[1] Below this, differences start to emerge. An area of uniform housing all built at the same time is usually called an *estate* or *housing estate* in British English; *estate* is the preferred term in British English for areas that contain multiples of the same sort of building: other examples include *council estate* (AmE *housing project*), *industrial estate* (AmE *industrial park*), and *trading estate* (AmE *business park*). Aside from its legal uses, *estate* in American English has much more limited currency. In the context of real property, and aside from the fixed collocation *real estate*, it conjures up something quite grand: *O. J. Simpson's Brentwood estate*. In the US an area of similar houses built at the same time is called a *development* or *housing development*; a more recent coinage is to call such areas *communities*, though this is mainly a marketing term. *Gated community* is now the standard term for a (usually high-dollar) development with controlled access for residents. A larger area newly opened to building that may con-

---

1. Though note the variable use of *village*, discussed in chapter 4.

tain multiple developments is often called a *subdivision* because it comes into existence by changes to zoning laws that applied to a larger division of land.

American English conveniently notes an area bounded by streets on all sides as a *block*. Most American towns and cities are built on grids, typically with orientation to the cardinal compass points, with uniform blocks in all directions; thus the term is so ubiquitous that it serves as a distance marker (*three blocks away*) and is used as shorthand in journalism to denote an approximate address: *the 4800 block of N. Washtenaw Ave.* means one of the houses in the block where the numbers range from 4800 to 4899 on the named street. This is sufficient to locate a spot in the minds of residents, since most US cities have a grid-based house numbering system. No such thing exists in British English, where *block* is usually a synonym for *building*. It occurs in *office block* (AmE *office building*), *tower block* (AmE *high-rise*), *block of flats* (AmE *apartment building*), and *mansion block* (an architecturally significant luxury apartment building of a kind found mostly in London).

Types of Dwellings

Names for the kinds of places where people live vary considerably in the two dialects. Styles of dwellings differ as well, and the niche that each place occupies in the cultural imagination is not necessarily the same as its seeming functional equivalent in the other dialect. Discussion of these names therefore follows, after this brief table of rough equivalents:

DWELLINGS

American	British
apartment	flat
high-rise (apartment building)	tower block
single family house	detached house
townhouse, row house	terraced house
apartment hotel, residence hotel	service flats
trailer, manufactured home	caravan

As noted above, *apartment* and *flat* are equivalents in a general way for a dwelling within a building that has accommodation for more than one household. American English distinguishes *condominium* (*condo* for

short) as an apartment that is owned outright rather than rented from a
landlord. Condominium sometimes refers to the entire building, and a
building that *goes condo* is one that converts from rented to owned apartments. *Flat* makes its way into American English in the compounds *two-
flat, three-flat, six-flat*, etc., meaning a building that contains two, three,
six, etc., apartments, and in *railroad flat*, a now old-fashioned type of
apartment consisting of a row of similar rooms opening onto a long corridor. Some parts of the US, notably New York, also have *co-op apartments*,
co-ops for short, in which the building is owned by a corporation that consists of the tenant-shareholders. British English has no distinct terminology for a rented, as opposed to an owned flat. Interestingly, each dialect
uses the other's preferred term as a sort of value-enhanced alternative;
thus, one can find very expensive *apartments* for sale in parts of London,
and a current luxury development on Baltimore's waterfront is being marketed as *European flats*.

British governments until recently have been much more in the business of building and owning housing than American ones, and as a result
the number and kinds of people who live in *council estates* are not really
comparable to those who live in *housing projects* in the US, which are
mainly substandard, inner-city slums. *Council flats* and *houses*, while rarely
luxurious, are often seen as desirable because of their low rents and guaranteed maintenance. Starting in the 1980s tenants in these flats were allowed to buy them. *Ex-council* is used to denote a flat or house in a council
estate that is now privately owned.

American houses vary considerably in style owing to the variety of cli-
mates and cultural milieus they are built in. A few styles are popular
throughout the country and are identified in real estate advertising by a
convenient shorthand. A *Victorian* is a house around a hundred years old
(or a newer house in this style) of brick or wood frame construction, two
stories at least, and often with ornate, decorative wood features inside and
out. A British Victorian house is quite similar in style, though with smaller
rooms and nearly always made of brick. A *Queen Anne* is less ornate than a
Victorian, but similar in style and often includes a wrap-around porch. A
ranch house, ranch, or *rancher* is a one-story, relatively modern house, in a
rectangular or L-shape. A *Cape Cod* is usually one and a half stories, wood
frame construction, with a gabled roof and dormer windows. A *colonial* is
rectangular, usually two stories, with shutters (not usually functional), sash
windows divided into small panes (not usually genuine), and typically with
fireplaces. A *saltbox* is two full stories high in front and one story high in

back with a sloping roof descending toward the front and back and the ridge toward the front of the house. A style currently in fashion among those who can afford it is derided by others as *McMansion*: a large family house that borrows randomly from various styles, needlessly proliferates gables, and presents a façade of ostentatious wealth.

In Britain, a common dwelling even more humble than the flat is the *bedsit* or *bedsitter*, a room or small suite of rooms in a house with shared facilities, such as a kitchen or bathroom. Flats come in a wider variety of styles than can be found in the US, and have the descriptions to prove it. A *converted flat* is one that was carved out of a building formerly serving some other purpose—typically as a single family house. The opposite is a *purpose built* flat, one in a building that was built to contain only flats (a *block of flats*). Some such buildings in Scotland of a particular style and vintage are called *tenements* and many of these have been refurbished to a high standard, though it is unlikely they could ever be marketed to someone from the US under this name, where a tenement is always a shabby, inner-city apartment building. A *maisonette* is a flat that occupies more than one floor of a building and has its own separate entrance from the street.

A feature of property common in Britain and not much encountered in the US is the distinction between freehold and leasehold. *Freehold* is the British English term for owning of real property outright, and corresponds to American English *fee simple*, though this term is rarely used outside of legal and technical real estate contexts. A *leasehold* property is one in which the owner enjoys complete possession and use of the property but the freehold belongs to another. The leaseholder pays a nominal annual *ground rent* to the freeholder, and the leases are usually very long-term affairs, such as one hundred years. Recent UK governments have encouraged the conversion of leasehold properties to freeholdings.

Houses in Britain vary less in style than those in the US, owing partly to the similarity of climate and partly to a tendency toward conformity to architectural styles of the nineteenth century. The commonest feature of urban domestic architecture is the *terraced house*, which shares walls with similar houses on each side; it is like an American *row house*, though without the associations of urban poverty that may accompany that term in American English. One socioeconomic step up from this is the *semi-detached house* (*semi* for short), attached to a mirror-image house on one side but open on the other; it is like an American *duplex*, though far more prevalent in the UK. A *detached house* is free-standing without attachment to another dwelling. Because detached houses are the exception rather than the rule in Britain, owning or living in one is perceived as a mark of worldly success; the term carries this association and amounts to quite a lot more than the sum of its parts. By contrast, the American English near equivalent *single-family home* is merely a descriptive term.

A British English *villa* is a detached house in a residential area, usually in Victorian or Edwardian style. An *end-of-terrace house* is intermediate between a terraced house and a semi, being the last house in a terrace and therefore open on one side. A *mews* property is one converted from or in a street that once consisted of stables. Besides the omnipresent *Victorian* houses, common British architectural styles include *Georgian* (generally flat facades, large windows, and some neoclassical features), *Tudor* or *mock-Tudor* (showing large, exposed wooden beams contrasting with white-painted plaster filling, which is called *half-timbering*).

It is common in many parts of the US to have an entire story of a home six feet or more below ground level; this part of the house is called the *basement*, and if habitable, it may be noted as a *finished basement*. It is normally called a *cellar* if it has earthen walls and floor, and this is now only found in older houses. An entire story well below grade is less common in the UK, and might be called either a cellar or a basement. More common is a floor of the house three feet or so below grade; when it is a separate dwelling it is marketed as a *garden flat*. The flat above it is typically noted as having a *raised ground floor*. The story of a house or any other building above the nominal ground floor is the *first floor* in British English, the *second floor* in American English, and so forth upwards.

Bed and breakfast (*B and B*, *B & B*) exists in both dialects and mainly describes the comfortable, often quaint rural hideaway where overnight paying guests can experience local color and a cooked breakfast the next day. In the UK, urban B & Bs are also used as accommodation for the vast numbers of people requiring it at government expense, such as refugees and asylum seekers. This gives a different connotation entirely for the term in British English. The naive American might think that someone described as "living in a B & B in Tottenham" was enjoying an idyllic existence, rather than living in indifferent squalor, which is more likely to be the case. The nearest American English equivalent for this sort of B & B is the *welfare hotel* or *transient hotel*; the technical term in American English is *SRO housing*, where the "SRO" stands for "single room occupancy," not "standing room only." Corresponding informal and disparaging terms are BrE *dosshouse* and AmE *flophouse* or *fleabag*.

Features of Dwellings

There is considerable variety in the names of rooms and housing features between American and British English; many of the terms are encountered most frequently in real estate advertising, whence some have made their way into ordinary speech. The first short table is a list of straightforward equivalents. The second table lists terms in property descriptions that are most likely to be unfamiliar or misunderstood, along with near equivalents where they exist. American advertisers are in the habit of saying that properties *feature* their various qualities; British property sellers claim that their properties *benefit from* the various things found there.

EQUIVALENT FEATURES OF HOUSING

American	British
baseboard	skirting board
clapboard	weatherboard
closet	cupboard
downspout	downpipe
exhaust fan	extractor fan
lot	plot
sunporch, Florida room	conservatory
transom[1]	fanlight, transom window
yard	garden[2]

[1] This word is the source of the American idiom *over the transom,* meaning "unsolicited": *a sampling of responses from the public that came over the transom.*

[2] British English uses *garden* for any of the property connected to a house that is cultivated, even a lawn. American English uses *yard* in this sense, and uses *garden* specifically for areas where a particular sort of planting is done: *a flower/vegetable garden.*

British English uses *fire* generally for what American English would distinguish as a *fireplace,* an *electric heater* (sometimes *electric fire* in British English), and a *gas heater* (sometimes *gas fire* in British English).

UNIQUE FEATURES OF HOUSES

Term	Source	Meaning (and near equivalent)
airing cupboard	UK	a closet built around a boiler or hot water heater where damp clothes may be hung to dry
basin	UK	a sink in any room that is not the kitchen

UNIQUE FEATURES OF HOUSES *(continued)*

Term	Source	Meaning (and near equivalent)
boiler[1]	UK	a gas-burning heat generator that circulates hot water to a radiator system and sometimes supplies hot water
cable	US	a connection to a cable television provider
cathedral ceiling	US	a high, vaulted ceiling
central vac	US	an electric hoovering system built into the house
cloakroom	UK	a small room containing a toilet; a *half-bath*
commode	US	toilet [becoming dated]
deck	US	an outdoor wooden platform at floor level for sitting outside or dining in good weather
double glazing	UK	windows with two panes of glass
drawing room	UK	dated or elegant variation of reception room
Eurokitchen	US	fitted kitchen with white appliances
fitted kitchen/bathroom	UK	a kitchen/bathroom in which the cabinets are built to the walls [normally taken for granted in the US]
full amenities	US	doorman, garage, and laundry facilities in an apartment building
great room	US	ostentatiously large *reception room*
half-bath	US	a room with a sink and a toilet
hutch	US	a built-in cabinet with a glass front
laundry	US	a washer and dryer in a house; a laundry room with coin-operated machines in an apartment building
loo[2]	UK	less refined designation for *cloakroom*; a *half-bath*
mixer tap	UK	a faucet that mixes input from hot and cold water sources [taken for granted in the US]
powder room	US	marketing term for half-bath
rec room, family room	US	a large room for the pursuit of indoor recreation
reception room	UK	a room suitable for receiving guests; nearest American equivalent is living room
siding	US	vinyl or aluminum covering in overlapping horizontal strips on the outside of a house
sitting room	UK	a room with couches and chairs where people can sit
wet bar	US	a drinks bar that includes a sink

[1] In American English *boiler* is used mainly as the heating furnace of a large commercial building.
[2] *Loo* generally does the work of American English *toilet* and *bathroom*, standing for both the porcelain fixture and the room where it is conventionally located.

Both countries support a thriving market in upgrading existing dwellings. *Refurbishment* is the preferred British English term for this, *renovation* is preferred in the US. A building in the US that has been completely demolished and rebuilt on the inside, or the process of doing this, is called a *rehab* or *gut rehab*. British English for this process is *conversion*, and the result is a *converted property*.

There is also a mechanism whereby properties in both countries can be designated as architecturally significant and therefore worth preserving in their original state, or some minimally altered version of it. In the UK this is an industry that keeps many builders, lawyers, and civil servants busy; dwellings so designated are called *listed* buildings or properties and are divided into *Grade I* (buildings of outstanding interest) and *Grade II* (buildings of special interest), with some finer shadings of status attached to these. No such building can be demolished or altered without special permission. There is no standard terminology for this practice in American English since rules governing it are mainly at the state or local rather than the national level.[1] *Designated landmark* and *landmark status* are both widely used.

Items for the Home

These two tables set out (1) household items that are mainly known by their trademark name in either country, and (2) household items, including furniture, that go by a different name in the two dialects.

HOUSEHOLD PRODUCT TRADEMARKS

Trademark	Source	What is it?
Anglepoise lamp	UK	desk lamp with a sprung, flexible arm
Ansaphone	UK	telephone answering machine
Biro	UK	ball-point pen
Blu-tack	UK	sticky blue-colored clay for attaching posters, etc.
Chubb	UK	deadbolt lock
Entryphone	UK	apartment-to-front-door intercom system
Hoover	UK	any vacuum cleaner
Lilo	UK	inflatable air bed
Plasticine	UK	similar to Play-Doh
Play-Doh	US	similar to Plasticine
Polyfilla	UK	similar to Spackle
Scotch tape	US	similar to Sellotape

1. An exception are those on the *National Register of Historic Places*, administered by the National Park Service.

HOUSEHOLD PRODUCT TRADEMARKS *(continued)*

Trademark	Source	What is it?
Sellotape	UK	similar to Scotch tape
Spackle	US	similar to Polyfilla
Thermos	US	vacuum flask

Dresser is more or less interchangeable in American English with *chest of drawers*, though if in a bedroom it is more likely to be called a dresser. In British English, a *dresser* (also *Welsh dresser*) is a storage device with drawers or cabinets below, and open shelves above, and is therefore the same as American English *hutch*, with the difference that a hutch can be built-in as well as movable.

The terms *decorating* and *redecorating* have similar application in both dialects, though in British English they can mean as little as painting or wallpapering. Americans use these terms specifically if that's all they're doing, and use the more general terms for a room makeover that includes changing several other items of décor as well as the color of the walls.

HOUSEWARES AND FURNITURE

American	British
clothes pin	(clothes) peg
comforter	duvet
couch	settee, divan →
crib	cot
extension cord	flex
flashlight	torch
floor lamp	standard lamp
hassock, ottoman	pouffe
highboy	tallboy
nightstand	bedside table →
sheer curtains	net curtains
thumbtack	drawing pin
trundle bed	truckle bed
valance	pelmet

The Money End of Real Property

Tenants on both sides of the Atlantic *rent* their dwellings. American landlords *rent out* their properties, or *rent* them *to tenants*, whereas British landlords *let* their properties. Advertising reflects this difference in usage: the US has *apartments for rent*, Britain has *flats to let*.

Householders wishing to buy or sell a property usually deal with *estate agents* in the UK, *Realtors* in the US. *Realtor* is a trademark and technically applies only to agents who belong to a national association; but in fact nearly all agents do, and the term is used ordinarily without any awareness of its trademark status by buyers and sellers. Another acceptable term in American English is *real estate agent*. Commissions for agents in the US can be five times higher than those in the UK, and many Americans therefore try to sell their own properties, bypassing agencies, through a number of established channels. These have attracted the general designation *FSBO*, sometimes pronounced "FIZ-bow," an initialism from *for sale by owner*.

Most purchasers of homes in both countries obtain a *mortgage*. Building societies are the most popular source for these in the UK; sources vary in the US. Three federally chartered corporations are associated with home financing and expanding home ownership in the US whose names are in general circulation. They are *Fannie Mae*, which securitizes and guarantees mortgages as well as assisting homebuyers and the mortgage industry in various ways; *Ginnie Mae*, which issues bonds that are backed by home mortgages; and *Freddie Mac*, which operates a secondary market for mortgages.

The default type of mortgage in the US, and the one that is assumed is nothing more specific is stated, is a fixed-rate thirty-year mortgage; in the UK it is a variable-rate thirty-year mortgage. Variable-rate mortgages in the US are not the standard but are common enough, especially among buyers with little money or during times of high interest rates; they are called *adjustable-rate mortgages*, or *ARMs*. In the UK some buyers may acquire an *endowment mortgage*. It is a complicated financing scheme, marketed as an investment vehicle, wherein a mortgage is linked to an endowment insurance policy. The policy matures when the mortgage is due, and its payout is used to repay the capital of the mortgage, which in the meantime has received debt-service payments only. Homeowners in both countries enjoy tax relief on mortgage interest. This is handled as an itemized deduction from income in the US, and administered in the UK under a system called *MIRAS*, for "mortgage interest relief at source."

The sale of property in the UK is normally handled jointly by estate agents and solicitors, one of each acting on behalf of buyer and seller. This business makes up a substantial part of many solicitors' workloads and is called *conveyancing*. In the US real estate sales are typically handled by the agents only, one for each party (the *buyer's agent* and the *seller's agent*, who split the commission), but lawyers may also be involved, especially on high-end properties. The point of no return—or at the very least, of costly and complicated return—in the sale of property in the UK is called the *exchange of contracts*; in the US it is the signing of a contract. The concluding event in the sale of property, when it actually changes hands, is called *completion* in British English, and *settlement* in American English, though the term *closing* is also used. After this process, it's time for everyone to *move*, as it is in American English, or *move house* as it is in British English.

Three terms figure often in British real estate transactions that are either unknown or not fixed in American English, probably owing to the extreme volatility of the property market in the UK and the frequent buying and selling of particular properties:

- **chain.** A situation in which the ability to buy a new property is dependent on selling one currently held. The shorthand designation *no chain* is used in advertising to alert buyers to a possible quick and easy sale.
- **gazump.** As a seller, to renege on a previously agreed price, refusing to sell until a higher price is met; as a buyer, to offer a price higher than one already accepted by the seller in order to get the property. It is usually reported from the point of view of the original bidder, who *gets gazumped.*
- **gazunder.** As a buyer, to refuse to stand by an offer you made in a rapidly declining housing market.

Addresses

The format of street and postal addresses can be a source of minor confusion for the transatlantic visitor or correspondent. The prevailing conventions in both countries provide about the same amount of specificity, and an understanding of the shorthand used in addresses makes them more easily placeable. Both countries follow the convention of proceeding from the particular (person) to the general in writing addresses, with the *post code* (British) or *ZIP code* (American) being the last item displayed in the address, at the lower right:

American format	British format
Mr. John Doe	John Doe, Esq
3434 Park LN	8 St Botolph Rd
Dallas, TX 75209-1066	LONDON E10 3BT

The *Esq* following the addressee's name in the British address is an abbreviation for the courtesy title *esquire*, to which every male addressee is entitled. It is never spoken, but *squire* is used as a friendly or humorous form of address between men who don't know each other well. *Esq* in American English following a name usually denotes that the person is a lawyer.

AMERICAN CONVENTIONS

The US Post Office has official abbreviations for the fifty states and some other destinations, as follows:

US POST OFFICE DESTINATIONS

AE	Armed Forces Europe		MP	Northern Mariana Islands
AK	Alaska		MS	Mississippi
AL	Alabama		MT	Montana
AP	Armed Forces Pacific		NC	North Carolina
AR	Arkansas		ND	North Dakota
AS	American Samoa		NE	Nebraska
AZ	Arizona		NH	New Hampshire
CA	California		NJ	New Jersey
CO	Colorado		NM	New Mexico
CT	Connecticut		NV	Nevada
DC	District of Columbia		NY	New York
DE	Delaware		OH	Ohio
FL	Florida		OK	Oklahoma
FM	Federated States of Micronesia		OR	Oregon
GA	Georgia		PA	Pennsylvania
GU	Guam		PR	Puerto Rico
HI	Hawaii		RI	Rhode Island
IA	Iowa		SC	South Carolina
ID	Idaho		SD	South Dakota
IL	Illinois		TN	Tennessee
IN	Indiana		TX	Texas
KS	Kansas		UT	Utah
KY	Kentucky		VA	Virginia
LA	Louisiana		VI	Virgin Islands, US
MA	Massachusetts		VT	Vermont
MD	Maryland		WA	Washington
ME	Maine		WI	Wisconsin
MH	Marshall Islands		WV	West Virginia
MI	Michigan		WY	Wyoming
MN	Minnesota			
MO	Missouri			

These abbreviations are supposed to be written as shown, that is, in capital letters and with no periods, but deviations from this form are usually not fatal. Likewise for the following officially accepted postal abbreviations:

US POST OFFICE ABBREVIATIONS

APT	Apartment	PKWY	Parkway
AVE	Avenue	PL	Place
BLVD	Boulevard	PLZ	Plaza
CIR	Circle	RD	Road
CT	Court	RDG	Ridge
CTR	Center	RM	Room
DR	Drive	SQ	Square
EXPY	Expressway	ST	Street
HTS	Heights	STA	Station
HWY	Highway	STE	Suite
IS	Island	TER	Terrace
JCT	Junction	TPKE	Turnpike
LK	Lake	TRL	Trail
LN	Lane	VLY	Valley
MTN	Mountain	WAY	Way

A common abbreviation in American addresses is the symbol #, which in addresses it is read as *number* or *apartment number*.

The US *ZIP code* comes in two versions, the short-hand five-digit one, and a longer one with four digits appended to the first five after a hyphen: 21158 vs. 21158–1406, for example. The last four digits are meaningful to postal employees only. The first number of the first five digits gives a rough geographical fix: ZIP codes starting with 0 are in the Northeast, and numbers increase from there toward the south and west, ending with ZIP codes beginning with 9 for the West Coast and Alaska.

BRITISH CONVENTIONS

British addresses follow a few conventions that may be opaque to un-schooled North Americans. No grid-based house numbering system exists in most British localities, so a house number, when present, gives no indication of its relative distance from anything, except perhaps the *top* or *bottom* of the street it is on (it is generally a matter of purely local knowledge which end is which). Many addresses in Britain in fact have no house number at all because houses or buildings have names that are recognized as official addresses by the Post Office.

An acceptable British postal address must contain the following:

- addressee (person or business)
- a building name, or a house number and street name
- post town (see below), preferably in capital letters.
- post code (see below)

It is common for named buildings in cities to be identified by street as well, for example, Clifton House, Worship Street.

A great deal of information is packed into the short string of letters and numbers called a *post code*. These are normally written as two short strings separated by a space, e.g., E8 3BP or SN11 0PE. But there are in fact four fields in the post code, as illustrated here:

EC | 2A | 7 | JX

Field 1 (EC in the example). One or two alphabetic characters. An identification of the *post town* (main sorting post office) where the address is located. The following codes are reserved for London: *N, E, S,* and *W* correspond roughly to geographic sections of the capital; the combinations *EC, NW, SE, SW,* and *WC* also exist, where *C* stands for *central*. Post town codes for the rest of Britain are roughly mnemonic and are based on letters from the name of the town, typically first, first and last, or first and second: *M* for Manchester, *BN* for Brighton, *EH* for Edinburgh, *YO* for York, etc.

Field 2 (2A in the example). One or two characters, numeric (except for central London where the numeric districts are subdivided). These are normally connected with particular delivery post offices.

Field 3 (7 in the example). A district or neighborhood within the delivery area of a single main post office.

Field 4 (JX in the example). Two letters that identify a group of up to eighty addresses within a district or neighborhood.

The amount of information is specific enough in a post code that, together with a house number, it is sufficient for identifying an address to a post office. However, it is customary for a postal address to include all the usual information noted above. For approximate locations it is conventional to give the first two fields of the post code, especially in cities; this shorthand identifies a neighborhood, and for those familiar with the various areas of London particularly, half a post code can suggest volumes about housing, socioeconomic level, and lifestyle.

It is not required to give the county name when the post town and post code are present, but in fact people typically write the county name in addresses. Many of these have unpredictable abbreviations.

UK COUNTY ABBREVIATIONS

Bedfordshire	Beds	Middlesex	Middx
Berkshire	Berks	Northamptonshire	Northants
Buckinghamshire	Bucks	North Yorkshire	N Yorks
Cambridgeshire	Cambs	Nottinghamshire	Notts
Gloucestershire	Glocs	Oxfordshire	Oxon
Hampshire	Hants	Shropshire	Salop
Hertfordshire	Herts	South Yorkshire	S Yorks
Lancashire	Lancs	West Yorkshire	W Yorks
Leicestershire	Leics	Wiltshire	Wilts
Lincolnshire	Lincs		

It is also not required to distinguish towns or villages whose names are duplicated elsewhere in the country, since a correct post code will eliminate this ambiguity. However, it is customary to give additional location information for obscure locations, or those that share a name with some other place, with the word *near* (*nr.*), thus "Heddington nr. Calne."

Common abbreviations for street designations vary from those in American English, and there are a few common designations for residential streets not typically found in the US.

BRITISH STREET ABBREVIATIONS

Arc	Arcade	Mans	Mansions
Bdy	Broadway	Mkt	Market
Boul	Boulevard	Ms	Mews
Circ	Circus	Par	Parade
Clo	Close	Pas	Passage
Flds	Fields	Prom	Promenade
Gdns	Gardens	Ri	Rise
Grn	Green	Vill	Villas
Ho	House	Wd	Wood
Junct	Junction	Wk	Walk
La	Lane	Yd	Yard

The commoner abbreviations are the same as in American English, though usually written upper and lower case and not followed by a period: *St*, *Rd*, *Ct* (Court), *Sta* (Station).

Mail for a person without an address, sent to a post office in the hope that said person will collect it, is sent to *General Delivery* in the US and to *Poste Restante* in the UK.

CLOTHING

After the lengthy foregoing presentations it may be some relief to find that the differences between the two dialects relating to clothing are rather simpler. The trade and technical designation for clothing in American English is *apparel*, although this word doesn't have much conversational currency. In British English it is humorous, formal, or obsolete; *clothing* is used instead. Ready-to-wear clothes are designated *off-the-rack* in American English, *off-the-peg* in British English. Made-to-measure clothes are *custom-made* or *tailor-made* in American English, *bespoke* in British English.

Many clothing terms can be treated as straightforward equivalents:

CLOTHING

American	British
coveralls	overalls
crew neck	turtleneck
cuff [on pants only]	turn-up
derby	bowler
fedora	trilby
galoshes	Wellingtons, wellies
hiphuggers	hipsters
jumper	pinafore dress
nightgown →	nightdress
panties	knickers
pantyhose	tights
parka	anorak[1]
pump	court shoe
sneakers	trainers, plimsolls [*dated*]
stocking cap	woolly hat
suspenders	braces
sweater	jumper
sweater set	twinset →
swimsuit →	bathing costume [becoming *dated*]
turtleneck	polo neck
tuxedo[2]	dinner jacket
undershirt	vest

CLOTHING TERMS *(continued)*

American	British
vest	waistcoat[3]
wingtip [shoe]	brogue

[1] *Anorak* has cultural connotations in British English that are not associated with *parka* in American English. Because of their popularity with trainspotters (see chapter 9), they may denote someone who is socially inept, obsessively studious, or extremely unfashionable.

[2] *Tuxedo* can also designate the entire outfit, including the trousers.

[3] British English uses *bulletproof vest* in preference to *b. waistcoat*, perhaps in deference to the American flavor of this garment.

British English uses *trousers* as the most general term for the usually full-length, lower-body garment that American English designates *pants*. Though *trousers* is also used in American English and Americans don't give it any particular connotations, they generally prefer pants about 3 to 1. *Pants* in British English mainly means *underpants* or *knickers*; thus, *He isn't wearing any pants!* would cause rather less alarm, though greater powers of discernment to notice, in British English than in American English. The pants/trousers distinction persists in some compounds (AmE pantsuit, BrE trouser suit) and in the idiom *wear the pants* (BrE *wear the trousers*), but British English conforms to American English in *Capri pants*, *hot pants*, *ski pants*, and *smarty-pants*, perhaps because trousers would sound absurd in these compounds. The opening at the front of such a garment is called a *fly* in American English, the *flies* in British English, whether it consists of buttons, snaps, or a zip.

Similar confusion can arise around the word *shorts*, which in both dialects is used of trousers that stop at or above the knees, but in American English can also designate men's underpants. British English has the charming euphemism *smalls*, now becoming dated, to designate underwear generally.

Frock as a synonym for dress has very limited circulation in American English and is often used whimsically in other than very dated contexts. It appears more often in British English but is nearly always marked by irony or humor, except in some fixed collocations: *posh/party/girlish frocks*.

Some other terms associated with sewing, fashion, and accessories are straightforward lexical variants:

SEWING AND ACCESSORIES

American	British
inseam	inside leg

SEWING AND ACCESSORIES *(continued)*

American	British
nail polish	nail varnish
run [in a woman's stocking]	ladder
snap	press stud
spool [of thread]	reel [of cotton]
zipper	zip

American English uses *dry goods* to designate textiles generally, especially at the retail level. British English calls this *drapery* or *haberdashery*, though haberdashery is closer to what American English terms *notions* (products for sewing such as thread, buttons, ribbon, etc.). *Haberdashery* in American English, by contrast, is a men's clothing store or the line of merchandise sold there, though this term is now quite dated.

A few accessories for the hair also go by different names in the two dialects, given in this table along with other hair-related terms.

HAIR AND ACCESSORIES

American	British
bangs	fringe
barrette	hair slide
bobby pin	hair grip, kirby grip
braid *n, v*	plait *n, v*
headband →	hairband
sideburns	sideboards
tease *v*	backcomb

Brand(ing) Success

The following trademarks have become synonymous with the item of clothing or fabric that they designate in their country of origin. The list omits those widely known in both countries (e.g., Levi's, Birkenstocks). All items are used generically and are often found not capitalized.

CLOTHING AND FABRIC TRADEMARKS

Trademark	Source	What is it?
Babygro	UK	baby's one-piece coverall stretch garment
Barbour	UK	dark green water-repellent jacket popular with the rural gentry

CLOTHING AND FABRIC TRADEMARKS *(continued)*

Trademark	Source	What is it?
Dacron	US	crease-resistant polyester; Terylene
Doc Martens	UK	thick-soled shoes mainly for the under-thirty set
Hush Puppies	US	soft-soled suede shoes; BrE *brothel creepers*
Jockey shorts	US	men's briefs
Pertex	UK	breathable fabric for camping gear and clothing
Terylene	UK	crease-resistant polyester; Dacron
Viyella	UK	fabric made of twilled cotton and wool
Weejuns	US	casual mocassins
Windbreaker	US	windcheater
Y-fronts	UK	men's briefs

CHAPTER EIGHT

Transport(ation)

This chapter examines differences between British and American English connected with vehicles, the way they travel, and the things they travel on, with some short diversions into pedestrian and other forms of travel. The differences are mainly ones of vocabulary arising out of usage and historical preferences, and foremost among these is the most general term. Britain had a system in the nineteenth century called *transportation*, by which Australia was largely populated with the political and criminal rejects of the UK and Ireland. This program proved so successful that the term for it was essentially retired from British English and allowed to rest on those laurels. Now British English uses *transport* to talk about the general phenomenon of moving people and things, while American English uses *transportation*. *Transport* in American English (aside from verbal uses) is mostly for more concrete rather than abstract meanings—*the transport of military and government passengers*—and for certain specialized vehicles—*a troop transport*. It is also used attributively in preference to transportation in several contexts, particularly in biology—*a transport link/protein*.

THE MOTOR VEHICLE

Lexical variants abound for different sorts of road vehicles. Here are the commonest ones:

179

VEHICLES

American	British
bicycle, bike →	push bike
coupe	coupé →
dump truck	dumper (truck), tipper lorry
dune buggy →	beach buggy →
fire truck, fire engine	fire engine →
flatbed truck	low-loader
garbage truck	dustbin lorry, bin lorry, dust cart
high-profile vehicle	high-sided vehicle
horse trailer	horsebox
lemon	Friday (afternoon) car
moving van	removal van, pantechnicon
salt truck	gritting lorry
sedan	saloon
semi, semitrailer, 18-wheeler	articulated lorry, artic, juggernaut
station wagon	estate car
tow truck	breakdown lorry, breakdown van
trailer [for accommodation]	caravan

Motor serves as an informal word for *car* in British English; the closest American English equivalent is perhaps *wheels*, though this is now a little dated. As a technical and trade term *automobile* and *auto* are the preferred terms in American English and occupy many slots in compounds (*auto parts, auto theft, the automobile industry*) that are taken by *motor* in British English (*motor insurance, motor racing, the motor trade*). The adjective *automotive* is also frequent in American English, nearly unused in British English. *Truck* and *lorry* are interchangeable in many other obvious compounds that are not noted in the table above between the two dialects.

A number of road and other vehicles based more or less on the car are sufficiently modified in one country or the other to deserve a unique name unfamiliar in the other dialect:

VEHICLES UNIQUE TO ONE COUNTRY

Vehicle	Source	What is it?
bubble car	UK	small three-wheeled road vehicle with a seat for the driver enclosed in a domed canopy
curtain sider	UK	semitrailer consisting of a frame with nonrigid, removable sides, or this attached to a tractor

VEHICLES UNIQUE TO ONE COUNTRY *(continued)*

Vehicle	Source	What is it?
low-rider	US	car with a very low chassis, sometimes achieved by special hydraulic jacks, and usually ornately decorated; also, a driver of one of these, or the subculture associated with it
milk float	UK	small, battery-powered flatbed truck for delivering milk to homes
RV	US	recreational vehicle; any vehicle classified as being mainly for recreation and usually requiring a special license plate
skidoo, snowmobile	US	motorized vehicle for driving on snow with a caterpillar track and skis on the front
Welcome Wagon	US	a car that alerts new residents in an area to local businesses by supplying them with sample products; a trademark, though often used generically
Winnebago	US	trademark for a motorized vehicle that incorporates a caravan

Car parts, though functionally identical in both countries and in many cases exactly identical (in the products of multinational automakers) often go by different names. This table also includes a small number of tools that have applications beyond the automobile.

CAR PARTS AND ACCESSORIES

American	British
back-up lights	reversing lights
carburetor	carburetter
fender	wing, mudguard
high beam, brights	full beam
hood	bonnet
jumper cable	jump lead
license plate, tag	number plate
low beam, dims	dipped beam
muffler	silencer
oil pan	sump
tire	tyre
trunk	boot[1]
windshield	windscreen

[1] This term gives rise to *car boot sale*, an event in which people sell items from the trunks of their cars; there is no American English equivalent, though an American hearing the term might think that this was a sale of wheel clamps, since boot is the American English term for this device.

The sides of a car are called simply *left* and *right* in American English, or occasionally *driver's side* and *passenger side*. British English more often uses *nearside* (for the side nearest the curb, i.e., the left side in the UK) and *offside* (for the right side). A car battery with no charge is *dead* in the US, *flat* in the UK (these apply equally to other kinds of batteries). The lowest gear in a manual transmission is called *low gear* in American English, *bottom gear* in British English. Finally, American English uses *gas* or *gasoline* where British English uses *petrol*; the terms persist in all compounds (*gas/petrol pump/station/tank*).

Roads and Highways

There are functional equivalents of the various kinds and systems of roads in the two countries; the overall networks are more or less analogous in terms of their coverage and redundancy, and so are best described in terms of direct comparison.

Britain has a system of *motorways* that serve the same function as the US *Interstate Highway* system: conduits for long-distance, relatively uninterrupted travel. All such roads in Britain are named with an *M* prefix; that is, the *M-1*, the *M-2*, the *M-25*, etc.; the definite article is always used. The US interstate highways all have an *I* prefix, that is, *I-10*, *I-695*, *I-70*; the definite article is never used unless the highway name is the first term of a compound: *driving on I-95*, *the I-90 corridor*. Motorways and interstate highways all have at least two lanes in each direction with a physical barrier between them; the general British term for these is *dual carriageway*, the American is *divided highway*. When this barrier consists only of concrete blocks in the shape of an inverted Y in cross section, they are called *Jersey barriers* in American English, with no strict British English equivalent. American English uses a number of other terms that all correspond to the British *motorway*; these are either regional variants, or they may reflect whether a particular highway requires drivers to pay (*turnpike, tollway, tollroad*), or whether the highway is in or near a city (*expressway*). Other terms that a British editor or reader can easily lump under the notion of motorway are *superhighway* and *freeway*.

Highway is a more inclusive term in American English than any British English counterpart but probably has its closest equivalent in *arterial road*, that is, a road that serves as a major connection between points. Such a road that encircles a metropolitan area in the US is usually called a *beltway*; the British term is *ring road* or *orbital*. Access and exit from such roads is via *on-ramps* and *off-ramps* in American English, *slip roads* in British English. A restaurant along the side of a major thoroughfare better known for its convenient location than for its food is a *transport café* in British English, a *truck stop* in American English.

In the US, the interstate highway system largely replaced and upgraded the former national system of roads whose constituents are now called *US highways*. These roads typically travel through, rather than around, metropolitan areas, require occasional or frequent stops, may not be divided, and may have only one lane in each direction. They are the functional equivalent of roads in Britain that carry an *A* prefix; that is, the *A-1*, the *A-40*, etc.; as with motorways, the definite article is always used: *an accident on the A-5*. US highways in the old system may carry the same numbers as interstate highways and are distinguished from them with a *US* prefix, that is, *US 66*, *US 30*. Informally and locally, these may also be prefixed with the word *Route*, thus *Route 66*, *Route 30*; the definite article is not used. The general rule for US Interstate Highways and the older US highways is that even-numbered roads run east and west, odd-numbered roads run north and south.

Functional equivalency breaks down below this level, owing to the different systems of administering roads. Britain has roads prefixed with *B*, which are secondary to the *A* roads; the US has highways that are built and maintained by states rather than any national authority, and these are distinguished from other roads that may carry the same numbers by prefixing the name or abbreviation of the state, thus *Maryland 496*, *NM 616*.

Transatlantic visitors in the US or the UK will notice the very different ways of handling roads that intersect. The place where this happens is usually an *intersection* in American English and a *junction* in British English, though junction is also used in American English for the places where highways meet. The older term *crossroads* now gets more figurative than literal use in both dialects, but is also likely to be used of an intersection of small, unimportant roads, or roads where traffic is not controlled by lights or other means. British English has the term *box junction* for an intersection with a yellow grid painted where the roads meet, indicating the vehicles should not enter it unless they have a clear exit. The same practice exists in the US, but without the name.

The classic British way to handle the logistical problem of roads intersecting is the *roundabout*, in which drivers from all directions enter a common circle and part from it at the point where the road they wish to take continues. Though present in the US—especially in the Northeast where the term for these is *rotary*—they are not very common, and are called *traffic circles* in most other US locales. By contrast, roundabouts are so common in the UK that they come in different varieties: a *mini-roundabout* is simply a white circle painted in an ordinary intersection, to indicate that traffic should circle before it turns. A *dual roundabout* is a confusing juxtaposition of two roundabouts that an American behind the wheel should never attempt unassisted. In all cases traffic proceeds in a clockwise direction in the UK, and goes *counterclockwise* in the US, or *anti-clockwise*, as the Britons would have it. *Circus* is occasionally used in the names of these junctions (*Oxford Circus, Piccadilly Circus,* though somewhat confusingly, since traffic at both of these well-known locations no longer follows a circular pattern). American English would use *circle* rather than circus in a similar context (e.g., *DuPont Circle* in Washington).

THE ROAD ENVIRONMENT

The road environment includes a few other features that may be unfamiliar to the foreign visitor, or called by a different name. The finished surface of concrete or asphalt that cars drive on is the *pavement* or *blacktop* in American English; a road with such a surface is a *paved* road. The same surface is called *roadway* or *tarmac* in British English; dictionaries note the latter as a trademark though it is often found uncapitalized. A British road with tarmac is a *metalled*, or sometimes a *made* or *made-up* road (the material used to make the surface is sometimes called *metalling* or *road metal*). A road lacking this is usually called an *unmade road* in the UK, a *dirt road* in the US.

ROADS AND DRIVING

American	British
billboard	hoarding
cattle guard	cattle grid
curve	bend →
detour	diversion
guard rail	crash barrier
median (strip)	(central) reservation
overpass	flyover
parking lot	car park
pass [*verb*]	overtake
pedestrian underpass	subway
shoulder	verge

ROADS AND DRIVING *(continued)*

American	British
sidewalk	pavement
speed bump	sleeping policeman
traffic jam	tailback
turn lane	filter
turn signal, blinker	indicator

The UK makes extensive use of *bollards* to control the flow of traffic: upright posts, usually of flimsy plastic, that direct traffic away from or around an area. These have no specific name in American English. The phenomenon in which drivers who are traveling in one direction slow down to look at an accident in traffic going the other way, thereby creating a *traffic jam* (BrE *tailback*), is called *gaper's block* or *rubbernecking* in American English, with no equivalent in British English.

There is comforting similarity between the wording of road signs in the US and the UK, which goes some way toward alleviating the distress that many feel at seeing everyone driving on the wrong side. A few minor differences:

ROAD SIGNS

American	British
Grade	Gradient
Do Not Enter	No Entry
New Traffic Pattern	Changed Priorities
Pavement Ends	Road Surface Ends
Roadwork	Roadworks
Yield	Give Way

The initialism *HGV* on British road signs is for *heavy goods vehicle*. *HOV* in the US is a *high-occupancy vehicle*, one carrying two or more people and so able to use designated lanes for faster travel. *HAZMAT* as an acronym for *hazardous materials* is well established in American English and catching on in British English.

There is little difference between *street* and *road* between the two dialects as they are used in the names of particular thoroughfares, though British English is a little more inclined to use *road* in urban settings than American English is. *Avenue*, on the other hand, is more popularly used in street names in American English than in British English, though without any consistent pattern, and not necessarily designating a business street as it often does in British English. A few other terms designating streets show differences between the dialects, mostly in form of abbreviation, are discussed under "Addresses" in the previous chapter.

The Car, the Driver, and the Law

Functional equivalency is the rule for nearly all the legal aspects of cars and driving in the US and the UK, and differences are mainly of terminology. Americans acquire a *driver's license*, Britons a *driving licence*. American cars display a *license plate* or *plates* or sometimes *tags*, British cars display *number plates*. The temporary plates used by car dealers are called *dealer plates* in American English, *trade plates* in British English.

In the US, license plates are issued by individual states, each of which governs its numbering system. Some states require one plate and some two. The plates are usually associated with car owners rather than with cars, and can be transferred. The British system is national and is based on the assignment of a number plate to a particular car for the life of the car, which is officially its *registration, registration mark*, or *registration number*. The alphanumeric system reflects the year of the car's manufacture, and so a certain status attaches to driving a car sporting the latest letter at the beginning of the plate number, which represents a *new registration* or *late registration* car. The initial letter of the number plate, since it is an indication of relative vintage, gives rise to a shorthand system of characterizing a car that tells its approximate age: thus a *T-registration Ford saloon*, a *V-reg Mini*. The abbreviated form is pronounced *rej*. This system was revamped in late 2001, and a new numbering system that identifies both a car's age and region of registration came into place.

Many US states allow drivers, for a fee, to choose the combination of letters and numbers that appear on their license plates; these are called *vanity plates*. A more complicated system exists in the UK: deviation from the standard alphanumeric system is not allowed, but many letter and number combinations either spell out or resemble known words, and these are considered valuable. A system exists for transferring the assignment of a particular registration from one vehicle to another, and a thriving industry facilitates this trade, in which *cherished registration numbers* change hands for vast sums of money. The law governing this is charmingly called the *cherished transfer scheme*.

US states vary in their requirements for determining the roadworthiness of a car; some require periodic inspections and others do not. The UK has a uniform requirement that is usually referred to as the *MOT*. The letters are an acronym for the (now reorganized and renamed) Ministry of Transport, and refer to that body's requirements that a vehicle pass a periodic inspection. A car that passes its MOT is issued an *MOT certificate*.

The most popular organization in the US to which motorists subscribe for emergency road service is the American Automobile Association, *AAA* (called *triple-A*). There are two competing counterparts in Britain, the Royal Automobile Club (*RAC*) and the Automobile Association (*AA*).

People who drive while under the influence of alcohol are called *drunk drivers* in the US, *drink drivers* in the UK. The associated crime is *drink-driving* (BrE) or *drunk driving* (AmE), though the commoner terms in the US for this are *DUI* (for "driving under the influence") or *DWI* (for "driving while intoxicated"). A summons issued for a driving or traffic violation may be called a *citation* in American English; *ticket* is used in both dialects. A minor accident is a *fender bender* in American English, a *prang* in British English.

THE RAILS

Though the distinction is not hard and fast, British speakers generally prefer *railway* in all instances where Americans prefer *railroad*. The vocabulary and associations of traveling by train are more firmly established in the British mind than in the American because of the more frequent, more extensive, and generally better rail service available in the UK. One evidence of this is that in British English, the word *station* alone is understood to mean *railway station*, or to use the more usual American term, *train station*.[1] Inside these, Americans proceed to the *ticket office* or *window*, and Britons to the *booking office*. British English designates the area where passengers board and detrain as a *platform*; it may also be called a *track* in US train stations. The comings and goings of trains constitute what Britons usually call a *timetable*, and Americans a *schedule*. Trains stopping at intermediate destinations between origin and terminus are said to *call* at such stations in British English; American English uses *stop*.

The units that make up a train are generically called *cars* in American English; those that carry people are usually *carriages* in British English, otherwise *wagons*, except the one that carries baggage (AmE *baggage car*),

---

1. *Depot* is also used in American English for these buildings, especially historical ones or ones that have been restored.

which is the *luggage van*. The *Pullman car*, an American invention, has no exact British English equivalent; *saloon carriage* comes closest. A British *dining car* is an American *diner*. Trains that carry raw materials or merchandise are *freight trains* in the US, *goods trains* in the UK; thus American English *freight car,* British English *goods wagon* or *goods truck* or *goods van*. An American *boxcar* is a British English *covered wagon*. The *caboose*, a standard feature of a US freight train, is not always present on UK goods trains but is called a *brake-van* when it is.

The term *piggyback*, though of informal origins, is now a standard term in American English for denoting containers that can move by road or rail: *piggyback freight, a piggyback yard*. This term has not caught on in British English, where *container* or *containerized* is used.

The driver of a locomotive is an *engineer* in American English, a *driver* or *engine driver* in British English. The person in charge of passengers on the train is a *conductor* in American English, a *guard* in British English. A few other rail terms are straightforward equivalents:

RAIL TERMS

American	British
baggage check, baggage room	left luggage
day coach	open carriage
freight yard	goods yard
gondola	open wagon
grade crossing	level crossing
redcap	porter
roadbed	permanent way
siding	loop line
switch	points
switchman	pointsman
switchyard	shunting yard
tie	sleeper
tracklayer, section hand	plate layer

An *Amtrak train* in the US is an intercity passenger train; all such services are operated by the government-chartered and -subsidized company Amtrak. All other trains carrying passengers are commuter trains run by local or regional transportation authorities. *British Rail* is now fading from usage in British English since its breakup in the 1990s and replacement by several publicly held railways that cooperate with the company called *Rail-track*, which owns the tracks and rights of ways and is responsible for their maintenance.

OTHER MEANS OF TRAVEL

The de facto rule for pedestrian traffic in the US is that walkers should cross streets only at intersections. Anything else is called *jaywalking*, a legal offense in some jurisdictions though one that is rarely prosecuted. Someone alleged to have been "picked up for jaywalking" is understood to have been the target of police on some other reason, or is being harassed by the police. Pedestrian traffic in Britain is largely controlled by two types of crossing: the *zebra crossing*, in which walkers cross the street on a pattern of black and white stripes, lit at either side by a flashing amber light called a *belisha beacon*; pedestrians always have the right-of-way here. The other crossing is the *pelican crossing*, controlled by a pedestrian-activated button that turns on a red light to approaching traffic. In the absence of these, British English has the *lollipop man* (or *lady*) who halts traffic with a round placard to allow schoolchildren across the road. The nearest American English equivalent is *school crossing guard*.

Public Transport(ation)

LOCAL TRAVEL

British English uses *bus* for the large multipassenger vehicles that carry people short distances within a metropolitan area and *coach* for the same sort of vehicle if it carries people between cities. American English uses *bus* for both of these. *Greyhound* or *Greyhound Bus*, though only one of many companies that operate long-distance buses in the US, is sometimes used generically for this kind of travel. An analogous UK institution is the *National Express*.

Urban underground trains are mostly called *subways* in the US, though *metro* is used in some cities, such as Washington and Baltimore, while other cities use a local acronym, such as BART in San Francisco or MTA in Boston. Cities where the trains run on an elevated platform, such as Chicago, use *el* for *elevated train*; usage is loose however, because the same line may go from subway to elevated. The same phenomenon can be seen with

London's *Underground*, or *Tube*, which runs mostly underground but often at ground level and sometimes on elevated platforms. Many American cities now have systems called *light rail*, comprising rail cars that run on a dedicated, separate railway system within cities and their suburbs. These have largely replaced or been built in preference to a system of vehicles that run on rails imbedded in streets, for which American English uses *streetcar* and *trolley* or *trolley car* and British English uses *tram*, although tram also has considerable currency in American English.

LONG DISTANCE TRAVEL

American travelers typically make *reservations*; British travelers make *bookings*, or book their tickets. The travel in question is more likely to be called a *trip* in the US, a *journey* in the UK; *journey* has a slightly formal ring in American English and would not be used, for instance, of a subway ride, although British English will have you taking journeys on London's Underground. A ticket to a destination that includes the trip back to one's point of origin is a *round trip* in American English, a *return* in British English. A variant is the *day return*, a return ticket for a journey to be completed on the same calendar day and often offered at a discount. A ticket without the return portion is a *one-way* in American English, a *single* in British English.

Dictionaries seem to draw greater distinctions between the dialectal differences in usage between *baggage* and *luggage* than speakers and writers do. In fact both terms are used in both dialects, interchangeably in many contexts and compounds, and misunderstanding rarely arises. There are a few preferences: the empty cases, especially when offered for sale, are always *luggage*. Once packed for a trip, American English is slightly more inclined to call them *baggage* and this is reflected in several compounds: *baggage claim/handler, excess/checked baggage. Carry-on* in American English collocates preferentially with *baggage* but is also seen with *luggage* and *bags*. British English shows similar patterns with baggage (but has *baggage reclaim* rather than *baggage claim* in airports). British English has a slight preference for *unattended luggage* over *unattended baggage*.

Vehicles for Hire

American English *car rental* and *rent-a-car* have gained considerable ground in British English because of American-based rental companies that operate there, but *car hire* is the more traditional British English term.

This is sometimes specifically noted as *self-drive*, suggesting perhaps that the standard is chauffeur driven. Both *taxi* and *cab* are used interchangeably in both dialects; these vehicles wait for passengers at a *taxi rank* in Britain and a *taxi stand* or *cabstand* in the US. A further distinction exists in taxis in the UK because of the widespread use of *minicabs*: ordinary cars that are used as taxis but must be ordered in advance, have fixed fares over fixed routes, and are not allowed (in principle) to pick up passengers who hail them on the street[1]. This has given rise to the retronym *black taxi* or *black cab* to designate proper, hailable taxis with meters, which were traditionally all black.

The Movement of Goods

The American English use of *shipment* and *shipping* as a general terms for the movement of goods, no matter what the means, is encroaching on British English, where traditionally there has been a distinction between goods that move by sea (for which these words are used) and goods that move by other means (for which *consignment* and *forwarding* are more common). The American English phrase *shipping and handling* (*S&H*) is usually given as *postage and packing* (*p&p*) in British English.

Consignment has a specialized meaning in American English to designate goods whose ownership is not transferred to the person offering them for sale until they are actually sold. The seller in this case has the goods, typically antiques, works of art, or other high-end merchandise *on consignment*, in a business designated as a *consignment shop*, which operates on percentage-based commissions.

---

1. The American term *gypsy cab* denotes a more or less equivalent conveyance, although gypsy cabs in the US don't generally enjoy the respectable status afforded minicabs in the UK; this may be because they operate mostly in neighborhoods that ordinary taxis deem unprofitable or too dangerous.

CHAPTER NINE

Sport(s) and Leisure

This chapter describes the main varieties of *sports*, as the Americans call them, or *sport*, as the Brits call it, that are followed avidly in one country and relatively unknown in the other. As well as being the sources of a great deal of terminology that is completely opaque to the uninitiated, sports jargon is productive of many metaphors that make their way into general usage, particularly in the case of cricket and baseball. These are described alongside the sporting situations that inspire them. The dedicated student should be able to make sense of sports reportage with aid of the profiles given below. Following this, there is a diversion into other forms of leisure generally requiring less exertion.

SPORTS

Sports Bodies

This table identifies sports bodies that are often not expanded in reportage because they are known to all likely readers. Many appear in later sections of this chapter.

SPORTS BODIES

Body	Source	What is it?
FA	UK	the Football Association, governing body of soccer
FIFA	UK	the international governing body of soccer

SPORTS BODIES *(continued)*

Body	Source	What is it?
MCC	UK	Marylebone Cricket Club (London)
MLS	US	Major League Soccer
NBA	US	National Basketball Association
NCAA	US	National Collegiate Athletic Association
NFL	US	National Football League
NHL	US	National Hockey League
PFA	UK	Professional Footballers' Association
UAA	US	University Athletic Association
UEFA	UK	governing body of soccer in Europe

Baseball

No sport provides more figures of speech to American English than baseball; acquiring a thorough understanding of how it works and all the metaphors derived from it is essential to anyone who would try to pass themselves off as a native. Two teams of nine players alternate at *batting* (when they can score) or *fielding* (when they try to stop the other team from scoring), on a playing area called a *diamond*, so named because of the arrangement of the *bases* in the corners of that quadrilateral shape. The area enclosed within this diamond is the *infield*. The larger area within which the game is played, including the *outfield* (area outside the diamond) and the spectator area is called a *ballpark*. Metaphorically, something that's *in the ballpark* is reasonable or acceptable. A *ballpark figure, estimate*, or the like is an approximate one (i.e., not so inaccurate as to be out of the ballpark).

A *batter* scores by making a *run*, that is, running around the diamond, touching each of the three bases, and returning to *home plate* where he started. This is typically done in stages, as described below. But before running, the batter has to hit the ball that is *pitched* to him by the *pitcher* of the opposing team, from a raised spot in the middle of the diamond called the *pitcher's mound*. The batter stands just to the side of home plate. When he *steps up to the plate* he is ready to bat, and this phrase is used figuratively of someone to indicate that he is ready for action. A successful hit that allows the batter to run and reach at least the first base is called a *base hit*. A base hit that allows the batter to get to first base is called a *single*; to second base a *double*; to third base a *triple*; and to run all the way around the bases (and thereby score one point), a *home run*. Figuratively, to *score* or *hit a home run* means to have a major success.

Fixed metaphors derived from this part of the game include (*not*) *getting to first base with someone*, which means (not) making a beginning in an interpersonal process that promises to make further progress. Getting to *first*, *second*, or *third base* with a man or a woman means specifically to reach various benchmark stages in successful seduction. To *cover all the bases* means to attend to everything that is necessary. To be *off base* is to be very mistaken, or seriously deviating from reasonable expectations; this is derived from the fact the a runner who is not touching the base is vulnerable to being put out. To *touch base* with someone is to make contact, however briefly; this idiom is now well established in British English as well.

More often than not, a batter's turn *at bat* does not result immediately in a base hit. Other typical outcomes are a *ball*, in which the officiating referee (the *umpire*) deems that the pitch was not worthy of trying to hit. The batter may also swing at the ball and miss; this is called a *strike*, but it is also a *strike* if the umpire judges that the pitch was a good one and the batter chose not to swing at it. A ball that arrives over home plate and between the chest and knees of the batter is considered hittable; this is the *strike zone*. The batter may hit a *foul ball*, in which the struck ball goes outside the area described by the baseball diamond and the batter is not allowed to run[1]. Finally, the batter may hit a ball that is caught before bouncing by a member of the fielding team; when this happens, the player is *out* (his turn at batting has ended).

A batter is also out after three strikes, in which case he is said to have *struck out*. The figurative meaning of *strike out* is to fail, especially at the last possible opportunity to succeed. After four balls, a batter *walks* (advances) to first base, even though he has not hit the ball. A pitcher will sometimes intentionally walk a particularly good batter, to prevent his making a hit that would score runs.

As a player bats, the umpire behind home plate keeps track of the number of balls and strikes. This is called the *count*, and is always indicated with balls first, strikes second: 2–0 means two balls, no strikes, and is read as *two and oh*. A count of 3–2 is a *full count*, since one more ball would result in a walk, and one more strike would result in an out.

The players on a team take their turns at bat in a fixed order; when the order is finished they start over again. An exception to this is the use of a *designated hitter*, who bats in place of the pitcher. Coaches may also instate

---

1. Although *cry foul* is probably not originally associated with baseball, it is what the umpire does to designate that a ball is foul, and the figurative meaning of "protest loudly at wrong or injustice" is commoner in American English than British English.

a *pinch hitter* according to fixed rules at a time when a hit is particularly needed. By extension, a pinch hitter is someone called upon to act on behalf of another in a critical situation: *the president sent in his best diplomatic pinch hitter; US astronaut Michael Foale pinch-hitting in a spacewalk for the ailing Mir commander Vasily Tsibliyev*. A *switch-hitter* is an ambidextrous batter, or informally, a bisexual.

When a batter has made a successful hit and is on one of the bases, he is then called a *runner* or *base runner*. Then another batter from the same team takes his turn at bat. If he makes a base hit, this allows the runner on first base to advance at least to second base. In this way, there may eventually be a runner on each of the three bases; in this case it is said that the *bases are loaded*. This phrase is used metaphorically to mean that a situation is ripe for some dramatic or definitive development.

As mentioned, a batter is out after three strikes. A batter may also *fly out*, when the ball he hits is caught by an opposite team member; a runner may be *tagged out*, when an opposite team member touches him with the ball when he is between bases; or he may be *forced out*, if the player defending the base he is running toward is already in possession of the ball. After three players from a team are put out, the teams change sides.

The job of the fielding team is to stop or impede all the foregoing scoring activity. The defending team plays eight positions besides the pitcher: the *catcher* (informally, the *backstop*), who crouches behind home plate and catches pitched balls that are not swung at; three *basemen*, one each at first base, second base, and third base; three *outfielders*, who play far out in right, center, and left field, ready to catch *fly balls*. Since most batters are right-handed their balls tend to fly into right field; thus *left field* has acquired metaphorical status as a position or direction that is surprising or unconventional. A person or idea that is *way out in left field* is wildly incorrect or mistaken. Finally there is the *short stop*, who plays between second base and third base, where many hit balls go.

A game consists of nine innings, an *inning* being an instance of each team taking a turn at bat and remaining there until three players are out. the first half of the inning is called the *top*, the second half is the *bottom*. At the bottom of the seventh inning, spectators observe the *seventh-inning stretch* by standing up and strethcing. Two games played back-to-back are a *doubleheader*. A *whole new ball game* is in fact not a new game at all, but the same game with very changed expectations, usually following a big change in the scores. The phrase has wide figurative use to denote a situation in which expectations or the course of progress are radically altered.

There are two *major leagues*, informally *big leagues*, comprising all the teams that compete nationally. From this, the adjective *major-league* has come to mean "in the most important class." Teams compete with others in their own league throughout a regular playing season. The top team in each league becomes the *pennant champion*. These two teams then go on to play in the yearly *World Series*. Most professional players start out in the *minor leagues*, whose teams are attached to smaller cities. These are disparagingly called the *bush leagues*, and by extension the adjective *bush-league* means inferior and amateur. *Little League* is the organized summertime game for children, and is used figuratively and disparagingly of anything adult.

Numerous statistics are kept on teams and players for purposes of comparison and recording achievement. Each inning has recorded *runs, hits, and errors* that count in favor of or against one team or the other. An *unearned run* is one scored off the other team's error, rather than off a hit. Another common statistic is the *batting average*, a ratio expressed to three decimal places of the number of base hits to the number of times at bat. In general, someone's batting average is their proportion of successes, and batting averages greater than three hundred (300) are considered good. Someone who is *batting a thousand* is succeeding constantly without failure. In baseball this would mean scoring every time at bat; no one actually does this.

Much attention in baseball focuses on the activity of the pitcher, since his actions are most influential on the outcome of the game. Before pitching the ball, the pitcher *winds up*, that is, makes preparatory movements with his pitching arm; these movements are a pitcher's trademark to some degree. *Windup* gets some figurative use to denote words or actions that are preparatory to something else (*Her windup made me think we were going to get a lecture*), but this can interfere with the more usual, non-baseball meaning of windup, i.e., *conclude*. He may *throw a curve ball*, one that is difficult to hit; this has the figurative meaning of taking someone by surprise in order to gain advantage. Or he may *throw a fastball*, one that is pitched at maximum velocity; this has the figurative meaning of gaining an advantage by acting very quickly, before an opponent can react. A single pitcher does not usually pitch for an entire game but is relieved at some point, usually when his continued success is doubted. The pitchers on a team are called the *bull pen*, which is also the name of the area where the relief pitcher warms up, and by extension, a name for a group of valued talent.

Several figures of speech originating from the bat in baseball or cricket now have mainly figurative use, and are suitably treated here, before we leave one sport and go to the other:

BAT IDIOMS

Phrase	Source	Meaning
bat a thousand	baseball	succeed constantly without failing
carry one's own bat	cricket	outlast all others [e.g., in a competition]
go to bat for sb	baseball	make efforts critical to sb's success
keep/play a straight bat	cricket	play fair; play by the rules
off one's own bat	cricket	on one's own inspiration or effort
right off the bat	baseball	immediately

Cricket

Cricket shares the trait with baseball of being the most civilized and subtle of national sports passions. It is governed by precisely written laws, and by extension anything not in keeping with traditional standards of fairness and rectitude is *not cricket*. There are a few terms in common with baseball, having slightly different meanings. It is played between two teams of eleven players each who alternate *batting* (when they can score) and *fielding* (when they try to stop the other team from doing so). Which side will bat or field first is determined by *the toss* at the beginning of a match. *Batsmen* work in pairs, each standing in front of an object called a *wicket* that consists of three vertical stakes (*stumps*) joined by crossbars (*bails*) at the top. The batsman is said to be *at the wicket*. His job, besides trying to hit the balls *bowled* to him and score some *runs*, is to defend the wicket (keep it from being dismantled by the ball). The *bowler* (from the fielding team) bowls the ball at the wicket, attempting to dislodge the bails from the stumps, which would put the batsman *out*. This constitutes *taking a wicket* for the fielding side, and *losing a wicket* for the batting side. The expression *on a sticky wicket* means in an awkward or tricky situation, arising out of the difficulty of batting on a wicket that has been drying after rain.

The area between the two wickets, where batsmen run, is officially called the *pitch*. *Queering someone's pitch* means to spoil their plans or chances of success, especially secretly or maliciously. Various markings on the pitch called *creases* indicate different limits for players or the ball. A player *at the crease* is batting; by extension, this expression means performing in a demanding situation, or called upon to do so. Thus Margaret

Thatcher in 1990, "I am still at the crease though the bowling has been more hostile lately."

In addition to being put out by the falling of the wicket (*out bowled*), a batsman may be put out or *dismissed* as follows:

OUT IN CRICKET

Method	Meaning
out Caught	when the ball he hits is caught by a fielder; one easily caught is called a *dolly*
out Handled the ball	when either batsman willfully touches the ball in play with a hand or hands not holding the bat
out Hit the ball twice	when the batsman hits the same bowled ball twice
out Hit wicket	when the batsman dismantles the wicket himself with the bat or a body part
out Leg before wicket (LBW)	when the batsman stops the ball from dismantling the wicket with his leg, in front of the stumps
out Obstructing the field	when either batsman willfully distracts the opposing side
out Stumped	when the wicket-keeper dislodges the wicket while the batsman is out of his ground—his place in front of the wicket—but not running
out Timed out	when the batsman fails to appear at the crease within a defined limit
Run out	when the fielding team dislodges the wicket while the batsmen are running and have not regained their ground

The cricket field, or *ground*, is roughly circular with the pitch at the center. For the purpose of describing positions on the field it is divided in half down the axis of the pitch; the side of the field behind the batsman, as he stands at the crease, is *leg* or the *leg side*. The side of the field that the batsman faces, and toward which his toes are pointing, is *off* or the *off side*. The fielding team play positions that go by an astonishing variety of names, and the names are shorthand in cricket reporting for where a hit ball goes. The table gives the meaning of the main terms:

CRICKET FIELDING POSITIONS

Term	Position
backward	behind an imaginary line passing through the stumps at the batsman's end and at right angles to the wicket
cover	in front of the batsman on the off side

CRICKET FIELDING POSITIONS *(continued)*

Term	Position
deep	far from the batsman, near the boundary
fine	behind the wicket, near the line of flight of bowled balls
long-off	far behind the bowler on the off side
long-on	far behind the bowler on the leg side
mid-off	near the bowler's position on the off side
mid-on	near the bowler's position on the leg side
short	near the batsman
silly	very close to the batsman
slip	behind and near the batsman on the off side
square	level with the batsman on the leg side

These are combined to produce such combinations as *deep square-leg, silly mid-off*, and *backward short-leg*.

As with the pitcher in baseball, much attention focuses on the bowler in cricket. He may bowl a *googly*, a ball that is difficult to hit because it curves. By extension a *googly* is a situation that takes someone by surprise. A ball that swerves from the leg to the off side is an *outswinger*; one going the other way is an *inswinger*. A bowler who takes three successive wickets with three successive balls does a *hat trick*, a term that has extended to many other sports to denote three consecutive wins, goals, scores, and the like. A bowler is said to *beat the bat* when he bowls a ball that the batsman fails to hit, often because it moves deceptively. It is a bad thing for a bowler to *throw* the ball; this means he did so with a forbidden bent arm action. A player who can both bat and bowl well is an *all-rounder*, a term that seems to apply more in cricket than any other sport.

If the batsman manages to hit the ball some distance, he runs toward the opposite wicket (still carrying the bat), while his partner runs toward him. Each pass from one end to the other constitutes a *run* for the batsman who hit the ball. While this happens, the fielding team attempts to return the ball to the bowler or to the *wicketkeeper*, who is another fielding player stationed behind the batsman's wicket. The ball is *dead* when this happens and the runners cease. Additional runs can also be awarded by a *boundary* when the ball or the player retrieving it goes beyond the limit of the grounds. This is good for four runs if it bounces before this happens; otherwise it is called a *six*, and good for six runs; thus the expression *hit someone for six*, which means to affect them severely. Runs may also be awarded in various penalty situations; those that do not arise from hitting the ball are called *extras* and are not credited to the batsman. These include *byes*, runs scored off balls that passed the batsman without being hit. A batsman scores a *century* when he reaches one hundred runs in a single innings.

A number of verbs describe the movement of the ball in cricket based on the batsman's way of hitting it; all of these can take as a direct object either the ball or the bowler (e.g., *sweep the ball, sweep the bowler*):

HITTING THE CRICKET BALL

Verb	Meaning
cart	hit the ball powerfully, sending it a long way
cut	strike the ball with the bat held horizontally, sending it to the off side
edge	hit the ball with the edge of the bat
glance	deflect the ball with the bat held at an angle
snick	deflect the ball with the edge of the bat
sweep	hit the ball on the leg side by bringing the bat across the body from a half-kneeling position

Two team *captains* have the primary role in setting the well-mannered tone of the game and keeping their players in line if there is a need to. A game consists of one or two *innings* (the noun is both singular and plural) for each side; a slang term for innings is *knock*. An innings consists of all the players on one side batting once, each player batting until he is put out (or in rare cases, when he may retire not out). When a side has finished its innings it is *all out*. However, a team captain may *declare* an innings (end it) for his team before all the men have batted. This is reported along with the score, along the lines of "the Caribbeans declared their second innings at 322." Normally teams alternate batting and fielding, but a team that is trailing disastrously according to fixed rules may be required to have a *follow-on* innings, batting twice in a row. A division of the game within the innings is an *over*, a sequence of six balls bowled by one bowler from one end of the pitch. An over in which no runs are scored is a *maiden* or *maiden over*. The next over begins with another bowler, from the opposite end.

The winning team is the one scoring the greater number of runs in their innings. If the result is reached while the winning team is batting, the win is stated as the number of wickets yet to fall, that is, the number of batsmen who, were it not for the team reaching a superior number, could still take their turn at bat. Thus, a result may be stated as winning a game by eight wickets. If the result is reached while the winning team is fielding, the result is stated as a *win by runs*. An incomplete game abandoned for lack of time is called a *draw*, regardless of the score.

The game is presided over by two *umpires*, who generally stand at either end of the pitch. They rule on various aspects of the play, including *giving* a batsman *out* or *not out* (i.e., declaring that he is dismissed, or is still batting). The bowler or a fielder will ask the umpire to adjudicate in a situation where he feels the batsman may be out with an appeal of "how's that?" sometimes rendered *"howzat?"* in the press and used figuratively as an expression of dismay at a questionable official opinion. The umpire gives a decision on the appeal of either *out* or *not out*.

The match of greatest importance is played between England and Australia for the *Ashes*, which is in effect the sacred relic of the international game, possession of which follows the victors. It is played for every two to three years.

Matches can last from one to five days, and consist of one or two complete innings, in which all eleven players have the opportunity to bat. An innings is finished when ten of the eleven players on a side have been dismissed. A shorter version of the game is a *limited-over match*, in which each team competes in a match with an agreed number of overs per innings, usually forty or fifty. Professional cricket in the UK is called *county cricket*, played by eighteen professional teams. In international cricket, which takes place among England and most of the Commonwealth countries it used to rule, matches are called *test matches*, or sometimes just *tests*. The visiting team are referred to as *tourists*. The two venues most associated with cricket and usually identified only by their names are both in London: *Lord's*, which is the headquarters of the Marylebone Cricket Club (*MCC* in headlines), and the *Oval* in southeast London.

(American) Football

Most of the English-speaking world uses *football* to mean the game that Americans only call soccer. American football was developed in the nineteenth century, combining some elements of soccer and rugby. The professional game is played on a rectangular field 120 yards long and 160 feet wide with goals at either end. There are parallel lines extending across the field at regular intervals, giving the whole field the appearance of a grid and giving rise to the name *gridiron*, which is used as an elegant variation for the field or the game itself. The size being familiar to most Americans, *football field* is often used as an approximation to other sizes (*a tunnel about two football fields long*). For comparison, it is about the same size as a minimum regulation soccer field, and about 15 percent smaller than a minimum international competition soccer field.

An area at either end of the field is an area ten yards long called the *end zone*, each of which contains a rooted structure called the *goalpost*, which is topped by a crossbar that supports two upright posts (the goalposts). Other locations on the field are identified by reference to the nearest yard line and the team defending the nearest goal, e.g., *the Packers' 10-yard line, the Ravens' 27-yard line*. Opposing teams of eleven players each try to score *touchdowns* or *field goals* (see below), which normally come after long and arduous attempts to move the ball down the field toward their opponent's goal.

The team that is in possession of the ball has the possibility of scoring; they are called the *offense* (pronounced OFF-ence); the other team, who tries to prevent this and to gain possession themselves, is called the *defense* (pronounced DEEF-ence). A game consists of four quarters of fifteen minutes each. The clock is stopped whenever the ball is not in play, so games take generally two hours or more. A long break is provided in the middle of the game, called *half-time*.

A game begins by one team (the kicking team) *kicking off* to the other, that is, kicking the ball toward them at their end of the field. From this phenomenon, *kick-off time* has come to mean the time that something begins. The team kicked to is the receiving team; their object is to move the ball to the goal back at the end of the field whence it came. The ball makes progress by a player running with it (*rushing*), or by a player passing the ball to another player who has run ahead. A *touchdown* (six points) is scored when the offense gets the ball across the defense's goal line, which is the beginning of the end zone. This entitles the scoring team to try for an extra point, called a *conversion*, by kicking the ball between the goalposts. Three points can be scored by doing this when the offense has had their last play and are about to lose possession of the ball (a *field goal*). The only other scoring possibility is a *safety*, wherein the defense can score by tackling the player with the ball in the player's own end zone. This is a sort of functional equivalent of an *own goal* in soccer.

The offense's progress toward the other team's goal is checked by the man with the ball being tackled, or by his running or being driven out of bounds. This is the occasion for a *down*, when the offensive players regroup and consider their next play. A team in possession is allowed four downs, during which time they must move the ball a total of ten yards forward. If they are unable to move this distance within four downs, they forfeit possession of the ball. Every time they move ahead ten yards they begin again with a *first down*. The situation of the offensive team is reported as a combination of (1) down and (2) yards to go before reaching another first down or the end zone. Thus, *second and six* means the team is on their second down and has yet to make six yards; *first and goal* means the team is on a first down and within ten yards of the goal line.

At the beginning of each down, players group along the *line of scrimmage*, the point on the field where play was last stopped, and from which progress forward is measured. Players must stay on their side of this line till play begins; a player who is on the wrong side of the line of scrimmage is *offside* and earns a penalty. A play begins by a player (the *center*) passing the ball backward between his legs (*snapping the ball*) to the *quarterback*, the key player whose actions mainly decide the course of play. The quarterback can either run forward with the ball, but more commonly he passes it off to a nearby player who runs with it (a *running back*), or he passes it forward to a player who has run down the field for this purpose (a *receiver*). The defense attempts to spoil all of this by *tackling* the player with the ball, or preventing any other player from running forward or receiving a pass (*blocking*). If a player who is carrying the ball or trying to catch the ball drops it, this constitutes a *fumble*, and any player who can get the ball then gets possession of it for his team.

Once the ball has been passed it cannot be passed again during that play. It must then be advanced by running (*rushing*) toward the opponents' end zone, always with defensive players in hot pursuit.

The professional game is now played entirely within one league, the *NFL*. The thirty-two teams it comprises are sometimes referred to as *franchises* since they are in fact franchised by the league. Top college football players who aspire to compete for selection in the NFL form a pool each year which is the basis for a *draft*, in which the players are chosen by different teams in the NFL in turns, ensuring that new talent is distributed evenly. A similar system operates in professional basketball. Players in their first year with a professional team are *rookies*.

Various championship games at different levels of the college sport are played late in the season, all identified as a *bowl* of some kind: the *Rose Bowl*, the *Orange Bowl*, the *Cotton Bowl*. The professional championship game, played in late January, is the *Super Bowl*, and almost has the status of a national holiday.

Rugby

Rugby (BrE *informal: rugger*) has a small and elite following in the US but is not generally known; it is avidly followed in all countries of the UK and in France, as well as South Africa, New Zealand, and Australia. Traditionally there have been two divisions: *Rugby League*, the professional game, and *Rugby Union*, the amateur game, with slightly different rules and followings. The game is played on a rectangular field of a size similar to soccer or American football. There are some other similarities to American football, except that the ball, similarly shaped but larger and white, cannot be passed forward, only sideways and backward (but it can be kicked and carried forward). Teams of fifteen (Rugby Union) or thirteen (Rugby League) defend opposite goals, which are surrounded by the *in-goal area*. The teams are about equally divided into *forwards*, who try to gain possession of the ball, and *backs*, who try to move it forward by developing running plays. The game begins with one side kicking off to the other.

There are several ways to score, the points being awarded varying between the divisions. A *try* is accomplished when the ball is grounded in the opponents' goal area. A *drop goal* is scored by *drop-kicking* the ball (kicking it on the bounce) over the goal crossbar. As in American football, a *conversion* is an opportunity for extra points after a try. A *penalty* gives a team against whom a rule has been contravened an attempt at a conversion-type opportunity to score.

The players frequently mentioned in reportage are as follows, with their principal function:

RUGBY PLAYERS

Position	What does he do?
fly half (Rugby Union)	standoff half (Rugby League) forms a link between the scrum half and the three-quarters [who occupy positions behind the forwards]
hooker	forward who tries to hook the ball, from the front row of the middle of the scrum
lock	forwards in the second row of the scrum
number 8 (Rugby Union)	forward at the back of the scrum
scrum half	back who puts the ball into the scrum
wing	also called flankers; forwards positioned on the outside

Play stops when a try is scored, the ball goes out of play, or an infringement occurs. The ball goes out of play if it goes *into touch*, that is, it crosses the border of the field and is dead. This is an occasion for a *line-out*, in which the ball is thrown back in to two competing, jumping lines of forwards. By extension, to *kick* something *into touch* means to reject it firmly or out of hand: *a suggestion that a subcommittee be formed was kicked into touch by the chairman.*

Play also stops when a player who *knocks* the ball *on* moves it forward improperly, giving rise to a *knock-on*, for which his team is penalized. If a player is in front of either a teammate who has the ball or who last played it and that player is interfering with play, he is declared *offside*; this is an occasion for a scrum or a penalty.

The ball is generally put back into play after an infringement by means of a *scrum* or *scrummage*, a formation of players from each of two teams that face each other, each team trying to get possession of the ball placed between them. This resembles a scene of mortal combat and by extension *scrum* means a disorderly crowd of people or things. Injuries in rugby are rife, giving the game a reputation of being rough. *Rugby player*, besides its literal meaning, is used to denote someone very strongly and thickly built, rough looking, or seemingly impervious to pain. Other opportunities for sustaining injury while face down in the mud are the *ruck*, formed when opposing players try to gain possession of the ball on the ground, and a *maul*, formed (in Rugby Union) around a player with the ball. The player with the ball may be *tackled*, as in American football, and must give up possession when this happens.

Association Football

Soccer, called *football* or formally *association football* in the UK, is acquiring, at long last, a following in the US and it is to be hoped that language describing how the game is played will make its way into American vernacular before long. The organization of the professional game is considerably different from the way American Football is organized and so deserves a short discussion.

Teams are organized in *clubs*, each of which has a diehard following; the clubs are organized in a four-level hierarchy consisting of the *premier league*, and three numbered *divisions*; movement within this hierarchy is based entirely on performance. A sufficient number of wins enables a club to be *promoted* to the next highest league; too many losses results in *relegation*, or descent to a lower level. There are various championships, the most important being the *FA Cup*, played each year in May at *Wembley* Stadium in London; the media cliché for the knockout competition preceding this is the *road to Wembley*. In addition the three leading teams in the premiere division get a chance to compete for the annual *European Cup*, against top teams from other European countries. Finally, a national representative team plays international matches, competing in a European competition every four years and the *World Cup* again every four years if the team manages to qualify for the competitions through doing well in a series of qualifying matches. Various aspects of play in the premier league are denoted by the noun *premiership*, often used attributively: *premiership action/matches/leaders*.

The playing area for football (soccer) is usually called a *pitch* in British English, and games are usually called *matches*. In football and other sports, color-coded uniforms go by the uncount noun *strip* in British English: *a player in Chelsea strip, the club's newly designed strip*. These are simply called *uniforms* in American English. Players are usually called *footballers*, a term not used in American English.

Other Games with Balls

Several other games are common enough in one country to be known to everyone while being mostly unknown in the other.

The principal games played on a billiards table in the US and the UK are different and occupy quite different cultural niches, and so merit a small exposition. *Snooker*[1] in the UK is a fully-fledged sport, with its own celebrity players, televised tournaments, and doping scandals. It is played mainly in clubs that are frequented by men of the working class, though someone of the middle class or with pretensions to it wouldn't be out of place there, and the televised professional sport is widely followed. *Pool* in the US, on the other hand, when not played privately in homes, is associated with barrooms, roadhouses, and *pool halls*, all perceived to be frequented by unsavory types where you would be as likely to witness a drug bust or get your teeth knocked out as you would to find a playing partner. The expression *behind the eight ball* (vulnerable or in danger) from pool is known but not very frequent in British English. The infrequently played

---

1. The American English informal verb *snooker*, "deceive or dupe," is not definitively related to the game and has no appreciable currency in British English.

billiard game called *carom* in American English is called *cannon* in British English.

The game of *bowls* has a firmly-rooted niche in British culture that is not found in the US, where the game is called *lawn bowling*, though it is seldom played. Other ball games known primarily in one country and not the other include:

BALL GAMES

Game	Source	What is it?
dodge ball	US	players stand in a circle and try to avoid being hit by a large ball thrown at them; a children's game
goalball	UK	a game for the visually impaired using a ball with bells in it
kickball	US	like baseball, but the ball is kicked rather than batted and can be thrown at a player to put her out
net ball	UK	like basketball without dribbling, with seven on a side; mostly played by girls
pelota	UK	game of Iberian origin played in a walled court with basketlike handheld nets; known in the UK mainly from holidays
real tennis	UK	forerunner of tennis, played in an enclosed court; small but avid upper-class following
rounders	UK	similar to baseball, played mainly in schools
softball[1]	US	baseball with a larger, softer ball; an amateur and leisure game
stickball	US	informal baseball with improvised bat and any sort of ball
tetherball	US	two players attempt to wind a rope fixed to the top of a pole in opposite directions by hitting a ball attached to the other end of the rope

[1] Proper baseball is sometimes called *hardball* to distinguish it from this game. By extension, *hardball* describes any tough, uncompromising situation: *hardball politics/tactics/questions; a company that can't afford to play hardball with the union.*

Different Ways of Saying Nothing

Idioms for noting a score of zero differ between American English and British English: *6–0* written as a score in any sport, without further context, would be read as "six to nothing" by an American and "six, nil" by a Briton. *Zip* and *squat* are slang American terms for zero that are frequently used to report scores. *O* is spoken in reporting the count in baseball (see above). A *duck* or *duck's egg* is British English slang for a zero score, originating with cricket; to be *bowled for a duck* or be *out for a duck* means not to score in one's innings. To *break one's duck* means to score for the first time in an innings. American English has *goose egg* with the same meaning, though without related phrases and idioms. A game in which one team does not score is called a *shut-out* in American English; the winning team *shuts* the other *out*.

British English also occasionally uses *nought* in place of zero when pronouncing scores and numbers: *nought point seven three, nought to six*. American English uses *zero* or *O* in these cases.

The Sports Calendar

The following table sets out the cherished sporting events in the US and the UK that happen at the same time each year and are widely discussed, as well as being the subject of special coverage in the media. Those whose titles are self-explanatory (e.g., *NBA Playoffs, London Marathon*) and those well-known internationally (*Wimbledon, Kentucky Derby*) are omitted, unless the name conceals something locally known about the event.

SPORTS CALENDAR

When	Event	Where	What is it?
mostly January	Bowl games	US	championship games for college football including the Hula Bowl, Orange Bowl, Sugar Bowl, Rose Bowl, and Fiesta Bowl
late Jan. or early Feb.	Super Bowl	US	National Football League championship game; takes place on *Super Bowl Sunday*
Jan. or Feb.	Six Nations Rugby	UK	includes England, Scotland, Wales, Ireland, France, and Italy; victory of any UK nation over the others is Britain's *Triple Crown*
February	Daytona 500	US	kickoff race for the Winston Cup, highest accolade of NASCAR racing
March	Iditarod	US	1000-mile dogsled race, Anchorage to Nome, Alaska
March	Crufts	UK	mother of all dog shows; televised
March	the Boat Race	UK	traditional rowing race on the Thames in London, between Oxford and Cambridge universities
April	the Grand National	UK	a steeplechase, run at Aintree, near Liverpool; an occasion for betting
May	Stanley Cup National	US	binational ice hockey championships; includes Canadian teams

SPORTS CALENDAR *(continued)*

When	Event	Where	What is it?
May	FA Cup Final	UK	the national football championship played at Wembley, in London
May (first Saturday)	Kentucky Derby	US	horse race in Louisville, KY; *Derby Day* in AmE refers to this
May	Preakness	US	horse race in Pimlico, MD, two weeks after the Kentucky Derby
late May	Indy 500	US	Indianapolis 500; 500-mile race for rear-engine cars in Indianapolis
June	Derby Day	UK	horse race at Epsom, Surrey
June	Belmont Stakes	US	horse race at Elmont, NY, three weeks after the Preakness. The American *Triple Crown* consists of winning these two plus the Kentucky Derby.
June	Royal Ascot	UK	Horseracing at Ascot, Berkshire; showcase for fashionable hats
July	Henley Regatta	UK	boat racing on the Thames; obligatory for fashionable aristocrats
August	Cowes Week	UK	yachting on the Isle of Wight
August	the Glorious Twelfth	UK	August 12, when grouse season begins
October, etc.	hunting season	US	has various meanings; the default is elk or deer season, which normally begins in October
October	World Series	US	Series of seven games for the national baseball championship
October or November	homecoming	US	occasion for alumni to return to a high school or college that usually includes a home football game; high schools elect a *homecoming queen* in a beauty-pageant type event
December	Varsity Match[1]	UK	rugby between Oxford and Cambridge

[1] *Varsity* in American English denotes the top level of play in high school or college sports, as distinct from those games played by lower classmen.

Regular matches played between competing teams in football, rugby, cricket, etc., as part of the regular season's play are called *fixtures* in British English. The nearest American English equivalent is *league game* or *conference game*, indicating a game whose outcome counts toward a team's standing. British English uses *friendly* to describe a game that is not part of regular season play. American English has various terms for describing extra-season play, such as *exhibition* and *preseason*. *Post-season* is usually used in American English to describe games leading to a championship, after the games of the season have all been played and the standings of various teams are determined.

The competitive sports grouped under the term *track and field* in American English is called *athletics* in British English. A short, televised repetition of a sports event immediately after it has happened in real time is called an *instant replay* in American English, an *action replay* in British English.

LEISURE

Gambling

Extensive systems exist in both countries whereby members of the public are persuaded to part with money on the slim chance of winning more as a form of amusement. Where this is organized in casinos around games of chance, it is normally called *gambling* in the US, *gaming* in the UK, though gaming is also the preferred technical term for this activity in American English. Betting and wagering of other kinds is organized differently in the two countries and regulated at different levels. In the UK, nationwide *betting shops*[1] can be found in high streets where wagers can be placed, mainly on horse races and sporting fixtures, but also on any number of other events imagined to have some degree of predictability, in the world of sports, entertainment, politics, and weather. One taking part may be said to *take a flutter* (place a small bet) on a horse or some other event, and is sometimes called *punter*, a widely used slang term for anyone making or contemplating a wager.

In the US, this form of betting is only allowed in some states, where it comes under the collective term *OTB* for *off-track betting*; it is almost exclusively on the outcome of horse races. Perhaps filling the void created by a lack of legal institutions, illegal gambling operations sometimes called *numbers* or *numbers games* operate in some cities, usually operated by organized crime and preying on the poor.

The demimonde of horse racing and the betting that surrounds it enjoy higher profiles in the UK than in the US. This is perhaps because of their association with the British aristocracy, on the one hand, and American organized crime on the other. Details of the extensive jargon of horseracing are beyond the scope of this book, but a few terms deserve mention because they are known even to nonbettors in the two differently organized systems.

1. *Turf accountant* is a humorous or euphemistic variation.

A percentage of stakes from races in the US are distributed to bettors on the horses that finish first, second, and third in a race. These horses *win, place,* and *show,* respectively. *Place* is also used (in both dialects) to indicate the achievement of any of these three horses, and may include the fourth horse in larger UK races, but a *place bet* is specifically for the second-place horse in American English, and any of the places in British English. A few other terms are generally known in one dialect and have some application beyond horse racing, either in other competitions or in figurative use:

BETTING ON HORSES

Term	Source	What is it?
accumulator	UK	bet on a series of races in which the winnings from one are staked on the next
bet across the board	US	bet on the same horse to win, place, or show
each-way bet	UK	bet on a horse to win or place; pays twice if the horse wins; also called *both ways*
forecast	UK	bet on the first two finishers to win and place in exact order; like AmE *perfecta,* but not limited to horses
morning line	US	List of odds on a group of horses in a race determined by the handicapper before the race [frequent figurative use: *The morning line puts the proposal's chance of success at 3–1.*]
perfecta	US	bet on two horses to win and place in exact order
tricast	UK	bet on the first three finishers in exact order; AmE *trifecta*
trifecta	US	bet on the first three finishers in exact order; figurative use as three of anything

Daily double has the same meaning in both dialects. Those seeking more detail can find glossaries online at the sites of various US tracks (some links from www.interbets.com) or of UK bookmakers (e.g., www.ladbrokes.com).

The UK also has an extensive legal system for betting on the outcomes of soccer games; this is called the *pools.* It lost considerable popularity when the *National Lottery* was introduced but still has an avid following among working-class men. A betting *pool* in American English is similar though less sophisticated and usually organized among a small group of mutual acquaintances. The UK's National Lottery has rules similar to lotteries operated by nearly all state governments in the US; some of which go under the name of *Lotto*. What American English dubs *slot machines* or *one-armed bandits* are called *fruit machines* in the UK, where they are relatively unregulated and can be found nearly everywhere; in the US they are subject to state regulations and are normally found only where other sorts of gambling are permitted.

The Drinking Life

Venues allowing consumption of alcohol on the premises conform to a handful of different types in the two countries and go by different names, some overlapping confusingly. The British *pub* is the most distinct institution; it normally has two parts, the *public bar* and the *lounge bar* (also called the *saloon* or *saloon bar*); the latter usually has more comfortable seating and more expensive drinks. A day or evening spent going from pub to pub is called a *pub crawl*; the nearest American English equivalent is the verb *barhop*. Many pubs serve food; when it is characterized as *pub food* this is usually an indication that it is merely adequate, often consisting of frozen, prepared dishes that are microwaved and served. A competing type of drinking establishment in the UK is the *wine bar*. It eschews the traditional sign and décor of the pub in favor of more modern features and offers a wide selection of wines.

Bar is the most general term in American English for social places to drink; it covers everything from the seediest neighborhood dive to expensive hotel lounges. *Lounge* is typically used for a bar that is part of another business, such as a restaurant or hotel, or a large bar that also features entertainment. *Tavern* is often used for small neighborhood bars. *Saloon* is associated mainly with the historical Wild West and is not permitted in the names of bars in some states because of its notorious past, although in others the name is used to evoke this atmosphere. An American *roadhouse* usually features dancing or entertainment and later, fistfights, and is typically located outside a town on a highway; this contrasts with the British English use of *roadhouse* which describes a quiet pub by a country road. A *bar and grill* has a rudimentary food service, usually featuring steaks, on the premises. A current trend is the *microbrewery* or *brewpub*, which makes its own specialty beers on the premises.

Playing Cards

These terms are equivalents in the two dialects:

PLAYING CARDS

American	British
blackjack	pontoon
deck [of cards]	pack
face card	court card
jack →	knave
solitaire	patience

The British children's card game *happy families* is more or less equivalent to US *authors*, both of which are becoming dated in this age of electronic stimulation.

Other Games and Activities

The majority of games and leisure activities that are known in both countries go by the same names in the two dialects. Here are some differences.

TOYS, GAMES, AND LEISURE PURSUITS

American	British
barhop *v*	pub crawl *n*
checkers	draughts
chinese checkers	chinese chequers
grab bag[1]	lucky dip
horse show	gymkhana
horseshoes	quoits[2]
jump rope	skipping rope
jungle gym	climbing frame
lawn bowling	bowls
miniature golf	crazy golf
pick-up-sticks	spillikins
shell game	thimblerig →
shuffleboard	shovelboard
tic-tac-toe	naughts and crosses

[1] *Grab bag* has considerable figurative use in American English that is not found with *lucky* dip in British English. The main meanings are (1) a mixed assortment of items: *a book that is a grab bag of excerpts from letters, journals, and diaries;* and (2) a collection of valuable things free for the taking: *a bill that was a special-interest grab bag for the pharmaceutical and agrochemical industries.*

[2] *Quoits* is played with rings rather than horseshoes, but is otherwise similar.

What American English dubs *bowling* is called *ten-pin bowling* in British English to distinguish it from the more common nine-pin variety, which is also called *skittles*. The objects to be bowled down in these games may also be called *skittles* in British English but always *pins* in American English. British English distinguishes between *angling* (fishing with a rod and line) and other kinds of fishing, a distinction that is not much known, and rarely remarked, among Americans.

A few pastimes deserve mention because of their uniqueness or cultural associations in each country. *Trainspotting* does not exist in any organized way in the US and only came to the attention of Americans through the book and film of the same name, which give little clue as to what it is: the subculture and activities of *trainspotters*, who find pleasure and meaning in collecting the numbers of locomotives, which they travel to various locations to spot. Adherents of the cult are assumed to be obsessive, not very sociable, and they almost undoubtedly wear anoraks. In the US *basketweaving*, though it has no organized following, is used as an example (no doubt unfairly) of an activity that requires no initiative or intelligence, and thus as a activity of last resort for a person who has failed at everything else. In the Western US and Canada, a *stampede* is an event, usually annual, that combines a rodeo with various other amusements such as a carnival, dancing, races, etc.

Traveling Amusements

The phenomenon that most Americans call a *carnival* is a *fun fair* in British English, i.e., an amusement with rides that travels from place to place, often in conjunction with some other celebration. The main British English sense of *carnival* is of a celebration taking place at a regular time each year, especially before the beginning of Lent (though this is not particularly celebrated in Britain), and the late summer West Indian celebration in London called in full the *Notting Hill Carnival*. The "regular celebration" sense is distinguished in American English as an uncount rather than a count noun: *Last year they went to carnival in Rio*. A worker for the traveling type of carnival occupies an identifiable sociological niche in American English and is called a *carny*.

Moving Pictures

Learners' dictionaries of English are fond of drawing a fast distinction between *film*, the designated British English term, and *movie*, the American English one. Usage does not support such a clear-cut distinction and in fact both words have considerable currency in both dialects. *Movie* is clearly preferred by Americans when talking about the most popular form of the entertainment, the full-length feature film, and British English is increasingly comfortable to use *movie* interchangeably with *film*, especially for the products of Hollywood—where in fact must such products come from. The term *TV movie* (*TVM*) is mainly American. The American English trade and technical term *motion picture* is frequent in industry literature but rare in conversation, and relatively unattested in British English. A short film advertising one of these that is released before the film itself is usually a *preview* in American English, a *trailer* in British English, though both terms have currency in both dialects and *trailer* is especially preferred among film cognoscenti in the US.

It is equally common for dictionaries to label *cinema* as a mainly British English term, both for the place where films are shown (AmE *movie theater*) and the art, industry, or academic discipline of films. In fact *cinema* has considerable American English currency in both of these senses, but with several qualifications. Particular movie theaters often incorporate the word *cinema* into their names, but it is rare for American speakers to say that they are going to the (or a) cinema; instead they go to *the movies* or a movie. For the second meaning, the industry or phenomenon of film, American English uses *Hollywood* to designate the mainstream American industry (*a scriptwriter/scandal/megadeal in Hollywood, a Hollywood celebrity/executive/persona*), but *cinema* or *film* for all that lies outside Hollywood (*New Zealand/Russian cinema, cult directors of independent film*). These patterns are about the same in British English. The contemporary exercise of bringing all this into one's home via expensive, state-of-the-art sound equipment and large-screen TV is called *home theater* in American English, *home cinema* in British English.

The rating systems for films in the two countries are complementary, as shown in the following table. These are assigned in the UK by the British Board of Film Classification, which issues each film a *certificate*, giving rise to designations in British English such as *12 certificate, 18 certificate*. US movies are evaluated and given a *rating* by the MPAA, or Motion Picture Association of America; the equivalent American English shorthand is *G-rated, R-rated*, etc.

FILM RATINGS

Rating	Country	What is it?
G	US	general audiences; no age restrictions
U	UK	universal viewing; no age restrictions
PG	US and UK	parental guidance suggested
12	UK	no one under 12 permitted
PG-13	US	no one under 13 admitted without an adult
15	UK	no one under 15 permitted
R	US	no one under 17 admitted without an adult
NC-17	US	no one under 17 admitted
18	UK	no one under 18 permitted

X is no longer an official classification in either country but is still used informally for the most restrictive classification of films. A classification of *NR* (not rated) for an American film either means that the makers declined to pay the fee required for a rating, or that they were sure of getting an NC-17 anyway and so didn't bother.

The Theatre

Americans may mean *movie theater* when they say *theater* but if they are attending a live theater performance they go to *the theater* or to a play. Terms describing the various locations in an auditorium vary considerably in American theaters and are not as standardized as those in Britain, perhaps owing to the social significance that attached in the past in Britain to being seated in a particular area. In general, these equivalents hold:

THE THEATER AUDITORIUM

American	British
main floor, orchestra	stalls
(first) balcony	dress circle
upper balcony, second balcony	upper circle
aisle	gangway
parquet	orchestra stalls
parterre, parquet circle	rear stalls

Where present, a *loge* in a US theater is usually a separated section at the front of the first balcony, an isolated dress circle; in British theaters it is a private box. A *mezzanine*, where present, is the first seating higher than the main floor and as such is another dress circle equivalent. *Gallery* is used in both dialects for the highest, cheapest seats, informally called the *Gods* in British English and the *peanut gallery* in American English.

Traditional US theaters and movie theaters have a *marquee*, a lighted sign projecting over the sidewalk with two vertical facades on which the current feature is advertised. When present on a British theatre this is called an *awning*, though this usage is not fixed. A *marquee* in British English mainly means a large, usually rented tent used for a ceremonial occasion such as a wedding.

The main meanings of the term *concession* in relation to entertainment have quite different meanings in the two dialects. In American English a *concession* or *concession stand* is a business set up within larger premises, often an entertainment venue, where a product is sold, such as refreshments, souvenirs, or literature. The products offered by such an enterprise may also be called *concessions*. In British English *concessions* is used to indicate discounts available to various classes of people attending events, such as pensioners or the unemployed. American English uses *discount* for this meaning.

A break between the acts of a play is called an *intermission* in American English, the *interval* in British English. A performance for which there are no more seats available is indicated with a sign that says *Sold Out* in American English, and usually *House Full* in British English.

Pantomime

The Christmas *pantomime* or informally, *panto* in the UK is unknown in the US, where pantomime is simply a full or formal version of *mime*. British pantomime is a highly stylized comic play, produced around Christmastime and based loosely on a fable or fairytale, with many stock players, some of whom appear in drag. It is an outing for families during the holiday season.

Tickets

Booking office appears in British English as the theater location where tickets may be bought or reserved, but *box office* is the preferred term in both dialects and the only one with figurative uses (*a box-office hit*). As with travel tickets, Britons *book* and Americans normally *reserve*. Last-minute tickets available at a staggering premium are sold by *scalpers* in the US, (*ticket*) *touts* in the UK; these terms apply to theater tickets as well as tickets for other sorts of entertainment.

CHAPTER TEN

What You Don't Say

The likelihood of committing inadvertent yet mortifying linguistic gaffes is not nearly so great among English speakers of different dialects as is it between speakers of altogether different languages, but there are still considerable opportunities for the British or American speaker to put his foot in his mouth while on the other side of the ocean. This chapter treats words that may pack an unexpected punch when used transatlantically, as well as contexts that may require a kind of linguistic circumspection that is different from what is likely to come naturally to the innocent abroad. Language that falls under the heading of political correctness is also treated here. While it is not the intention here to supply the prankster with linguistic ammunition, it is impossible to treat this subject without spelling out a good number of terms that many speakers would find disquieting (at the least) to encounter in print or conversation. Those with the most tender sensibilities are advised to turn away now.

SCATOLOGY

Parts of the Body

Various words with many other jobs to do are called into service as slang for private parts of the body in both dialects. These differ to some degree between the two countries. American English slang words for penis that might conceivably appear in innocent British conversation include *cock, dick, dong, doodle, dork, meat, pecker, peter, putz, rod, tool,* and *weenie*. Without awareness of these, the Briton might not understand the American's declining an invitation to a hot mouthful of spotted dick (see chapter 7). The American must also be assured that the British child's enthusiasm for Blue Peter (see chapter 11) is not anything to be concerned about. Similarly, the now rather old-fashioned British admonition *keep your pecker up* (keep your spirits up) should be used sparingly in speaking to Americans, unless more evidence of virility is wanted. By the same token, British English *clever dick* (AmE *wise guy*) might better be avoided in the company of Americans.

British words for the same organ include *joystick, knob, plonker, prong, todger, wang,* and *willie*. Of these, only the last is likely to present an obstacle in American English, since Willie is a common diminutive for Will or William. Statistics are not available, but it seems reasonable that the queues forming outside British cinemas for *Free Willie* when it was first released had an air of festivity about them that was missing from the American ones. For reasons to be explained by someone specializing in another field, half of the foregoing terms are also used, in their dialect, to designate a man of inferior intelligence. Vulgar terms for female genitalia are largely the same in both dialects and so don't bear repeating here, though the variable use of *fanny* must not be overlooked (see below).

The commonest appliance for the male organ, the prophylactic sheath, goes by a number of names that normally do not pass into polite conversation, or do so only accompanied by blushes or tittering. Both dialects use *condom* in technical, antiseptic contexts. The main American English slang term is *rubber*, which has made considerable advances in British English, displacing *johnnie* to some degree, and also making the prevalent British English use of *rubber* (a pencil *eraser*) difficult to use without double entendre. *Trojan*, a common trademarked name in the US, provides an opportunity for puns in American English. In British English, the trademark *Durex* acts in a similar fashion.

British English *arse* is the equivalent of American English *ass*, the vulgar slang term for buttocks and thereabouts. Many of the same phrases and compounds exist in both dialects, and they are deemed to be equally vulgar. British English has *ass* at its disposal for nonoffensive use and the media are fond of spinning off variations on the modified quotation from Dickens, "the law is an ass." This is less frequent American English, where impunity with the use of *ass* is only guaranteed when sanctioned by a biblical context.

The British English expression *arse over tit* is a vulgar way of saying "end over end." British English also has *arse bandit*, an unflattering term for a gay male. American English has *candy ass*, a coward.

Bottom is the more socially acceptable British English term for the buttocks, followed by *bum*. *Behind* and *rear end* win out in American English, which also makes playful use of *tush* and *tushie* (from Yiddish) and *fanny*. The word *fanny* is especially to be avoided by Americans when speaking to Britons. A light-hearted phrase such as "get your fanny over here" could cause the greatest offense, since in British English the word is vulgar and taboo slang for the female genitalia. The strap-on container called a *fanny pack* in the US is a *bum bag* in British English.

The testicles are put into figurative service in both dialects, though under different names and for different effects. *Balls* can have the meaning "nonsense" in British English, but it is also used in all-male conversation in both dialects as a metonym for courage. Spanish *cojones* is similarly used in American English. *Bollocks* is acceptable in informal British English for its various figurative uses, i.e., to mean "nonsense," or as an expression of annoyance. A *bollocking* is a severe reprimand. A *balls-up* or *cock-up* (BrE) is the same as a *snafu* in American English. Other names for these vital organs without significant figurative uses are *knackers* and *goolies*, both British English, and *nuts* American English.

Women's breasts are respectfully and technically so called in both dialects, and many of the same ruder terms are also shared. Britons might not recognize *hooters*, a vulgar American English term (though also the name of a restaurant chain); the singular denotes a car or other kind of horn in British English. Americans can be assured that a British driver with his hand on the hooter is well within the bounds of proper conduct.

Activities and Excretions

The favorite British English rude slang term for masturbate is *wank*; in American English, it is *jerk off* or its variant *jack off*. These apply mainly to men. The corresponding terms of contempt for a useless or despicable character, also applied mostly to men, are *wanker* and *jerk-off*. The less common British English verb *toss* shows up more often in the contemptible term *tosser*. None of these terms passes in polite society.

British English has the useful verb *bonk* and verbal noun *bonking* to describe the sex act in an informal and inoffensive way that is acceptable, such as in feature journalism. The verbs *roger* and *shag* and their corresponding gerunds are slightly less acceptable, but not quite as vulgar as *screw* or as the f-word, which have the same status in both dialects. American English has no similar terms deemed sufficiently respectable for appearing in mainstream journalism and resorts to circumlocution or technical terms when necessary. A Briton in want of this activity is said to be *randy*, which is generally not understood in American English, Randy being a moderately common man's given name. The American English word *horny*, with the same meaning, is not acceptable in polite conversation.

The phrasal verb *knock up* is vulgar slang in American English for "make pregnant." In British English it has a number of meanings. One is to knock on someone's door as a means of waking them. Many American tourists have been surprised by and skeptical of elderly hotel attendant's claims to perform this service for them every morning. *Knock up* also has the meaning in British English of "concoct" or "create in an impromptu fashion," thus *a chef who could knock up gourmet dinners in half an hour.* From this comes the adjective *knock-up*, meaning "improvised" or "provisional." Finally, a *knock-up* in British English is a brief period of practice before playing, especially in racquet sports; the nearest American English equivalent is *warm-up*.

Spunk in British English is a vulgar slang word for semen, and so the complimentary American English adjective *spunky*, or the approving observation that some has got a lot of spunk do not translate well without modification. The description of Sally as a "spunky gal" in the Stephen Foster lyric would hardly recommend her to most Britons, and might well leave them wondering how she got that way.

Piss is the vulgar word for urine in both dialects, though verbal and adjectival uses vary. *Pissed* (or *pissed off*) in American English means very angry; *pissed* (or *pissed up*) in British English means drunk. American English does not share the rude British directive *piss off* (go away). Finally, British English also has *take the piss*, meaning to mock someone derisively for amusement; this activity is called *piss-taking*.

Slang and euphemistic terms for vomit, noun and verb, overlap considerably between the dialects. *Hurl*, relatively recent in American English slang, is not as well established in British English, while British English *honk* is not so used in American English, where it usually means "sound your horn": the various American bumper stickers incorporating this verb, e.g. *Honk if you love Jesus*, might present a dilemma to the visiting Briton.

Much discussion surrounds the adjective *bloody*, mistakenly taken to be gravely offensive in British English but carrying only the literal meaning, "covered with or soaked in blood," in American English. In fact it is not deeply offensive in Britain, and is often used in light-hearted exasperation; it should only be avoided in polite or formal conversation. *Bloody-minded* is a British English expression for "stubborn" or "pig-headed" and is not of itself offensive.

It has not been the intention to supply a complete list of offensive words, only to list those that differ between the dialects or that might lead to misunderstanding. If you find that your favorite is not here, chances are that it is used in the same, equally vulgar way in both dialects.

DICTATES OF POLITICAL CORRECTNESS

The firestorm of political correctness in language and behavior that descended on the United States in the 1990s and rapidly spread throughout the English-speaking world continues unabated. Levels and areas of sensitivity vary considerably on either side of the Atlantic; it is prudent to know what words or phrasing may cause offense in one country that can pass unremarked in the other.

Ethnic and Racial Classifications

It has become increasingly undesirable to affiliate any person with a racial or ethnic group without also revealing a benevolent reason for doing so, and this is perhaps as it should be: geneticists remind us that the concept of race is arbitrary and has no basis in science. The prevailing categories of race and ethnicity in both the US and the UK are mainly historical in origin, were devised as a means of isolating and stereotyping minorities, and in most cases are no longer very accurate at describing any fixed phenomenon. All of that notwithstanding, the terms persist strongly in the minds of their users. All of the terms noted below as being best avoided can usually be used with impunity within the group that they designate, but are regarded as slurs when used by people not belonging to the group purportedly identified.

It is nearly always acceptable in American English to designate US citizens who are immigrants or who are of obvious foreign descent by a hyphenated compound: *Korean-American, Jamaican-American*. Corresponding forms of such compounds generally don't appear in British English, and the same idea has to be put across by explanation: *a Briton of*

Indian descent, a Jamaican with British citizenship. The single exception to the hyphenation rule in American English is *African American*, now the preferred noun for designating Americans who are descendants of slaves during the period of US slavery that ended in 1865 with the end of the Civil War. This term supplants *African-American, Afro-American, Colored,* and *Negro,* listed here in reverse historical order and in order of increasing offensiveness. Oddly, two of these terms persist in two high-profile US not-for-profit organizations, the United Negro College Fund and the National Association for the Advancement of Colored People. *Coloured* enjoyed a vogue fifty years ago in the UK but now is regarded as dated or offensive. *People of color* is used in both dialects to designate collectively those to whom the label *white* doesn't apply. *Black* is used dispassionately in both dialects to describe people of sub-Saharan African origin, but it is sometimes used offensively in British English to describe any foreigner whose skin color is darker than the old-fashioned British standard, for example, South Asians or Middle Easterners.

American Indian is a largely acceptable term in both dialects for a member of any of the native peoples of North America; *Native American* is the term adopted by the government and by many other bodies, though members of these peoples largely prefer American Indian. A term still in currency in Britain for these people, probably without disparaging intent, is *Red Indian*. This term is completely unacceptable in American English, as is *squaw* to denote an Indian woman. *Amerindian* enjoyed a vogue in American English but has now fallen from fashion; it still has some currency in British English. *Eskimo* as a designation for natives of Alaska and northern North America is disputed in American English with regard to its correctness; *Inuit* is now a more acceptable term, but *Eskimo* persists in British English, and in English generally as an acceptable term in anthropological use.

The designation *Asian* has no specific resonance in American English with regard to people, since it can characterize a person from any of dozens of countries making up a sizable chunk of the world's population. In British English, however, it is a standard though not very polite classification for people from the Indian subcontinent, or for Britons who are the children of these. The closest American English term to British English *Asian* is probably *subcontinental*, though this word is not widely in circulation. American English also has *Asian Indian* to distinguish from American Indian. For those from east Asian countries, American English may use the now slightly old-fashioned (and perhaps in some quarters, offensive) *Oriental*, but its use with regard to people is usually a marker for educated speakers that the user is either prejudiced, or not very sophisticated.

The country formerly known as *Burma* is still known as Burma in most of the UK press; US journalists generally make *Myanmar* the term of choice, while not addressing the fact that the new name has been put forward by an illegitimate government.

Hispanic is a convenient and acceptable catch-all American English term, both adjective and noun, for Spanish speakers and people of Latin American or South American descent in the US. *Latino* (masculine) and *Latina* (feminine) are equally acceptable. *Chicano* and *Chicana* as designations for Mexican-Americans enjoyed a vogue in the 1970s that has now mostly passed.

The term *Caucasian* to designate anyone other than peoples of the Caucasus is out of fashion in both countries, except in American English police jargon, where it is still used to designate white people of apparent European descent: *a female Caucasian approximately twenty years old found strangled.* Use of *Caucasian* in American English outside of this specialized technical context is usually loaded with racist overtones.

Terms of disparagement for various ethnic and national groups are largely the same in both countries and thus don't need airing here, since they cause offensive in equal measures wherever they are used. The term *Jew* is generally acceptable in British English as purely descriptive, but is sometimes not regarded so in American English, perhaps from the negative connotations of the slang verb *jew*. A better choice is *Jewish person*, or a rephrasing that eliminates the need for a noun all together.

Owing to a supposition that they started out with reference to slaves, two terms of American origin fall under the ax of political correctness, one in the US and one in the UK. *Nitty-gritty*, which can be used completely innocently in American English, is spuriously taken to have disparaging racial overtones in British English and is thus best avoided in totally correct speech and writing. The American *coon's age,* meaning a very long time, is to be avoided by those observing a similar standard. It is not used in British English.

Terms Relating to Religion

The designation *Black Muslim* for members of the Nation of Islam, formerly standard, is now found offensive by some in American English. There is no simple substitute, since *Muslim* alone is not adequately descriptive, in the minds of orthodox Muslims anyway. The adjective *Roman* in any but an historical context is not generally used in American English to refer to Roman Catholicism; it is so used sparingly, and usually disparagingly, in British English. *Mohammedan* is off-limits in American English as a term for a Muslim, though it appears with some regularity in the *Independent* in the UK as an apparent elegant variation on *Muslim*.

Terms Relating to Sex and Sexual Orientation

The most stringent rules dictated by feminism have now passed in both countries and it is now possible to refer to a group of mature women as *ladies* in both countries without giving offense. Designating an individual woman as a *lady* is acceptable in British English and is in fact the formula used in the House of Commons, e.g., "the honourable Lady," for members to refer to female members. *Lady* is less acceptable in the US for designating an individual woman though it is rarely found offensive by mature women.

Terms of disparagement for gay people are likewise common in both Britain and the US, though all of them are used jocularly, or even affectionately, within the gay community. *Fag* is slightly more common in the UK as a slang term for a cigarette than as a disparaging term for gay man, the main American meaning. Except for the cigarette meaning, *fag* and *faggot* can hardly be used in British English without double-entendre or self-consciousness in any of their traditional senses. It is, however, still possible to find in the freezer case of British supermarkets a product called *faggots in gravy;* they are liver meatballs, not really part of the American diet, and surely never to be sold under that name, even if they catch on! *Rear-ender* is a slang (and disparaging) British English term for a gay man, but in American English it is the usual term for describing a car accident involving one car colliding with the back of another.

People with Disabilities

The trend in American English over the past quarter century has been to abandon terms that are interpreted as being disparaging or discriminatory for people who suffer from some mental or physical handicaps. No sooner do the terms acquire unambiguous denotation than they are replaced by new terms that have more positive associations. *Cripple* and *crippled* were long ago discarded, and replaced by *handicapped*. This term persists in technical usage to refer to devices and facilities (*a handicapped toilet/parking space*) but is seen as increasingly unacceptable when applied to people. They are said to *have disabilities*, or preferably, to be *challenged* in some way: thus *developmentally challenged, physically challenged*. *Differently abled* has also appeared as a term to designate the disabled that removes all stigma (and transparency of meaning for the unschooled). *Retarded* is likewise no longer acceptable for describing children or adults with mental capacity that has not developed with their age; they now are said to have *learning disabilities*. British English has not gone quite so far in abandoning more traditional terms, but the influence of American English has made all of its developments along these lines clearly understood in Britain.

Misunderstood Minorities

Visitors from either side of the Atlantic may have difficult comprehending sensitivities to particular populations that do not receive such special treatment at home. The main areas to note are as follows.

Unemployment and Welfare

In the UK great care is taken lest any stigma attach to the unemployed, who are sometimes called *unwaged*. They are offered discounted admission to many entertainments; this may be indicated on a sign by the code *UB40*, the name of the government-issued form such people possess; or they may be actually identified with the form: *tickets are £7, £5 for students and UB40s*. This, despite the fact that severance pay (or the *redundancy package* as it sometimes is in British English) in general is far beyond what any American would dream of, and unemployment benefits are generally more liberal and longer-running.

This phenomenon reflects that widely held American belief, absent in Britain, that everyone should be able to pick herself by the bootstraps. More grist for this mill can be found in the different associations attending the word *welfare* in the two dialects. In American English it is thought of mainly in relation to the government-provided benefit to unemployed and largely unemployable adults, though *welfare* is not officially a part of the name of any of these programs, which in any case are being largely phased out. Leading American English collocates with *welfare* are *reform, mothers*, and *overhaul*. In British English, on the other hand, *improving, contributory*, and *foundation* get high marks for lining up with *welfare*. The creation of the *welfare state* is seen by many Britons as a milestone in human social progress; in the US, even the use of the term *welfare state* is usually a signal that somebody is about to trash it.

ABORTION

The polarization caused by the issue of abortion in the US cannot be overstated to the visiting Briton and it is a topic that any peace-loving person would avoid. Those conscripted into a conversation about it should know what terms to use and avoid, since they will stamp the user as belonging to one side or the other. The camp favoring abortion availability is usually comfortable calling themselves *pro-choice*; they are called *pro-abortion* by their opponents. Those who favor a ban on all abortions, usually for religious reasons and from the belief that life begins at conception, call themselves *pro-life* or *right-to-life*; they may be called *anti-abortion* or *anti-choice* by their opponents. Some other terms in use, none of which is baggage-free, include the following:

AMERICAN ABORTION TERMINOLOGY

Term	Usage
abortion rights	term used by pro-choice advocates to characterize their position under the 1972 Supreme Court decision (*Roe vs. Wade*) that legalized abortion in the US
abortionist, abortion doctor	pro-life term for doctor who performs abortions; pro-choice term is often *clinician*
partial birth abortion, PBA	used mainly by the pro-life group, but also in US legislation; late (after 20 weeks) abortion involving partial extraction of the fetus before it is aborted. Technical terms: *D&X abortion, intact dilation and extraction (IDE)*
unborn child, unborn life, pre-born child	pro-life terms for fetus

The term *informed consent*, which has many applications in medicine and law both in American English and British English, is lately being used specifically in the US with reference to abortion, in proposals that doctors should be required to give women contemplating an abortion quite detailed information about medical assistance benefits, the financial responsibilities of the father, and abortion alternatives, as well as descriptions of the developing fetus.

CHAPTER ELEVEN

The Stuff of Life

Grouped in this chapter are discussions of topics from everyday life where differences between the two dialects do not amount to a chapter-length treatment. The reader will be excused for finding this an inelegant solution to organizing the subject. The intention is to include as much as possible of the material likely to be encountered in reading and listening, even if it means packing some of it into an omnibus. The front seats go to a number of high frequency words that are not easily classifiable under a subject heading, but that show pervasive differences between the dialects.

PECULIAR PAIRS

The words discussed in the following paragraphs are encountered frequently in general contexts in both dialects. Common to them all is an area of overlap in the principle meaning between the dialects, along with areas, sometimes quite large, in which each dialect has a dominant sense for the word that is not found in the other. The words are mostly organized in pairs, with occasional expansion into other related terms; a single word heading in some of the paragraphs is one whose principal meaning is different in the two dialects, thus constituting a pair represented by a single form.

attach, fix

An early (1832) British visitor to the US complained that *fix* was one of a small handful of words that were in constant use by Americans for many purposes beyond those prescribed for it: "if anything is to be done, made, mixed, mended, bespoken, hired, ordered, arranged, procured, finished, lent, or given, it would very probably be designated by the verb 'to fix.'"[1] Perhaps this explains why American English largely abandons one of the oldest, and in British English the commonest meaning of *fix*, that is, "make fast." When two things are joined, especially by means of parts or devices designed for this, Americans usually *attach* one to the other, where Britons *fix* one to the other. Other American uses of *fix* that were decried by the early observer are now established (or shall we say, fixed?) in English generally and no longer regarded as Americanisms, except the idiom *fixing to + infinitive* (about to). Americans are as willing to *fix* a date as Britons, but *set* a date is more common in American English.

cart, trolley

Cart is the American English and *trolley* is the British English lexical variant for (a) the wheeled basket you use in the supermarket to collect your purchases, and (b) a wheeled piece of furniture with storage space. Under the influence of American e-commerce, the virtual version of (a) is more often a *cart* than a *trolley*, even on UK sites. Both dialects use *trolley* for a wheeled vehicle in a mine or factory used for transporting materials. *Trolley* is also used in British English for a wheeled hospital bed, the thing American English calls a *gurney*. (See also *trolley, tram* below.)

clever

The main meaning of *clever* in British English corresponds more or less to *smart* in American English; a merely descriptive term of intelligence: *All of their children are clever, even the cleverest pupils didn't get it*. American English would use *smart, bright*, or *intelligent* in these sentences, all three being more or less equal in meaning though slightly different in register. Like *scheme*, discussed below, *clever* in American English is often value-laden: it may indicate praiseworthy ingenuity (*a clever solution to a thorny problem*), deceptive craftiness (*clever publicity intended to disguise the product's shortcomings*), or impertinence (*Don't get clever with me!*) (See also *smart*.)

---

1. Quoted in Guy Jean Forgue, "American English at the Time of the Revolution," *Revue des Langues Vivantes* 43:253–269 (1977).

corn

Without a qualifying context, *corn* in American English denotes varieties of the plant *Zea mays,* especially *sweet corn*, the kind eaten as a vegetable, or *field corn*, the kind grown for animal feed and for its many uses in food products and industry. This is the sense implicit in the mainly American English compounds *corn belt, cornbread, corn cob, corn oil, corn syrup*, and many others. The British English word for this plant is *maize*, or occasionally *Indian corn*; the edible variety may also be called *sweet corn*. Without a qualifying context, *corn* in British English denotes any cereal crop, but especially the principal cereal crop of an area, and thus is likely to mean wheat in England or oats in Scotland. This is the sense of corn implicit in the compounds *corn circle, corn dolly, corn exchange*, and *Corn Laws*. Compounds like *cornfield* and *corn harvest* normally denote different things in the two dialects.

fall, autumn

American English uses *fall* in nearly all contexts to denote the season between summer and winter; British English uses *autumn* and regards *fall* strictly has an Americanism. American English, on the other hand, makes use of *autumn* as an elegant or euphonic variation. It is preferred if not obligatory in certain compounds (*autumn leaves, autumn equinox*) and used by writers, especially copywriters, to supply an air of refinement that *fall* seems to lack.

fancy

As a verb, *fancy* enjoys far wider use in British English than in American English. It is the verb of choice in British English in constructions where Americans would probably use *like* (*He's fancied her for the longest time but never asked her out*) or *feel like* (*What do you fancy for supper?*) In American English, the verbal use of *fancy* is always marked in some way (poetic, archaic, affected), except perhaps in the meaning "imagine": *a small town that fancies itself the alfalfa capital of the world.* Some US dictionaries give *fancy man* and *fancy woman* without labels, but contemporary usage is rare. Adjectival and noun use in the two dialects is similar, except that British English has the compound *fancy dress* where American English generally uses *costume* (~ ball/party/parade).

ground, earth

There are large areas of overlapping meaning in both dialects where these two terms are more or less interchangeable. In the context of electrical wiring only, *ground* is the American English and *earth* is the British English lexical variant for an electrical connection with zero potential between a device and the ground. Both words are also used as transitive verbs in this context.

homey, homely
Homey means homelike, evocative of the comforts of home, in both dialects, although British English prefers *homely* for this meaning. *Homely* in American English means physically unattractive, and is usually applied to girls and young women.

keen
American English uses a variety of words for different kinds of enthusiasm that British speakers are in the habit of lumping under the adjective *keen*. Thus British *She's a keen cyclist, We weren't that keen on going, keen supporters of more privatization,* while all possible constructions in American English, have a distinctly British ring. Americans would be more likely to use *eager, enthusiastic,* or *avid* in these sentences: *She's an avid cyclist, We weren't that eager to go, enthusiastic supporters of more privatization.* The common British English collocation *dead keen* is not established in American English; a close equivalent is probably *hot*. American English uses *keen* mainly in combination with nouns and mainly with the meanings "sharp," "acute," or "finely tuned": *keen interest/insight/observation/instinct, a keen eye/observer/sense.*

line, queue
An orderly group of people waiting for the same thing that each will experience in turn is a *line* in American English, a *queue* in British English. Americans so standing are usually *in line*, though *on line* is also heard, especially in the Northeast. Britons so configured are *in a queue*. The corresponding verbs are *line up* and *queue up*. Someone who tries to upset this natural order by joining the group at a place other than the back is said to *cut in line* in American English, *jump the queue* or *queue-jump* in British English. *Queue* is used exclusively in computer applications in both dialects.

lumber, timber
Both dialects can agree on a group of harvested or harvestable trees being called *timber*. Once cut down into usable boards, these remain timber in British English and this is reflected in some common compounds for which American English would be likely to use *wood* or *wooden*: *timber*

cladding/joist/flooring/merchant, sawn timber. Timber that has been processed becomes *lumber* in American English; thus *lumberyard, the lumber industry, scrap lumber.* The principal meaning of *lumber* in British English is "articles of furniture or other household items that are no longer useful and inconveniently taking up space." Such materials are kept in a *lumber room.* The related phrasal verb, *lumber* sb *with* sth is commoner in British English but exists in both dialects. American English alone has the *lumber* verb sense "cut and process timber" and this finds its way into common compounds: *the lumbering industry, a lumbering center.*

mad

The American English use of this adjective to mean "angry" was remarked on by visitors in the colonial period, although it has origins in English dialects with this meaning far earlier. It remains today the preferred colloquial word in American English for *angry*, especially in the constructions *get mad* and *mad at sb.* Americans normally use *crazy* in the contexts where Britons choose *mad*, i.e., to characterize mental imbalance especially as induced by circumstances—*it's driving me mad, things have gone a bit mad at work*—but these usages normally wouldn't raise eyebrows in American English, just as their substitutes with *crazy* wouldn't sound completely out of place in British English. For expressing wild enthusiasm, the American English idiom is *crazy about* and the British English one *mad on.* The preferences for these two words in the two dialects are not nearly as marked as those with many other words in this section.

mean

British English deems a person, proposal, plan, etc., that seems ungiving and uncharitable to a fault as *mean: It was mean of you to refuse the loan.* The American word of choice for this quality is *selfish*, or informally and more pejoratively, *stingy.* In American English *mean* is used mainly to denote cruel, malicious, nasty, selfish, or otherwise offensive behavior: *Why must you be so mean to me? She gets very mean when she's angry; a mean dog.*

ocean, sea

Both of these words enjoy wide usage in both dialects and both of them are fixed in a number of compounds (e.g., all proper names for bodies of water) and idioms (e.g., *at sea, plenty of other fish in the sea*); there is, however, a slight British English preference for *sea* in some contexts where American English uses *ocean* or some other word. British English usually uses *seabed* where American English would put *ocean floor*. *Oceanfront* and *waterfront* turn up more often than *seafront* in descriptions of property in American English; the opposite is true in British English. *Oceangoing* is American English and preferred to *seagoing*, which is the only choice in British English. Finally, Britons describe time near the water as being *beside the sea* where Americans would more likely say *at the beach*, *at the shore*, or *on the coast*.

overseas, abroad

Despite the fact that all foreign countries are overseas from Britain, *abroad* is the adverb of choice for describing them in relation to Britain while American English prefers *overseas*. Each dialect freely uses the word not preferred by it as a second choice as an adverb. *Overseas* is the adjective of choice in both dialects. Americans normally identify their immediate North American neighbors by name since they don't really qualify as being overseas.

part, little, bit, piece

All of these words can be used as nouns in either dialect to indicate a (usually) small part of something, but *bit* is preferred in British English (*I've lost the bit that goes on the end, She left out all the good bits, Do your bit, bit by bit, the end bit*) where Americans might be as inclined to use *part* or sometimes *piece* as an exact substitute: *the good parts, Say your piece, Do your part, part by part*. British English also shows a slight preference for *bit* in noun and adjective uses where Americans would be inclined to use *little*, though here the preference is not as strongly pronounced: thus British *The rain has let up a bit, It's getting a bit late*, American *The rain has let up a little, It's getting a little late*. Both dialects like "a little bit" as a submodifier: *it makes me a little bit nervous*.

rent, hire, let

British English typically uses *rent* for real property and *hire* for everything else, especially movable things, that are taken into possession and used for a fee, eventually to be returned to the owner. Thus, a *hire car* (AmE *rental car*), *plant hire* (AmE *equipment rental*), *hire a video/suit/helicopter*. American English tends to use *rent* for both real property and movables. The primary use of *hire* in American English is "engage for employment"; this exists in British English, but is usually the second choice after *take on*: *The firm has taken on three new accountants*.

There are also differences among these words from the point of view of the property owner: in British English the owner *lets* property or *hires out* equipment. The American owner *rents* or *rents out* both. The typical wording of signs advertising accommodation in the two dialects shows the distinction: AmE *house for rent*, BrE *house to let*. A point of agreement between the two dialects is in the phrase *for hire* that applies to an available taxi. British English has *hire purchase* for what American English calls *installment plan*.

repair, mend
Both of these verbs are common in both dialects, but their range of collocates—in this case, their objects—varies considerably. *Mend* enjoys wider use in British English as a general term and is typically used of, e.g., dishes, roads, and shoes, all items for which Americans would use *repair. Mend* in American English is the preferred term for the repair of fabric and clothing only. Figurative uses of *mend* are common in both dialects: *mend fences, mend your ways, mend a relationship.* Informally and colloquially, Americans use *fix* (discussed above in a different context) in nearly all the literal ways that Britons use *mend* or *repair.*

roster, rota
Roster does the work in American English that is divided between *roster* and *rota* in British English. Americans are inclined to use *roster*, or more informally, *sign-up sheet* for any list in which individuals share a responsibility in turns. This is usually called a *rota* in the UK, and the activity is called doing something *by rota. Roster* in British English, by contrast, normally has the narrower meaning of a list of persons along with the times that they are either responsible for or excused from something.

sanitarium, sanatorium
Both of these words now have a distinctly old-fashioned ring in modern English. *Sanatoriums* (or *-toria*) curiously seem to exist mostly in non-English speaking countries, where they are convalescent hospitals for those suffering from chronic diseases. *Sanitarium* is a mainly American spelling for the same thing, and is additionally associated with a number of American residential mental hospitals of the nineteenth and early twentieth centuries.

scheme
In American English the word *scheme* often carries the connotation of something deceitful or fraudulent: *a check-kiting/counterfeiting/Ponzi/*

pyramid scheme. For this reason, legitimate enterprises that British English would label schemes—*a pension/housing/export scheme, a scheme that will take people off the dole, a scheme to clean up the sewers in Glasgow*—get called *plans* or *programs* in American English: *a savings plan, a housing program*. The "value-free" use of scheme in American English is in terms denoting logical organization: *a classification/organizational scheme, the overall scheme of things*.

smart

Smart does the work in American English that *clever* does in British English: the standard word for describing someone who is intelligent or something that shows intelligence. A secondary use of *smart* in American English, "impertinent" (*smart remarks, don't get smart with me*), is usually handled by *cheeky* in British English, which is also known in American English but has considerably less frequency. Both dialects have *smart-aleck*, originally an Americanism and usually *smart-alec* in British English.

Smart in British English, on the other hand, is used mainly as an appreciative term about personal appearance, design, or fashion: *smart beachwear/suburbs/hairstyles*. This sense is also used in American English and is not remarkable in attributive examples like these, though a sentence along the lines of *He looked very smart* would not sound natural in American English. The use of *smart* in the "intelligent" sense turns up in British English mainly in compounds that are largely American imports such as *smart bomb, smart card, smart growth, smart money*, and *smart move*.

through

Through in American English as a stand-alone predicate, or followed by a *with* prepositional phrase, means "finished": *Are you through in there? Don't interrupt me till I'm through*. British English would use *finished* in this context. In British English, *through* as a stand-alone predicate, or followed by a *to* prepositional phrase, means "having progressed to the next level" and is typically used of competitors: *teams who are through to the last sixteen in the Worthington Cup*. Thus in the context of an elimination competition, British and American speakers are likely to mean exactly the opposite by the statement *They're through*.

vacation, holiday

Time taken off from work, ideally with pay from one's employer, is called a *vacation* by Americans and a *holiday* (or *hols, informal*) by Britons. The words are straightforward lexical variants in many constructions: *go on vacation/holiday, take a vacation/holiday trip, come back early from one's vacation/holiday. Vacation* has little currency in British English except as a fixed period in which schools or law courts are not in session; when used of schools, the informal form *vac* also appears. Both American and British English use *holiday* for all the other common senses of the word, such as national holidays and religious holidays. The compound *holiday season* in American English refers to the period from Thanksgiving up to the New Year. In British English, it denotes the period from just before Christmas until the New Year, and also refers to the period in summer, roughly July and August, when most people take their holidays.

wrinkle, crease

As both nouns and verbs, these words stand in both dialects for a visible sharp fold in fabric or paper, or the activity of creating one. American English tends to use *crease* and its compounds and derivatives where the fold in question is intentional or desirable, and *wrinkle* otherwise: thus *wrinkled pants, a wrinkle-resistant fabric.* This use of *wrinkle* exists in British English and is used especially of skin, but there is a marked preference for *crease*, whether the fold is wanted or not, in paper and fabric: thus *crease-resistant clothing, a skirt that's all creased up.* Whether the crease is a desirable one or otherwise is usually apparent from the context.

THE ARMED FORCES

The armed forces of the two countries mirror each other to some degree:

ARMED FORCES

American	British
US Army	British Army
US Airforce (USAF)	Royal Air Force (RAF)
US Navy (USN)	Royal Navy (RN)
US Marine Corps (USMC)	Royal Marines (RM)

The US *Coast Guard* is responsible mainly for peacetime defense of the US coastline; its system of rank and promotion is the same as that of the US Navy. The US Air Force was not organized until 1947; prior to that, military aviation was under the direction of the *Army Air Force.*

Tables attempting to equate the ranks in the two countries' armed forces are widely published as back matter in learners' dictionaries, for reasons about which one can only speculate: Are learners of English liable to be called up to serve on short notice? Will unredeemable *faux pas* result when the student of English fails to note the disparity in rank when seating a British Wing Commander and an American Brigadier General at a dinner party? It is likely that such comparisons are only of use on the battlefield, and in any case they change unpredictably. Presented here are general outlines that should assist the transatlantic reader in placing a military rank, with particular notes about terms that may cause confusion.

Commissioned Officers

The hierarchy and titles of commissioned officers of the two countries' armies and marines are identical from general down to Second Lieutenant with one exception: a British *brigadier* is at the level of an American *brigadier general*. The titles of naval and air force officers differ somewhat:

AIR AND NAVAL OFFICERS

US Navy	Royal Navy	USAF	RAF
Admiral	Admiral	General	Air Chief Marshal
Vice admiral	Vice-admiral	Lieutenant General	Air Marshal
Rear Admiral (Upper Half)	Rear-Admiral	Major General	Air Vice Marshal
Rear Admiral (Lower Half)	Commodore	Brigadier General	Air Commodore
Captain	Captain	Colonel	Group Captain
Commander	Commander	Lieutenant Colonel	Wing Commander[1]
Lieutenant Commander	Lieutenant Commander	Major	Squadron Leader
Lieutenant	Lieutenant	Captain	Flight Lieutenant
Lieutenant, Junior Grade	Sub Lieutenant	First Lieutenant	Flying Officer
Ensign	Midshipman[2]	Second Lieutenant	Pilot Officer

[1] *Wing Commander* and its informal abbreviation *Wingco* are sometimes used in British English to designate a bossy, take-charge personality.

[2] A *midshipman* in American English is not a naval rank but rather a designation for a military academy student in training for the Navy or Coast Guard rank of ensign.

Warrant Officers

In all services of both countries the rankings of warrant officers are obvious by their modifications, e.g., *chief warrant officer, warrant officer second class, etc.* The US Air Force has no warrant officers.

Lower Ranks

Ranks below the level of warrant officer are designated *non-commissioned officers* (*NCOs*) in all US armed forces; the lowest ranks are simply called *enlisted men* (or *women*). They are called *other ranks* in the British Army and Royal Marines, *ratings* in the Royal Navy, and *airmen* in the Royal Airforce. Note that *airman* (see next table) is a specific rank in the US Air Force. Attempts at one-to-one comparisons between ranks at these levels of the countries' forces are contrived at best because the number of levels do not correspond precisely. Here are separate tables presenting the ranks in descending order of each country:

NONCOMMISSIONED OFFICERS

US Army	US Navy and Coast Guard	US Air Force	US Marines
Sergeant Major	Master Chief Petty Officer	Chief Master Sergeant	Sergeant Major
Master Sergeant, Sergeant 1st	Senior Chief Petty Officer	Senior Master Sergeant	Master Sergeant, First Sergeant
Sergeant 1st Class	Chief Petty Officer	Master Sergeant, First Sergeant	Gunnery Sergeant
Staff Sergeant	Petty Officer 1st Class	Technical Sergeant	Staff Sergeant
Sergeant	Petty Officer 2nd Class	Staff Sergeant	Sergeant
Corporal	Petty Officer 3rd Class	Senior Airman	Corporal
Private 1st Class	Seaman	Airman 1st Class	Lance Corporal
Private	Seaman Apprentice	Airman	Private 1st Class
	Seaman Recruit	Airman Basic	Private

BRITISH OTHER RANKS

British Army	Royal Navy	Royal Air Force	Royal Marines
Staff Sergeant	Chief Petty Officer	Flight Sergeant	Colour Sergeant
Sergeant	Petty Officer	Sergeant	Sergeant
Corporal	Leading Seaman	Corporal	Corporal

BRITISH OTHER RANKS *(continued)*

British Army	Royal Navy	Royal Air Force	Royal Marines
Lance-Corporal	Able Seaman	Technician	Lance-Corporal
Private	Junior Seaman	Aircraftman	Marine

Officer Training

Both countries have officer training schools that are known by the name of their location:

OFFICER TRAINING SCHOOLS

Name	What is it?
Annapolis (MD)	US Naval Academy
Sandhurst (Surrey)	British Army officer training school
West Point (NY)	US Army officer training school

US Marines receive officer training at Annapolis. The US Air Force Academy is in Colorado Springs, CO, but is not synonymous with the city; likewise for Britannia Royal Naval College (Dartmouth, Devon), the Commando Training Centre Royal Marines (Lympstone, Devon), and the various venues for RAF officer training.

Military ID

The metal tags identifying members of the armed services are popularly *dog tags* in American English, though the proper term is *identification tag*. In British English it is *identification disc*.

Those Who Served

Former members of the armed services are always called *veterans* in American English; this term takes second place to *ex-serviceman* or *ex-servicewoman* in British English, grouped together under *ex-service personnel*. At the level of central government, their affairs are handled by the *Veterans Administration* (VA) in the US, an independent federal agency. In the UK they are looked after by the *Veterans' Advice Unit* of the Ministry of Defence, along with an undersecretary whose responsibility is veterans' affairs. The VA is comparatively a larger and wider-reaching organization, owing to the greater numbers of people it looks after and the fact that many of its direct responsibilities are handled by other public service bodies in the UK (such as the NHS). The VA operates many hospitals and nursing homes exclusively for veterans and also administers the *GI Bill*, a blanket term for many different pieces of federal legislation but mostly referring to a bill passed in 1944 that initiated the tradition of providing many housing, education, and healthcare benefits to US veterans.

The premiere private organizations in the US dealing with veterans are the *American Legion* and the *VFW* (*Veterans of Foreign Wars*), both of which operate local chapters in communities small and large all across the US. The British functional equivalent, similarly organized, is the *RBL* (*Royal British Legion*). The *American Legion* was chartered by Congress; the other two organizations operate as charities.

Major Wars

The main twentieth century wars are popularly called *World War I* (*WWI*) and *World War II* (*WWII*) in American English; the leading terms in British English are *First World War* and *Second World War*. Each dialect uses the other's first choice as its second choice. There are a few differences in the preferred terms used for various other historical conflicts, all of which take the definite article except when used attributively.

WARS

American	British
Afghan Wars	Anglo-Afghan Wars
Civil War	American Civil War
English Civil War	Civil War
Revolutionary War	War of American Independence

THE MEDIA

The manner in which international news media may have a cross-fertilizing effect on the two major varieties of English was discussed briefly in the introduction to this book. The way in which print and broadcast media in each country influences the language of that country is even greater, but I would argue, rather greater in the UK than in the US. Two factors responsible for this are (1) population and demographics: the fact that the UK is a smaller country both in terms of land and people means that in the media, as in many other areas of life, a degree of centralization is natural and practicable that would not work in the US; and (2) the nature of the regulation, ownership, and standards prevailing in media organizations are considerably different between the two countries. The reader who has come this far will perhaps be understanding if the author now mounts a soapbox (some may think it a high horse) to speculate briefly on the ramifications of these phenomena.

The overall effect of these two factors is, to my mind, not only a greater influence over language exercised by the UK media, especially in the area of usage, but also a generally beneficial, or at the very least harmless influence in the UK. This is a service to which the media in the US can make no such claim. The mainstream media outlets in the UK—television, radio, and newspapers—are generally uniform throughout the country. The BBC operates two television channels and six radio stations (see "Broadcast Media", below) that are available everywhere. One or more of the five quality newspapers (see "Print Media", below) are read by the majority of educated adults in the country every day. Together, these constitute a concentrated dose of what is for the most part considered, edited, and intelligently presented English to which a plurality of people are exposed.

While it is decried in some quarters of British society that the media, like everything else, is run by a small and elite Establishment clique, it is not observed often enough that this clique (if it is one) in fact maintains a very high standard of English that sets the tone for public discourse in the UK. In the US, by contrast, the choice of media outlets is vastly wider and more diffuse, while the standard of English prevailing in the majority of them is vastly worse. The result is that Americans find no model of English in the media that is worthy of emulating, and indeed they very often find models that they should warn their children against imitating. Anyone who doubts the difference between prevailing standards of language in the media need only tune into half an hour's worth of local news coverage on a US television station and start counting the grammatical errors, non sequiturs, and anacolutha that fly from the lips of reporters without any apparent awareness on their part. This does not happen with any editorially controlled broadcast program in the UK. It is also instructive to compare the speeches of MPs made during Prime Minister's Questions or during debate with those falling from the lips of Congressmen and Senators in legislative session or during congressional hearings. No one with any appreciation of grammatically spoken English, as it has evolved over centuries, could find the American version superior in such a comparison. The difference is down to there being a well-established standard for publicly spoken English in the UK that is missing in the US.

With that by way of introduction, we now look to the terminology sur-
rounding the mass-produced language in each country and the differences
therein.

Print Media

NEWSPAPERS

The major daily newspapers in the UK are national newspapers, while
Americans who read a daily newspaper probably read one published in
their own city, or the nearest city large enough to support one. The result is
that American newspapers have a much more parochial flavor, and play a
less influential role in national life, than their counterparts in the UK. The
New York Times, and to a lesser extent the *Washington Post* are the only US
newspapers that could compare favorably with British papers such as the
Daily Telegraph, the *Times*, the *Independent*, and the *Guardian*, in terms
of influence, and in breadth and quality of reporting. These four papers are
called the *broadsheets* or the *quality papers* in British English; the order in
which they are given here is roughly from conservative to liberal in outlook.
They are contrasted with the *tabloids*, daily newspapers in tabloid format
that take a more sensational and less intellectual approach to reportage.
The archetype of these is the *Sun*, and the British English term *Sun-read-
er* is code for a relatively uneducated, unreflective, young to middle-aged
man who is pro-British and enjoys lingering over the *Page Three Girl*, a
photograph appearing in the paper every day of a different topless model.
    In the US, *tabloid* is usually shorthand for what is more accurately
called a *supermarket tabloid*, a small weekly color newspaper typically sold
at the supermarket checkout and specializing in stories of questionable au-
thenticity about the moral transgressions of celebrities. The leading title,
and the one taken as representative of the genre, is the *National Enquirer.*
Some regular daily newspapers in the US are printed in tabloid format,
such as the *Chicago Sun-Times* and the *Rocky Mountain News*, but they are
not regarded as tabloids in the British English sense.
    Anonymous opinion in UK newspapers is expressed in *leaders* or *lead-
ing articles*; these are *editorials* in American English. Opposite the editorial page in US papers is the *Op-Ed* page, which typically contains signed
commentaries and feature articles. *Supplement* commonly describes the
extra parts of the Sunday newspapers in the UK, especially *colour supplement*, which corresponds to the American *magazine section*. The other
extra Sunday parts are usually called *sections* in American English.

MAGAZINES

A few titles in each country are noteworthy for the way in which they characterize the people who read them. These profiles may assist the transatlantic reader in unpacking the considerable cultural baggage that can accompany the mention of a magazine title or a description of a person as being a reader of a particular one. The list is limited to well-established titles that are not themselves suggestive of the magazine's content, and thus omits ones along the lines of *Gardener's World* or *American Cheerleader*.

MAGAZINE PROFILES

Magazine	Source	What is it?
Beano, the	UK	children's comic book in continuous publication since the mid-twentieth century, well known to every Briton
Billboard	US	premiere magazine of the music industry
Country Life	UK	showcase for the most expensive real estate in the UK; news of architecture, the arts, gardening, the countryside, field-sports, and wildlife as appreciated by rich people
Ebony	US	leading upmarket African-American culture magazine
Exchange & Mart	UK	advertisements for second-hand merchandise
Hello	UK	bright and cheerful articles, many about celebrities, mostly of interest to women
Loot	UK	advertisements for second-hand merchandise
National Review	US	leading forum for conservative opinion
New Republic	US	leading forum for moderate to liberal opinion
New Statesman & Society	UK	leading forum for liberal opinion
NME	UK	New Musical Express; premiere music weekly for the 15–24 set
Private Eye	UK	often hilarious political, literary, and artistic satire that walks a very narrow line between fact and vicious rumor; often the subject of law suits
Redbook	US	women's magazine; recipes for fattening desserts side-by-side with articles about how to lose weight fast
Soldier of Fortune	US	opportunities for mercenaries; stories of violent adventure. A favorite of gun lovers and members of the far right.
Tatler	UK	upscale society, celebrity, fashions, beauty
Variety	US	premiere magazine of the entertainment industry

The following titles are published in both the US and the UK in separate editions, but appeal to about the same demographic niche in each country: *Condé Nast Travel(l)er, Cosmopolitan, Elle, Esquire, FHM, Good Housekeeping, GQ, Marie Claire, Penthouse, Playboy, Rolling Stone, Vanity Fair, Vogue*. Many business and news magazines also publish under the same title in both countries. The *Spectator*, a weekly, is a leading forum of conservative opinion in the UK; the *American Spectator*, a monthly, is also conservative-leaning but does not enjoy the high-profile status of its British namesake. *Which?* magazine in the UK, and its many subsidiary titles, is the functional equivalent of *Consumer Reports* and its offspring in the US. *Issue* is used in both dialects for a particular edition of a magazine; *number* is equally common in British English.

Broadcast Media

TELEVISION

TV is the main American English and *telly* the main British English informal designation for television. British English distinguishes what it calls *terrestrial channels*, those broadcast from land-based transmitting stations that are receivable without any special equipment other than an *aerial* (usually *antenna* in American English, though *aerial* is equally acceptable). These are distinct from the various satellite and cable channels. The five terrestrial channels in the UK are BBC1, BBC2, ITV, Channel 4, and Channel 5. These all have distinct personalities in the minds of the viewing public; *Channel 4* in particular has a mandate to broadcast programs of interest to sectors of the population perceived not to be adequately served by the other channels, and it has a reputation of being in the hands of the artistic and cultural avant-garde.

The functional equivalent of these in the US are what American English calls *the networks*, namely, ABC, CBS, NBC, and Fox, the four channels that are available nearly everywhere without special receiving equipment. These are more or less indistinguishable in style of content; *Fox* is the newest of them and has the reputation of being willing to discard standards of taste, decorum, and integrity more readily than the others in an attempt to increase ratings. All the networks broadcast a national *feed* that their local affiliates then package into a schedule of programs for local consumption; the general rule is that each *media market* (there are hundreds in the US as a whole) has one local affiliate station for each of the four networks.

Broadcasting alongside the networks and complementing them in terms of content to an ever decreasing degree is *public television*, or *PBS*. It is supported by voluntary, though aggressively solicited contributions from the public and by corporate and foundation grants. At its best it rivals the quality of BBC television programming, and is in fact largely responsible for bringing successful British programs before the American public.

Many American broadcasting institutions spawned by the cable and satellite revolution are now known internationally, such as CNN and ESPN. More for local consumption is *C-SPAN*, two broadcast channels that televise Congress in session, congressional hearings, public speeches, news conferences, and other public gatherings of general interest.

American English uses *anchor* to describe the main presenter of a news program, whether it is a local or national one. Most of these are regarded as having minor celebrity status. Their functional equivalents in the UK are simply called *newsreaders*. Despite their more modest title, they are considerably more adept at unscripted conversation than their American counterparts.

SMALL SCREEN ICONS

The propagation of cultural icons via television is a bit lopsided between the US and the UK: everything that is truly successful in American television, whether good (*The Simpsons*) or bad (*Jerry Springer*) eventually gets syndicated and shown in the UK, resulting in Britons not only getting a relatively larger dose of American English, but also becoming familiar with a great many more American cultural references than Americans have an opportunity to do for British culture from British television. American networks tend to import only the funniest or the artiest, leaving much of what makes up the mainstream British diet of television untouched. A 2001 survey in the UK of the one hundred greatest TV characters of all time awarded spots on the list to more than a dozen Americans, or American creations. Of the winners who were not American, perhaps half a dozen are widely known to Americans, almost all of them via programs that have appeared on PBS. This table presents a few cultural icons from television, mostly British, that are the sources of frequent cultural allusions likely to be opaque to the foreigner:

TV ICONS

Item	Source	What/Who is it?
Alan Partridge	UK	talk-show host specializing in making viewers cringe with embarrassment or disbelief
Alf Garnet	UK	character from the defunct series *Till Death Do Us Part*; the inspiration for Archie Bunker in *All in the Family*

TV ICONS *(continued)*

Item	Source	What/Who is it?
Arthur Daley	UK	shady but likable used-car salesman from the now defunct program *Minders*
Blue Peter	UK	long-running children's program that attempts to educate and inform in a cheerful way; similar to *Mr. Rogers' Neighborhood* in the US.
Cilla Black	UK	chirpy Liverpudlian hostess of *Blind Date* and many other entertainment programs
Coronation Street	UK	long-running and popular prime-time soap set in north west England; thought to exemplify working-class life
George Dixon	UK	archetypal friendly and honest policeman from the defunct program *Dixon of Dock Green*
Leave it to Beaver	US	sitcom from the 1960s, exemplifying family life; parents were Ward and June Cleaver; children were Wally and Beaver
Mister Rogers	US	host of *Mister Rogers' Neighborhood*, a children's program that occupies roughly the same niche as *Blue Peter* in the UK
Ozzie & Harriet	US	50s and 60s sitcom, exemplifying family life from that era
Ruby Wax	UK	popular comedian who exemplifies and pokes fun at the excesses of her native US

RADIO

As in television broadcasting, the BBC dominates the radio airwaves in the UK, operating five radio stations that are receivable everywhere. The programming on each of these appeals to different sectors of the listening population, resulting in the fact that which radio programs a Briton listens to is often used to say something about who they are:

UK RADIO

Station	What is it?
Radio 1	pop music and brash DJs; geared toward young people
Radio 2	eclectic range of music and mainstream entertainment; the most listened-to radio in the UK
Radio 3	mostly classical music and the arts
Radio 4	news, cultural programs, plays, clever quiz shows, arts; a bastion of the middle classes
Radio 5	mostly sports

Radio 4 includes a daily half-hour soap opera called *The Archers*, which is a national institution with an avid following; it takes place in an imaginary farming community in the West of England and is a topical reference point that is used to characterize the vanishing ideal of rural English life.

Radio in the US is largely a local affair, with more many thousands of stations nationwide, some broadcasting no more than a few miles beyond their source. There are some nationally syndicated programs hosted by people who have become well-known because of this. Nearly all of them that have attained their icon status—and thus the ability to stand for a an entire portmanteau of values—have done so by offending large groups of people rather than through some exemplary quality. The best known examples of this are *Rush Limbaugh*, the ultraconservative talk-show host, a kind of nonthinking man's hero; *Dr. Laura Schlessinger*, the ultraconservative phone-in therapist who badgers her callers; and *Howard Stern*, the "shock jock" who flouts as many standards of taste and decency as the authorities will permit.

National Public Radio (*NPR*) does on the airwaves what PBS does on American TV, that is, provide high-quality programming that is not driven by the commercial concerns of privately owned radio stations. Its news and cultural programs are similar to what is broadcast on Radio 4 in the UK, which in fact has probably been its role model in many cases.

The radio frequency band is divided between FM and what American English always calls *AM*, the radio frequencies that British English and the rest of the Anglophone world call *MW* or *medium wave*. There is little broadcasting on shortwave and long wave in the US. *AM radio* is generally characterized as older, more local, more conservative, and of poorer quality than FM radio. All US radio stations are assigned *call letters*, three- or four-letter designations that uniquely identify each one; these start with W (mostly east of the Mississippi) and K (mostly west of the Mississippi), e.g., *WLS, KSLV*.

MEDIA BUZZWORDS AND ALLUSIONS

The uniformity and concentration of media outlets in the UK results in there being a code of sorts in reportage, based on fixed usages and allusions to events and quotations that all educated readers recognize; this recognition amounts to a cultural literacy that the American can only master by continuous exposure and study. The tokens and types that constitute this code could be the subject of an entire book; what is presented here is a primer only that should aid the transatlantic reader in navigating headlines and media pundits' cryptic remarks.

BRITISH MEDIA CLICHES

Cliché	Translation
be economical with the truth[1]	lie, or fail to provide information that would reasonably be given in a particular context
be seen to be doing sth	give the appearance of taking action, whatever the reality may be
refuse to be drawn on sth	decline to give an answer to a direct question
short sharp shock	a short, severe punishment intended to bring a person or institution to their senses

[1] This phrase, now firmly established in British English, was first used in 1986 by Lord Armstrong when arguing the government's case for the suppression of the book *Spycatcher* by Peter Wright.

The UK media are quite fond of two words little used in American English journalism to describe conflict: *row* is headline shorthand for any kind of conflict ranging from a minor disagreement up to a full scale confrontation. *Furore* (pronounced "fyu-ROAR-ri") is reserved for rows and scandals that are the subject of widespread condemnation: *the Salt Lake City corruption furore*. The American English version of this is the word *furor* and doesn't enjoy quite the circulation of British English *furore*. British newswriters are also fond of finding and pointing out a *knock-on effect*, for which the usual American English translation is *consequences*, or more journalistically, *impact*: *The measure was rejected because of its feared knock-on effects in manufacturing industry*.

The US mainstream media is less coded than the British one, and at the same time more widely disseminated; Britons making their way through the *New York Times* should have considerably less trouble than Americans deciphering the *Guardian,* and so no corresponding primer is presented for American English journalism. It is worth noting however that the associations attached to one particular word tossed around in the media are quite different between American and British English, and that word is *European*. The contexts in which this adjective is typically encountered differ considerably between the two dialects and reflect its very different connotations. Over the past quarter century or so, *European* in British English has come to be associated with the European Union, and specifically with its governing bodies and administration in Brussels: *European directives, the European Superstate*. The connotation is often negative, especially where *European* is contrasted with *British*, and in the frequent contexts in which the powers of the European Union are seen to threaten British sovereignty. This baggage would make it impossible for *European* to be used in British English in one of its most cherished senses in American English, that is, as a marketing term that bestows a vague aura of quality, sophistication, and elegance of design on a product. The usage is based on the fact that most Americans have never been to Europe, and many of those who have regard it as a vacation wonderland. It should never be assumed that products so marketed in the US have any connection with Europe at all: *European tanning beds, a luxury apartment with European-style kitchen.*

The word *welfare* also has quite different connotations when used in the US and UK media, and is discussed at the end of the previous chapter.

SMALL TOPICS

The remainder of this chapter is taken up by topics in which the differences between American and British English are treatable in brief, arranged hereinafter alphabetically by subject.

Items for Baby

The majority of clothing items and accessories for babies and very young children go by identical names in the two dialects. Here are a few differences:

ITEMS FOR BABY

American	British
(portable) bassinet, baby carrier	carrycot
baby carriage	pram, perambulator [*formal*]
crib	cot
diaper	nappy
pacifier	dummy
stroller	push chair
nipple [for a baby bottle]	teat

The body fat of children that usually disappears by adolescence is called *baby fat* in American English and *puppy fat* in British English. *Baby fat* in American English can also refer to the extra weight a woman puts on during pregnancy.

Music

American English uses a more memory-friendly system of terminology for the names of notes. Here are the equivalents.

MUSICAL NOTES

American	British
whole note	semibreve
half note	minim
quarter note	crotchet
sixteenth note	semiquaver
thirty-second note	demisemiquaver
sixty-fourth note	hemidemisemiquaver, quick note

A few other terms from the world of music are lexical variants in the two dialects.

MUSICAL TERMS

American	British
authentic cadence	perfect cadence
concertmaster, concertmistress	first violin, leader
deceptive cadence	interrupted cadence
English horn	cor anglais
flutist	flautist →
half step	semitone
Picardy third	tierce de Picardie
whole step	tone, whole-tone

The word *symphony* alone is not used in British English to designate an orchestra, as it sometimes is in American English. The protective cover for an LP record is usually a *jacket* in American English, a *sleeve* in British English.

The Natural World

Most plants and animals go by the same names in American and British English. Those that differ and are not already treated under food (chapter 7) include the following. With garden flowers in particular, there is a tendency for the name of an entire genus to be known mainly by the genus name in one dialect, and by the type species in the other, but with both terms having some currency in both dialects.

PLANTS AND ANIMALS

American	British	Taxonomic name
alfalfa	lucerne	*Medicago sativa*, legume family
canola	(oilseed) rape	*Brassica napus*, mustard family
cattail	bulrush, reed mace	genus *Typha*, family Typhaceae
columbine	aquilegia	genus *Aquilegia*, buttercup family
crane fly	daddy-longlegs	insect of the family Tipulidae
daddy-longlegs	harvestman	arachnid of the order Opiliones
four o'clock	marvel of Peru	*Mirabilis jalapa*, family Nyctaginaceae
German shepherd	alsatian	*Canis familiaris*[1]
impatiens	busy lizzie	genus *Impatiens*, balsam family
linden (tree)	lime (tree)	genus Tilia, family Tiliaceae
marijuana	cannabis	*Cannabis sativa*, family Cannabaceae
mercury	Good King Henry	*Chenopodium bonus-henricus*, goosefoot famly
New York aster	Michaelmas daisy	*Aster novi-belgii*, daisy family
scotch pine	scots pine	*Pinus sylvestris*
snapdragon	antirrhinum	genus *Antirrhinum*, figwort family
yarrow	achillea	genus *Achillea*, composite family

[1] Said animal is normally walked on a *leash* in American English, a *lead* in British English..

Sycamore is used in both dialects to refer to trees of various families. American and British English agree on the sycamore of the Bible, *Ficus sycomorus*. The tree more commonly designated in British English as a sycamore is what American English calls the *sycamore maple*, *Acer pseudo-platanus*. To most Americans, a sycamore is the plane tree *Platanus occidentalis* or other related plane trees, which are sometimes called *buttonwoods*; these are called *plane trees* in British English. In the UK the horse chestnut is informally called the *conker tree* and the nuts it produces are *conkers*, the playing pieces in a children's game.

The common bird referred to as a *robin* is a relatively large thrush in the US, *Turdus migratorius*, which the British dub the *American robin*. The UK robin is a smaller thrush, usually *Erithacus rubecula*. Similarly the *oriole* is a bird of the blackbird family in the US, appearing in several species, while *oriole* in British English denotes a family of passerine birds related to the starling.

The Nonprofit Sector

Both countries have a number of high-profile organizations whose names are immediately recognized by speakers and readers. The following table unpacks the commonest ones whose names are not transparent:

NONPROFIT ORGANIZATIONS

Name	Source	What do they do?
ACLU	US	American Civil Liberties Union; defender of constitutional rights, especially freedom of speech
ASH	UK	campaign against smoking
Barnardo's	UK	leading children's charity; operates some children's homes
Easter Seals	US	helps people with disabilities
Goodwill	US	helps people with disabilities and other disadvantages through direct donations and many charity shops; full name is Goodwill Industries International
March of Dimes	US	funds research for birth defects, infant mortality, low birthweight, and prenatal care
Mencap	UK	help for people with learning disabilities
NAACP	US	National Association for the Advancement of Colored People
Relate	UK	marriage counseling
Samaritans	UK	crisis line for suicide intervention
United Way	US	charity umbrella organization that distributes donations to various mainstream causes after deducting its administrative fees

The practice whereby charities raise money by selling donated second-hand goods is well-established in both countries. These outlets are called *thrift shops* in American English, *charity shops* in British English. The food charity Oxfam seems to have the greatest number of such shops in the UK, and *Oxfam Shop* is sometimes used generically to indicate this kind of business. In the US, both Goodwill Industries and the Salvation Army operate many such stores and they stand for the type, giving rise to such locutions as *I bought it at the Salvation Army, I gave it to Goodwill.*

The UK has *girl guides* rather than US-style *girl scouts*, though the parent organizations of these two groups are affiliated internationally.

Qualities of the Person

This list of words, many of them informal or slang, are commonly used in one dialect or the other to characterize people of a certain type; they are largely unfamiliar in the other dialect and so may require explanation.

WORDS CHARACTERIZING PERSONS

Name	Source	What sort of person?
barrow boy	UK	a working-class seller of wares from a barrow
berk	UK	a stupid person
blighter	UK	a hapless person who finds no success; like American schlemiel
blowhard	US	a person, usually a man, full of loud, empty talk
boffin	UK	a person with complex or arcane knowledge, such as a high-level scientist; wizard
brown-nose	US	a grossly obsequious person
buttinsky	US	a person who interrupts rudely
Caledonian	UK	a Scot
carrot-top	US	a red-haired person
chrome dome	US	a bald person; *cue ball*
cornball	US	a person overly fond of silly jokes, especially his or her own
cowboy	US/UK	AmE: the traditional Wild West type, or a reckless or irresponsible person; BrE: a dishonest or careless businessperson or contractor
den mother	US	a woman in charge of a troop of Cub Scouts; fig., nurturing woman in charge of many
dweeb	US	a boringly studious person
geezer	UK/US	BrE: slang for *man*; AmE: an old, usually lecherous man
Geordie	UK	a person from Tyneside
git	UK	a contemptible person, usually a man
goldbrick	US	a person who shirks responsibility; BrE *skiver*
Hoosier	US	a person from Indiana
klutz	US	a clumsy or awkward person
lager lout	UK	a man who is disorderly and drunk in public
momma's boy	US	mother's boy
oddbod	UK	an oddball
Okie	US	an unsophisticated person from Oklahoma
Old Etonian	UK	an alumnus of Eton College, a prestigious private school near Windsor

WORDS CHARACTERIZING PERSONS *(continued)*

Name	Source	What sort of person?
Old Harrovian	UK	an alumnus of the Harrow School, a prestigious private school in London
putz	US	a contemptible, worthless person
schlemiel	US	a hapless person who finds no success; like BrE *blighter*
schmuck	US	contemptible person; BrE *sod*
Scouser	UK	a person from Liverpool
scrubber	UK	a prostitute or promiscuous woman
skiver	UK	a person who shirks responsibility; AmE *goldbrick*
slapper	UK	a vulgar, usually middle-aged, overly made-up woman
sod	UK	a contemptible person; BrE *schmuck*
stage-door Johnny	US	a man who loiters at stage doors intent on romancing an actress
Stepford wife	US	a traditional, conservative, pre-feminist housewife
stirrer	UK	a one who stirs up trouble; vulgar version is *shit-stirrer*
Suzy homemaker	US	an overly proud or punctilious housewife
wonk	US	a person excessively devoted to a dull or arcane subject
yenta	US	a busybody or meddling woman
yob, yobbo	UK	a rude, noisy, aggressive young man

American English uses *Joe Blow*, *John Q. Public*, and *Joe Six-Pack* as stand-ins for a typical man and *John Doe* for an unnamed man; *Jane Doe* is the female counterpart. British English uses *Joe Bloggs* or *the man on the Clapham Omnibus* for the average man; *A. N. Other* is used to occupy a slot that will later be filled by a real person's name.

The descending order of British English informal terms for *man*, from the familiar and endearing to the despicable, is *mate, chap, bloke, sod, bugger, bastard*. In American English this scale is roughly *buddy, dude, guy, jerk, bastard, SOB*.

Powerful Places

The evocation of government executive power by *the White House* or *Number 10 Downing Street* is well known to both British and American speakers. A few other places in both countries stand for something more than buildings or addresses and may not be as well known to Transatlantic visitors:

POWERFUL PLACES

Place	Where is it?	What does it stand for?
Fleet St	London	British journalism
Foggy Bottom	Washington, DC	The US State Department
Harley St	London	expensive and specialist doctors
Lambeth Palace	London	authorities of the Church of England
Madison Ave.	New York	the advertising industries and its devices
No. 11 (Downing St)	London	the Chancellor of the Exchequer
Park Ave.	New York	opulent wealth
Sellafield	NW England	a nuclear power plant located there
Tin Pan Alley	New York	American musical theater
Wardour St	London	the British film industry
Whitehall	London	government ministries and civil service

The Post Office

Britons and Americans mean the same thing when they say *post office*, although the institutions are lopsided functional equivalents in the two countries: British post offices have facilities for a very large number of services, such as collecting benefits and paying bills, that are not available at US post offices. This point of coincidence is the tip of an iceberg of variant usage between the dialects in postal matters. In Britain, the *Royal Mail* delivers the *post*; in the US, the *Postal Service* delivers the *mail*. The common nouns *mail* and *post* and their identical verbs are lexical variants in the two dialects that are consistent in a number of compounds, each of which has minority status in the dialect where it is not the main form: thus British English *postman, registered post, postbox, postbag, post room* where American English normally has *mailman, registered mail, mailbox, mailbag, mailroom*. Both dialects use *post office, post office box,* and *parcel post,* though an American who rents a post office box in a post office probably calls it a mailbox. In addition to that receptacle, *mailbox* in American English can designate either of two other things: (1) a box for delivery of mail to a home or business that is mounted on a post or attached to a wall; and (2) a box in a public place where letters can be mailed. The functional equivalent of (1) in British English is *letter box*, which is more often than not a slot in a doorway; the equivalent of (2) is *postbox* or *pillarbox*, when the box is of a particular large, red, cylindrical variety.

Both dialects use *fan mail, hate mail, junk mail,* and *mail order.* Terms

that have entered the language since the computer age have largely left
post behind in both dialects: *mail merge, e-mail, snail mail.*

The UK postal service is operated by a publicly held company called
Consignia, which replaced the old Post Office Group and which operates
the *Royal Mail* (delivers letters) and *Parcelforce* (delivers packages), as well
as post offices and *sub-post offices* (small post offices located inside other
businesses) throughout the UK. Consignia also owns the trademark *Post
Office* in the UK. In the US the postal service is operated by an independent government agency called the *Postal Service* (*USPS*).

Wretched Refuse

Both dialects use *refuse* as the formal and technical term for rejected
and discarded items, but ordinary usage differs. *Rubbish* is the general-
purpose word in British English for the same thing; American English
prefers *trash* or *garbage.* Some American speakers distinguish between
these, using *garbage* to designate food waste, and *trash* for the rest. Receptacles for this are (*rubbish*) *bin, dustbin,* or simply *bin* in British English, *garbage can* or *trash can* in American English; there are many other
compounds made up with the preferred words in each dialect. Men who
collect these from houses are *garbage men* or more respectfully, *sanitation
workers* in American English, *binmen* or *dustmen* in British English. Both
rubbish and *trash* are used as transitive verbs in their respective dialects to
mean "criticize as worthless." For the meaning "damage or wreck wanton-
ly" (i.e., *rock stars trashing hotel rooms*), both dialects prefer *trash.*

The large construction-site sized receptacles for refuse are *skips* in
British English, *Dumpsters* (a trademark) in American English. All of this
eventually ends up in a landfill, informally called a *tip* in British English, or
a *dump* in American English. Both of these terms are used in their respective dialects informally to describe a household with less than desirable
standards of cleanliness.

Items no longer wanted but deemed too valuable to discard are recy-
cled in similar ways in both countries, using different words. One method
is the charity or thrift shop, already discussed above. British English has the
jumble sale, a sale of used items, usually quite tawdry and forlorn, under-
taken as a means of raising money for a charity. This used to be called *rummage sale* in American English, though that term has been largely
displaced, probably owing to the negative associations attending *rummage.*
The vogue terms are *yard sale, garage sale,* and *tag sale.* These may be held

by individuals, groups, or charities. The rapacious consumerism that prevails in American culture results in these being common events everywhere, especially in people's homes. British English also has *car boot sale*, an event in which individuals sell used goods from the trunks of their cars. The nearest American English equivalent is probably *flea market*, which also exists in British English.

With all due respect to the author Emma Lazarus, it is worth noting here for British English readers that the inscription at the base of the Statue of Liberty contains a brief poem, "The New Colossus," that is source of many an allusion in American writing, including the heading of this section. It ends with these lines (italics added, to highlight the inspirational collocations):

> Give me your tired, your poor,
> Your *huddled masses* yearning to breathe free,
> The *wretched refuse* of your *teeming shore*.
> Send these, the homeless, *tempest-tost* to me,
> I lift my lamp beside the *golden door!*

Religion

A small muddle exists in the UK in that it consists of four countries, two of which have established churches that are different from each other, and two of which have churches named for them but are not established. The *Church of England* (*C of E*) is the established church in England, and is part of the *Anglican* communion. (The only US church belonging to this organization is the Episcopal Church in American, commonly called the *Episcopal Church*). The *Church of Ireland*, the *Church in Wales*, and the *Scottish Episcopal Church* are all Anglican but not established. The *Church of Scotland* is Presbyterian and established.

The incumbent of a C of E parish is called a *vicar*, though he may have some other specific, church-bestowed title.[1] The bishops of the Church of England (more than two dozen) sit in the House of Lords and are called *Lords Spiritual*. Chief among these are the *Archbishop of Canterbury*, and the *Archbishop of York*. Either of these may occasionally get involved in social or political issues by making statements about the church's position.

---

1. This title is not used by the US Episcopal Church, which uses *rector*.

A group in the UK that gets rather more public attention than their small numbers would suggest is possible are the *Anglo-Catholics*, who are Anglicans favoring a form of worship very close to that of the Catholic church and who envision reunion with the Catholic church as an eventual goal of the Anglican church. They are more or less the same as *high church* Anglicans. Catholics make up a larger percentage of the US population (about 25 percent, as opposed to 15 percent in the UK) and play a higher profile in public life. *Catholic* is always considered an adequate designation in American English, without mention of Rome.

Traditionally there was a distinction between *church* (meaning the Church of England) and *chapel* (designating, disparagingly, other Protestant sects because their adherents were usually below the middle class). *Nonconformist* was also widely used, as noun and adjective, to designate these other Protestants. Because of the growing multicultural aspect of British society, and the very low rates of church attendance, this distinction is now confined mostly to earlier literature.

The US has no established religion, as this is expressly forbidden in the constitution. Despite this, the country is overwhelmingly Christian and religion plays a very obvious role in the public life of the country. The manifestations of Christianity in the US are an ongoing subject of interest in the British media since they are so different from what can be found at home, so a great deal of the terminology is already familiar in British English. The bewildering variety of Protestant denominations is as confusing to natives as to outsiders, but they do fall into camps in the popular perception and in media designations. The *Mainline Protestant* denominations, many of which have taken steps toward greater unity, are Presbyterian, Methodist, Episcopal, Lutheran, Disciples of Christ, and United Church of Christ. The last two are respectively nineteenth- and twentieth-century denominations of US origin. These churches are all Trinitarian and are described by some as "liberal Protestant," a not very accurate label that serves to distinguish them only from fundamentalist sects.

The following table presents some other denominations found in the US that have achieved a place in the national consciousness, while not being very well known in the UK. The list is not meant to be exhaustive, and exclusion from it should not be construed as oversight, but more likely the result of the sect being already as well-known in the Anglophone world outside the US as in it (as in the case of the Jehovah's Witnesses or the Branch Davidians):

AMERICAN CHURCHES

Church	Who are they?
African Methodist Episcopal (AME)	African American church formed in the early nineteenth century in response to racism in the Methodist church; methodist in doctrine and government
Christian Science	church founded by Mary Baker Eddy in the nineteenth century; it rejects conventional medicine
Church of the Brethren	Anabaptist denomination that grew out of the German Baptist Brethren; no relation to the UK Plymouth Brethren or its offshoots
Church of the Nazarene	Wesleyan-Arminian church, formed in the early twentieth century; extensive missionary work worldwide
Mennonite	Anabaptist Protestant sect that includes the Amish; various denominations
Unitarian Universalist (UU)	Noncreedal church formed from the union of the Unitarians and the Universalists in 1961

The principle divisions of Jewry in the US are *Reform, Conservative,* and *Orthodox*; these correspond to *Liberal, Reform,* and *Orthodox* in the UK, where the liberal branch is sometimes called *Liberal and Progressive.* Judaism in the US is more out and open, though probably no less stereotyped, than in the UK, owing mainly to numbers: the US has the world's largest population of Jews, who are three times more prevalent in the overall population than in the UK. If these figures have a mirror in language it is probably in the greater frequency of Yiddish words naturalized in American English that are either rare or unused in British English, or entered British English through American English: *glitch, kibitz, klutz, putz, schlemiel, schlock, schmooze,* and *tchotchke,* to name a few.

Telephone Talk

Functional equivalents and lexical variants are the rule between the telephone systems in the two countries, which differ very little in what they actually do. First, equivalent terms:

TELEPHONE TERMS

American	British
911	999
area code	STD code, dialling code

TELEPHONE TERMS *(continued)*

American	British
busy signal	engaged signal/tone
call collect	reverse the charges →
call forwarding	call diversion
Caller ID	caller display
cell phone	mobile phone
collect call	reverse-charge call
dial tone	dialling tone
information	directory enquiries
phone booth	phone box
prerecorded time message	speaking clock
toll-free number[1]	Freefone™
unlisted *adj, adv.*	ex-directory *adj., adv.*

[1] A synonym is *800 number* because originally all toll-free numbers used this area code; now several different ones are used.

All telephone numbers in the US and Canada follow a uniform format: (000) 000-0000, where the first three digits in parentheses are the area code. These sometimes do not have to be dialed for calls made within the same area code. Numbers and STD codes in the UK vary in length. When reciting a telephone number that contains doubled digits, Britons say, e.g., *double three* rather than *three three* as Americans would. Some British speakers use *treble* to prefix triple digits in telephone numbers; thus *treble four* rather than *four double four*. For Americans, it's *four four four*.

British English tends to use *ring* as a noun and verb for making telephone calls, since *call* in British English still largely retains its earlier meaning of appearing in person. In American English, *call* is preferred as both noun and verb for telephone use, though *ring* is also current. A radio or television program allowing listeners or viewers to telephone with their views is usually a *phone-in* in British English, a *call-in* in American English.

The symbol # that appears on telephone keypads is called the *pound sign* in American English, the *hash mark* in British English. The digits 2 through 9 have associated letters on American telephones that make it possible to convert some words to telephone numbers, and vice versa. This device is heavily used in marketing to provide a mnemonic device for various products and services; e.g., *dial 1-800-NEED-HIM* (for an evangelical Christian organization), or *dial 1-888 CARPETS* (for a carpet company).

For now, the phrase *on the telephone* can mean "having a telephone in one's home" in British English as well "talking on the telephone." The latter is the only meaning in American English and is about to win out generally in British English, since it is increasingly assumable in the UK that everyone is "on the telephone" or has a mobile. *Blower* is a common informal term for telephone in British English; *horn* is a less common one in American English, only in the phrase *on the horn*.

Expressions of Time

The majority of conventions, if not actually used in both countries, are easily understood and in most cases there is little chance of misunderstanding. These differences can be found:

DATES

The American convention is April 12, 2002; the British convention is 12 April 2002. The British convention has the advantage of no punctuation and proceeding from the unit that changes most frequently to the one that changes least frequently. Ambiguity can arise, however, when dates are written entirely in numerals: 12.04.2002 would be interpreted in American English as December 4, 2002. For materials to be seen in the other dialect, it is better to spell out the names of months in whichever format, or to adopt a variant of the British convention, in which the month is given in roman numerals: 12.IV.2002.

INCLUSIVE TIME

American English uses *through* to connect two named points in time when they are included in the overall period: *Tuesday through Friday* means Tuesday, Wednesday, Thursday, and Friday. British English doesn't thoroughly accept this handy convention and usually phrases it *Tuesday through to Friday* or *Tuesday through to Friday* or *Tuesday to Friday inclusive,* only the last of which is completely unambiguous.

CLOCK TIME

Both countries eschew the twenty-four-hour clock, though Britain is subject to influence of the European Union, which prefers it. The American convention is 8:19 p.m.; periods following *p* and *m* are optional. The British convention is 8.19pm; note that no space intervenes between the numbers and letters. The middle of the day is usually *noon* in American English, *midday* in British English. Thirty minutes past the hour is called, e.g., *two-thirty* in both dialects; British English also has, e.g. *half-three*. Minutes past the hour are designated with *past* in British English, *past* or *after* in American English. Minutes before the hour are designated with *to* in British English, *to* or *of* in American English.

FUTURE TIME

British English alone has the handy expression *Thursday week* to mean what American English would render as *a week from (this coming) Thursday*. The formula works with the days of the week, and also with *yesterday*, *today*, and *tomorrow*.

EVENTS PLACED IN TIME

These can be designated without the preposition *on* in American English: *Wednesday evenings I attend services, She's leaving Tuesday*. British English would phrase these *On Wednesday evenings I attend services, She leaving on Tuesday*, both of which are also acceptable in American English.

British English prefers *as from* followed by a date to indicate the time when something is beginning or put into effect: *The new clause would have the effect of abolishing, as from 1 April 1992, this 20 per cent*. American English uses *as of*: *As of now we will only consider completed applications*. British English has the adverbial modifier *gone* to mean "past" in informal and approximate mentions of time: *It's gone half nine*. The nearest American English equivalent is *just after*.

Fortnight as a designation for two weeks is widely understood but rarely used in American English. The four time zones that span the forty-eight contiguous US states have various shorthand designations. *ET* denotes Eastern Time, from which the others—Central, Mountain, and Pacific—can be deduced by subtracting one, two, and three hours, respectively. Full-blown abbreviations for all the time zones and all possible sorts of time are made with three-letter combinations consisting of the zone initial, the time type initial (i.e., either *D* for *daylight savings time* or *S* for *standard time*), and *T*: *PST, MDT, CST*, etc. *GMT* for Greenwich Mean Time is well established in American English, though its summer alternative *BST* (British Summer Time) is less well known.

Tools

Nearly all of these go by the same name in both dialects, with these exceptions:

TOOLS

American	British
box end wrench	ring spanner
crescent wrench	adjustable spanner
jackhammer	pneumatic drill
level	spirit level
lopping shears	loppers →
pruning shears	secateurs
wrench	spanner

APPENDICES

APPENDICES

Other Major Dialects

It is outside the scope of this book to provide a comprehensive treatment for world English's other major dialects, but it is hoped that a few notes about them, particularly in their relation to American and British English, will be of interest to readers of this book. There are a couple of patterns common to all the other major dialects: (1) historically early influence on them by British English that now is giving way to greater influence from American English, and (2) a general preference for British English spelling that shows intermittent accommodation of, or as some would have it, corruption by, American English spelling forms.

Australian English

The English spoken and written in Australia is rather later than any of the other major dialects in coming to be recognized as a dialect all its own. Early on, any deviations from British usage were simply viewed as incorrect. Only in the third quarter of the twentieth century was the *Macquarie Dictionary* published, taking upon itself the task of documenting Australian English as the national language. The dictionary today is in its third edition and has earned its place as the authoritative source of the nation's language. Given the historical connection of Australian English with British English, it is somewhat ironic that the first edition of the *Macquarie Dictionary* was built largely on a database that was American in origin and that supplied the foundation of a family of American dictionaries.

Australian English developed itself in the image of British English during the convict period, when the country was settled by convicts and their minders from the UK and Ireland. Uniquely among early exports of English, the tongue arrived in Australia as the language of both the ruling class and the subjugated class that they brought with them. The influence of aboriginal languages on Australian English has been negligible, except of course in vocabulary.

Spelling in Australian English up until the middle of the twentieth century followed the British English models in all respects, but with the increasing globalization of the English publishing market, printed sources imported from North America has led to increasingly common acceptance of American English spellings. The situation today is not rigid, and to some degree unique among major dialects: Australian English has thrown off the mantle of British English spelling as being the only proper one. For many classes of words, it permits either the preferred American or British English spelling, though the British English are found more often in print. The laissez-faire attitude to spelling—perhaps a reflection of the easy-going attitude prevailing in Australian culture—seems to extend to variant forms appearing within a single document: consider this excerpt from a recent Australian newspaper:

> "I think it's problematic to say you're a trained social worker as an explanation for particular decision-making when you're not *practising* in the specialist field and you haven't kept up to date," she told The Canberra Times. "Society changes so quickly, we can't *practice* using simply the material we learnt [at university]." (emphasis added)

In fairness, however, it should be pointed out that this kind of inconsistency can also arise quite naturally from a lapse of editorial attention, followed by the use of a spell-checker that is not equipped to distinguish nouns from verbs.

Although there are only one hundred or so words from Australian aboriginal languages that are found universally in English dialects, Australian English has understandably a great many more, numbering in the several hundreds. In other matters of word choice, there is greater correspondence between Australian English and British English than there is between Australian English and American English, but exceptions can be found: for example, Australians fill their cars with petrol, like their British cousins, but use *kerosene* to denote the other fossil fuel widely used in lamps and heaters that American English also designates as kerosene, but

British English calls *paraffin*. The foreign naturalist in Australia is bound for confusion: there can be found many flora and fauna bearing names from Old World and northern hemisphere genera and species to which they have no genetic relationship, but enough of a superficial resemblance that they inspired the original discoverer to so dub them.

Like most countries today in which English is the first language, Australia has become a multicultural society. For most of the twentieth century, the foreign-born in Australia were likely to have come from another English-speaking country, especially the UK; but today most of the foreign-born in Australia come from a country where English has second-language status at best. This has resulted in a marked decline in the influence of British English on Australian English, while the influence of American English increases via electronic and other means.

Canadian English

The close relationship between Canadian English and American English is not surprising in the light of a simple geographical fact: Canada shares international land borders with only one country, the US, and one of those borders is four thousand miles long. Several historical and present-day factors, however, contribute to an ongoing relationship of Canadian English with British English, and so it is perhaps more than any other major dialect a hybrid of the two main dialects in English, while also including many home-grown words and usages, especially borrowings from French and from Inuit and other Native American (or as Canadian English has it, First Nation) languages. Canada can claim the distinction of having the oldest English-speaking community in North America, on the island of Newfoundland, where the local dialect still bears many traces of its very early (sixteenth century) separation from "English English."

Although many of them were only a generation removed from England, Americans were prominent in the early settlement of nearly all areas of Canada and so from the outset, American speakers had a great influence on the development of Canadian English. But during this same time, Canada remained loyal to Britain politically, and self-consciously retained many British institutions, including many features of the language. The main spelling reforms that characterize American English had already been promulgated before Canada even won the right to self-government from Britain in the mid-nineteenth century. Canada is today one of the members of the Commonwealth of Nations that recognizes the British monarch as its sovereign. This fact keeps its English bound to the British English standard in many ways, most of them under the influence of officialdom. And while Canadians are bombarded by American popular culture unceasingly, they manage to maintain a much closer affinity with British popular culture than Americans do; several websites devoted to the popular British soap opera *Coronation Street* (a program largely unknown in the US) have Canadian addresses.

From the point of view of Canadians, Canadian spelling is an institution unto itself; but unfortunately for them perhaps, there are no spellings that are uniquely Canadian. All of them are either the same as American English or British English spellings, and so from a purely analytical point of view, Canadian spelling is a blend. The British English *-our* spellings win out over the American English *-or* spellings in most cases, though at least one Canadian dictionary lemmatizes the *-or* forms and most Canadians do not blink when these are encountered in print. Like some of their British counterparts, Canadian dictionaries lemmatize *-ize* rather than their "-ise" counterparts and Canadian newspapers use the *-ize* spellings. On the other hand, British English *-re* spellings predominate over American English *-er* ones in dictionaries and in print.

No one can dispute the close resemblance of the standard (mainly urban) Canadian accent to the standard American one: many English speakers from outside North America don't recognize the difference at all, and even Americans and Canadians in conversation may require several exchanges before a marker appears to one or the other. In matters of usage there are also far more coincidences between Canadian English and American English than between Canadian English and British English. Canadian newspapers often print Associated Press wire stories unedited, which usually results in unreconstructed American English appearing in print north of the border. US broadcast media are available unexpurgated in many of Canada's population centers. Thus Canadians are continuously subjected to both American and British forms, one in the media and one via educational institutions and official channels. The long-range prognosis is that Canadian English will hold its own against complete subjugation to American English, but only by self-conscious effort.

Indian English

As a dialect spoken in varying degrees by some thirty million people, Indian English ranks third among world Englishes in numbers of speakers and naturally has more "word-of-mouth" influence in Asia than either American or British English does. Though it is not a first language for many of the Indians who speak it, it is the lingua franca of the Indian diaspora, in Asia and around the world, as well as being a lingua franca in India.

No other major dialect of English better illustrates the ability of the language to grow beyond its traditional grammatical borders, and no other major dialect presents more of a challenge to the traditional arbiters of what is correct and not correct in English generally: the English spoken and printed in India is perfectly comprehensible within its language community, and the written form of it presents few obstacles to understanding for speakers of American English or British English, yet surprises abound. A perusal of the online editions of any of the English-language newspapers in India—and this is a highly recommended exercise for every devotee of English—will reveal many anomalies. The definite and indefinite articles appear and disappear adventitiously in many constructions. Consider: *Indian ports which handle almost 90 per cent of the country's imports and export cargo are undergoing modernisation programme of the infrastructural facilities* (*Afternoon Despatch & Courier*, Bombay). Every native American or British speaker would insert *a* before *modernisation* in this sentence, though the Indian writer has not seen the need for it. There is also considerable liberty taken with idioms and other phrases considered to be fixed in the two major dialects. Consider this excerpt from the *Times of India*: *only the revival of the Hindutva card can infuse a fresh life into a moribund organisation.* Speakers of American or British English would undoubtedly have used the fixed idiom "breathe new life." The use of commas to punctuate sentences in Indian English also shows no apparent pattern to the American or British reader, and there is a tolerance for run-on sentences that would have been the target of a crackdown by British or American primary school teachers, if they had only gotten there in time.

Like most other major dialects, Indian English is viewed by scholars to have within it a handful of major dialectal divisions, each of which carries with it sociological trappings. There are however patterns common to all of Indian English that distinguish it from other major dialects, and these are largely attributable to the influence of native languages. Identifying characteristics, in addition to seemingly eccentricities noted above, include the systematic use of stative verbs progressive forms (*We are wanting answers to our questions*); failure to invert the subject and auxiliary in question forms (*Why you are here?*); and the generalized tag form "Isn't it?" supplying the place of the inflected and conjugated tag forms (e.g., *Don't they?*,

Haven't you?, Didn't she?, etc.) that are a bane to learners of English everywhere. It is worth noting that this question tag is also found in Cockney speech (in the form "In'it?"), and seems to be gaining headway wherever English is a second language because of its irresistible simplicity.

Indian orthography follows British English to the letter and it is unlikely that American spellings will make any headway, although it is probably worth monitoring what effect the cottage industry of software code-writing in India, largely fueled by American companies looking for a good deal, may have on the English flowing in both directions as a result.

Irish English

Aside from the countries that make up the UK, no country other than Ireland can boast earlier sustained exposure to English, nor earlier establishment of an English-speaking population. Trade links between Great Britain and Ireland have existed for more than two millennia and as a result of these, and of early settlement in Ireland by Britons, English was widely established in Ireland by the twelfth century, when the shift from Old English to Middle English was nearly established. In the centuries that followed, Irish Gaelic reasserted itself as the main language spoken on the island, but a second and more enduring wave of settlements and invasions by Britons from the fifteenth century onward reestablished English and slowly began to supplant Gaelic as the first language of most Irish natives.

The physical proximity of Ireland to Great Britain and the long association of their peoples has resulted in the English of Ireland being a very near relation of British English. It is easy to lose sight of the fact that, as in South Africa and India, English in Ireland was a language imposed on a population who already had a language of their own; standard Irish English today deviates far less from British English in grammar and syntax than do the Englishes of those two countries. There are, however, some features of Irish English that have their roots in the Gaelic language that it displaced, and these, along with its unique pronunciation (which is also influenced by Gaelic) easily distinguish it from other dialects. Irish English features include (1) the tendency to answer a yes/no question with a sentence (*Does he live here? He does.*) rather than with a word, because there are no words for *yes* or *no* in Irish Gaelic; (2) plural forms for you, such as *youse* and *yiz*, perhaps reflecting the presence of their equivalents in Gaelic; and (3) using a pronoun and gerund following *and* to indicate the simultaneous occurrence of two events: *So in they come and us sittin' on the bed.* Many of these features can also be found in nonstandard or dialectal speech in the English of other countries that were the destination of Irish emigration; variant plural you forms abound in American and British regional speech, and using a sentence to answer a yes/no question is a common feature of Southern American English. The widespread elision of the g sound at the end of -*ing* forms, especially participles, in American rural speech is also likely to have been influenced by Irish immigration.

Irish orthography follows British English to the letter and it is unlikely that American spellings will make any headway. As in the case of India, there is a large volume of human and digital traffic between Ireland and the US in the field of high technology, but the competition for influence on Irish English by American English is considerable, owing to the close proximity of Ireland to the mother source. The historical influence of Irish speakers on American English, on the other hand, is indisputable. A few words of Irish origin are today commoner in American English than in British English, reflecting the influence of Irish immigration throughout American history and especially following the nineteenth century Potato Famine. These include *clabber, smithereens,* and possibly *moniker.* The jury is still out on the etymology of *shenanigan* but it has reasonable claim to being of Irish origin. The case for *shebang* is less convincing but marginally plausible.

South African English

English settlement in South Africa took place over a period that coincided largely with the convict settlement of Australia, and similarities in the Englishes in these two countries, particularly in pronunciation, is well documented. The situation in which English presented itself in South Africa, however, was far from being the relatively clean slate that existed in Australia, where the incomers encountered a fairly sparse and migrant population. In early nineteenth century South Africa there were already large settlements of Khoisan- and Bantu-speaking peoples, and the Dutch presence in the Cape Province was also well established, with Afrikaans already on its way to becoming a language separate from Dutch. In South African English today there is quite a lot of borrowing from Afrikaans, especially for items of local manufacture and features of the landscape.

Perhaps more than in any other country where English competes with other official languages (South Africa now has eleven), the use of English in South Africa is now and has always been politicized, and impossible to divorce from its socioeconomic and cultural trappings. It is the first language of only about 10 percent of South Africans, but two-thirds of these are white, and most of the rest are non-Black. Before the abolition of apartheid, when English was one of only two official languages (along with Afrikaans), it was inextricably associated with the ruling economic and political powers in the country, and mastery of it was viewed as a key to success. Today, while it is still dominant in many areas of public life, including commerce, the media, and to some degree government, it is not viewed as an "innocent" language; its historical and current use foster the perception that it contributes to the maintenance of unequal relations of power in South Africa.

Like most other Englishes that started out as de facto instruments of colonial domination, South African English follows British English in orthography, and in many items of vocabulary as well. Words that are not borrowings from Afrikaans or African languages are far likelier to have come from British English than from American English (*newsreader*, *beetroot*, *scone*, *duvet*). In fact the influence of American English on South African English today is negligible in light of the many other vivid and present forces that are currently shaping the language; these include Afrikaans, the indigenous languages, the English of the large community of Indians, and the traditional influence of British English.

Recently there have been suggestions that black South African English should be recognized as a separate major dialect, owing to its set of verifiably unique vocabulary, pronunciation, grammar, and syntax. Some see this as a way of validating the language of a disenfranchised class whose English is not quite the English of the traditional wielders of power, while others view it as a resurrection of apartheid through the back door, in academic clothing.

Idioms and Phrasal Verbs

This appendix treats: (a) idioms common to both dialects that vary only slightly in form; (b) common idioms with very similar meaning but quite different form in the two dialects; (c) phrasal verbs that fall into either of these categories, that is, differing only slightly in form between the two dialects, or with similar meaning but using different verbs in the two dialects. The business of equivalencies in these cases is not an exact science; it is often the case that an idiom or verb phrase in one dialect will have wider or more specific application than its counterpart in the other. The attempt here is to strike a balance between an oversimplified list and a treatise in tortured detail, though it must be said that there is scope for such a treatise; an exhaustive listing of the figures of speech in each dialect that have an approximate semantic cousin in the other would fill a book of their own.

Idioms

The idioms and expressions in this table exist in some form in both dialects, with slightly different wording, sometimes no more than the presence or absence of an article. They are arranged alphabetically by the first noun in the American column, or in the absence of a noun, by the first adjective, verb, or adverb.

IDIOMS AND EXPRESSIONS DIFFERING SLIGHTLY IN FORM

American idiom	British idiom
cash on the barrelhead	cash on the nail
thick as a board [stupid]	thick as two short planks
beat around the bush →	beat about the bush[1]
take the cake	take the biscuit
in the cards	on the cards →
happy as a clam	happy as Larry
one-shot deal, one-time (event, etc.)	one-off (event, etc.)
diamond in the rough	rough diamond
queer as a three-dollar bill	queer as a nine-bob note
in for a dime, in for a dollar	in for a penny, in for a pound →
put one's foot in one's mouth	put one's foot in it
take sth with a grain of salt	take sth with a pinch of salt
half-cocked	at half-cock
can't make heads or tails of sth	can't make head nor tail of sth
down at the heel(s)	down at heel
highway robbery	daylight robbery
home away from home	home from home
a man's home is his castle	an Englishman's home is his castle
blow/toot one's own horn	blow one's own trumpet
do a good/bad job	make a good/bad job
know-it-all	know-all
have a new lease on life	have a new lease of life
leave well enough alone	leave well alone
be of two minds about sth	be in two minds about sth
scream bloody murder	scream blue murder
a night on the town	a night on the tiles
on the nose	spot on
trade places	change places
not touch sth with a ten-foot pole	not touch sth with a bargepole
in the raw [naked]	in the buff
Rube Goldberg (invention, etc.)	Heath Robinson (invention, etc.)
by a long shot	by a long chalk
pull up stakes	(pull) up sticks
sleep in the streets	sleep rough
there's a sucker born every minute	there's one born every minute
head table	top table

**IDIOMS AND EXPRESSIONS DIFFERING
SLIGHTLY IN FORM** (*continued*)

American idiom	British idiom
tempest in a teapot	storm in a teacup
have another thing coming[2]	have another think coming →
(have a) green thumb	(have) green fingers
third time's the charm	third time lucky
step on sb's toes	tread on sb's toes
to top it off	to cap it all
take turns	take it in turns
shoot one's wad	shoot one's bolt
rub sb the wrong way	rub sb up the wrong way
throw one's weight around →	throw one's weight about
knock on wood	touch wood
make a world of difference	make the world of difference
if worst comes to worst	if the worst comes to the worst
upscale	upmarket →

[1] See "Prepositions" in chapter 2 for a discussion of *about* and *around*.
[2] This form of the idiom is far more prevalent in American English, though the British version is demonstrably the original, and in the view of some, the only correct form.

Idioms and Figurative Words Unique to One Dialect

This table sets out idioms that are unique to one dialect, equating them with an idiom or expression in the other dialect with identical or similar meaning. They are arranged alphabetically by the first noun in the left column, or in the absence of a noun, by the first adjective, verb, or adverb.

UNIQUE IDIOMS AND FIGURES

American idiom	British idiom
roll in the aisles	fall about laughing
when all is said and done	at the end of the day →
take the bull by the horns →	grasp the nettle
in a coon's age	for donkey's years
since day one	since the year dot
a bad deal; a bum steer	hard cheese
a dime a dozen	ten a penny
shoot oneself in the foot	blot one's copybook
like Grand Central Station	like Piccadilly Circus

UNIQUE IDIOMS AND FIGURES *(continued)*

American idiom	British idiom
beat sb by a hair's breadth →	pip sb at the post
knock holes in sth	drive a coach and horses through sth
iron-clad	copper-bottomed
jack shit, zip, zilch	sweet fa [fanny adams or fuck all]
never-never land →	cloud-cuckoo land
like mad, like crazy	like the clappers
give sth a once-over →	run the rule over sth
walking papers	marching orders[1]
take a powder	do a bunk, do a runner
take the rap	carry the can
in a row [consecutively] →	on the trot
send sb to the showers	dismiss early from competition
six of one, half-dozen of the other	much of a muchness
talk a blue streak	talk the hind legs off a donkey
get in/into a tizzy	get your knickers in a twist
be toast	have had one's chips
give sb a tongue-lashing →	have a go at sb
Voilà!	Bob's your uncle!
a washout	a damp squib
fifth wheel	gooseberry
you win some, you lose some	(it's) swings and roundabouts

[1] Far more use in sports for sending a player off the field than the American English gets.

Phrasal verbs

A phrasal verb is one that consists of the combination of a verb plus an adverb or preposition that have a significantly different meaning than the verb alone has. Examples include *bring up, goof off, wind down, take in, carry on, pan out.* There is no difference in the syntax of any of these verbs between the dialects; the differences arise either in the preference for one adverb or preposition over another, or of using entirely different verbs to mean the same thing. The verbs are alphabetized in the left-hand column.

PHRASAL VERBS

American	British
break in [a new car, engine, etc.]	run in
cater to sb	cater for sb
close out [a business]	wind up

PHRASAL VERBS *(continued)*

American	British
cut off [in traffic]	cut up
feel sb up [caress sexually]	touch sb up
fill out [a form]	fill in
fool around	muck about
get along [with someone]	get on [with someone]
get it on with sb [have sex]	have it off/away with sb
get by [manage]	rub along
get rid of →	get shot of
go bad [become rotten]	go off
gulp down	knock back
hang out [with sb]	knock about [with sb]
mess around with sb	mess sb about
put sb on [deceive]	have sb on
sell out [property]	sell up
settle into sth →	bed into sth
sign up [enlist or register]	sign on
stop in/by	pop in
take care of	look after
tee off [make angry]	brass off
tell on sb	sneak on sb
trip sb up	catch sb out

Measures and Numbers

Owing to its membership in the European Union, the UK is being increasingly compelled to metricize. Already litigation has resulted from greengrocers who would insist on selling their goods in pounds rather than in kilos, and decisions have gone against the traders who preferred the imperial measures; they have been dubbed "metric martyrs." The approaching and ironic result seems to be that the United States, Britain's most spectacular colonial failure, will be the only major nation in the world to continue using English imperial measures, even at the cost of allowing multimillion-dollar space vehicles to blow up because of failure to account for the differences between the two systems. Americans are still quite happy to use the *BTU* (British Thermal Unit), even with its imperial moniker; it has been mostly displaced by its metric cousins, the *joule* or the *kilojoule*, in the UK.

Metric units between the US and the UK differ in only one regard: spelling. Those ending *-tre* in British English end in *-ter* in American English: thus AmE *meter*, BrE *metre*; AmE *liter*, BrE *litre*.

Imperial Unit Differences

While sharing common names there are some differences among some imperial measures between the US and the UK that can catch the unsuspecting, particularly cooks, off guard. The *imperial gallon*, in declining use in the UK, is substantially larger than the US gallon; they hold 4.55 and 3.75 liters, respectively. The subunits of a gallon are all in common use in the US, that is *half-gallon*, *quart*, *pint*, and *cup*, each of which is half the volume of the previous one. None of the other named units here is much used in the UK except the pint (still the standard for beer and milk, though perhaps not for much longer), but it should be noted that a UK pint contains 20 ounces and an US pint contains 16 ounces. The American mnemonic rhyme "a pint's a pound the world around" is in fact not true!

Volume units larger than a gallon, the *peck* (2 gallons) and the *bushel* (8 gallons) have only historical or informal usage in the UK. As with other imperial units, they are conventionally slightly larger than their US versions. The bushel is still the unit of measure for many crops in the US (apples, wheat, potatoes, corn, oats, etc.); yields of these of these are typically given in *bushels per acre*. The UK measures such outputs in *tonnes per hectare*.

Metrication notwithstanding, Britons are still inclined to note their personal weight in the old unit of the *stone* (plural same), which is equal to 14 pounds: *a 10-stone woman who lost 5 pounds on the diet.*

A *hundredweight* is a unit of 100 pounds in the US, and of 112 pounds in the UK. Because of metrication this term is becoming strictly historical in British English, but the unit is still used for some agricultural commodities in American English.

Ton and *tonne* are both used in British English with different denotation. *Tonne* is reliably used to denote what American English usually calls a *metric ton*, that is, a unit of 1000 kilograms or 2204.62 pounds. *Ton* in American English always means a measure of 2000 pounds; in British English it may mean a *long ton* or a *short ton*. The *long ton* or *gross ton* is 2,240 pounds and is usually what is meant if the term *ton* alone is encountered. The *short ton* is the same as the American English *ton*. American English uses *gross ton* when it means the unit of 2,240 pounds. Contexts abound in which the reader of British English may be at a loss to know exactly which ton is meant, but since the word is typically used in contexts in which approximations only are given, the distinction is not usually terribly important.

Tons and *tons of sth* are the standard American English informal words to indicate huge quantities of something; these are also used in British English, where they compete with *loads*, *heaps*, (also found in American English) and *wodges*.

Cooking Measurements

Modern British recipes and cookery books normally give measurements in two scales, metric and imperial (usually using ounces). American recipes and cookbooks use a single system, based on imperial measures but adapted specifically for cooking. American cooks who wish to use British recipes can usually make mental conversions from the imperial measures given to the *cup* system (see below), based on there being 16 ounces to the pound. British cooks wishing to use American recipes can do the math if they wish, but it is far more sensible to invest in an inexpensive set of American *measuring cups* and spoons, which will work for all US recipes.

The American system of cooking is based on measures that can be derived from the *cup* (*c*) and the *teaspoon* (*tsp*). A *cup* of liquid measure is 8 fluid ounces; the weight of dry measures in cups varies according to the substance: recipes calling for a cup of sugar, flour, cocoa, etc., always mean that measure by volume, not by weight, and there is no easier way to determine this than to simply fill the container indicated to the top and level it off. A set of American measuring cups comprises the cup, half cup, third cup, and quarter cup.

A cooking *teaspoon* is about 5 ml and for cooking purposes is the same as a British teaspoon.[1] The American system also uses the *tablespoon* (*T*), which is equal to 3 teaspoons. These spoons are sold in sets (*measuring spoons*) that contain various fractions and multiples of the teaspoon and tablespoon.

Temperature

Temperatures in the Fahrenheit scale are on their way out as points of reference in British English, since the generation now becoming adults were weaned on the Celsius scale: weather forecasts always give preference to Celsius temperatures, with their Fahrenheit equivalents mentioned parenthetically if at all. The situation is the opposite in the US, where Celsius is preferred only in strictly scientific contexts. Normally no misunderstandings arise from the dual use of these systems when common sense is used: a day with temperatures *in the 70s* could only mean Fahrenheit, and temperatures that *soared to a sweltering 31 degrees* could never mean Fahrenheit. The only context that requires scrutiny is the phrase *below zero*, which in British English is mostly likely to mean only "below freezing," and in American English is likely to mean "below zero degrees Fahrenheit," or about -18° C.

1. Note, however, that the *teaspoon* in a set of British cutlery is considerably smaller than the teaspoon in a set of American flatware.

Paper Sizes

The UK uses the metric-derived system of paper sizes, based on A0, containing a square meter of paper, and its commonest representative *A4*, the standard size of paper for letters and computer printing. The American functional equivalent is *letter size*, which measures $8\frac{1}{2}$ by 11 inches. This table sets out the commonest sizes and their functional equivalents:

PAPER SIZES

Name	Metric Size (mm)	Size in Inches	Nearest US Size	Size in Inches
A8	53 × 74	2.07 × 2.91	business card	$2 \times 3\frac{1}{2}$
A7	74 × 105	2.91 × 4.13	index card	3 × 5
A6	105 × 148	4.13 × 5.83	microfiche	4 × 6
A5	148 × 210	5.83 × 8.27	5 × 8	5 × 8
A4	210 × 297	8.27 × 11.69	A (letter size)	$8\frac{1}{2} \times 11$
A3	297 × 420	11.69 × 16.54	B (ledger size)	11 × 17

A common US size not found in the UK is *legal*, which measures $8\frac{1}{2}$ by 14 inches and is used in preference to letter size for many legal documents. It is also sold in ruled, yellow pads called *legal pads* that are a favorite scrawling place for lawyers, writers, students, and many others. Before the inexorable march of metrication the standard paper size for office use in the UK was *foolscap*, which was both wider and longer than contemporary standard paper sizes. The name for it, which now has a slightly nostalgic ring, is more common today than the paper itself.

Big Numbers

The names used for numbers from 10^9 and upwards sometimes go by different names in the two dialects. The American English names are unambiguous. The British English terms in dated texts need to be questioned, as there is an increasing tendency since about the 1970s to adopt the American names, and different institutions may have different policies. The traditional distinctions are as follows, with the superscript denoting the power of ten, and also the number of zeros that follow the one:

BIG NUMBERS

Number	AmE name	BrE name [*dated*]
10^9	billion	thousand million[1]

BIG NUMBERS *(continued)*

Number	AmE name	BrE name [*dated*]
10^{12}	trillion	billion
10^{15}	quadrillion	thousand billion
10^{18}	quintillion	trillion
10^{21}	sextillion	thousand trillion

[1] *Milliard* may be found rarely as a competing term.

It is modestly assumed that the average English speaker will not have to deal with amounts in excess of these, but the pattern continues upward.

The Transatlantic Calendar

Laid out here is a chronological account of fixed special days throughout the year that may be poorly understood by Transatlantic readers and visitors. Also included are days recognized in both countries for the same thing, but with different customs or different vocabulary. Summary notes at the end explain terms that occur more than once.

TRANSATLANTIC CALENDAR

January 1	*New Year's Day* (UK bank holiday and US federal holiday)
January 2	*Bank Holiday* (Scotland)
January (third Monday)	*Dr. Martin Luther King Day* (US federal holiday, observing his birthday, which was the fifteenth)
February 2	*Groundhog Day* (US), traditional season prognosticator. If hibernating groundhogs emerge and see their shadow, winter will continue another six weeks. Not an official holiday. Its origins are connected with *Candlemas*, on the same day, now only observed in some churches.
February 14	*St. Valentine's Day*, in the US usually *Valentines Day*
February (third Monday)	*Presidents' Day* (US federal holiday), celebrates the combined birthdays of Abraham Lincoln (twelfth) and George Washington (twenty-second)

TRANSATLANTIC CALENDAR *(continued)*

February (movable)	*Shrove Tuesday*, also called *Mardi Gras* (especially celebrated in New Orleans), also called *Pancake Day* in the UK and celebrated with pancake races there (in which contestants run while holding a pan and flipping a pancake). Called *Fastnacht* in a few US areas with a high concentration of German descendants. Followed by *Ash Wednesday*.
March 1	*St David's Day* (Wales, which celebrates its patron saint)
March (second Sunday)	*Mothering Sunday* (UK), also called *Mother's Day*
March 17	*St. Patrick's Day* (US and Northern Ireland, where it is a bank holiday), the patron saint of Ireland who is celebrated with parades and "the wearing of the green," especially in US cities with a large Irish population (New York, Boston, Chicago)
March (third or fourth Sunday)	*British Summer Time* and US *Daylight Savings Time* begin.
March or April	*Good Friday* (UK bank holiday); *Easter; Easter Monday* (UK bank holiday except Scotland)
April 1	*April Fool's Day* UK celebrations are more elaborate, with the major newspapers and other media outlets running bogus stories
May (first Monday)	*Early May Bank Holiday* (UK), sometimes called May Day
May 1	*May Day*, celebrated in both countries in recognition of spring; an occasion for *Morris Dancing* in the UK, a traditional folkdance performed in costume. A small socialist or Marxist fringe in the UK marks this as *Labour Day*
May (second Sunday)	*Mother's Day* (US)
May (last Monday)	*Memorial Day* (US federal holiday), to commemorate the war dead and have blowout sales; *Spring Bank Holiday* (UK). In the US, unofficially the beginning of the summer season.
June 14	*Flag Day* (US), birthday of the US flag. Not a federal holiday
June (third Sunday)	*Fathers' Day*
July 4	*Independence Day*, also called *fourth of July* (US federal holiday), celebrates the signing of the Declaration of Independence in 1776 and the beginning of the end of English tyranny

TRANSATLANTIC CALENDAR *(continued)*

July 12	*Orange Day* (Northern Ireland Bank Holiday), celebrates the Protestant victory in the Battle of the Boyne, 1690
August (first Monday)	*August Bank Holiday* (Scotland)
August (last Monday)	*Summer Bank Holiday* (UK except Scotland) coinciding with this weekend is the *Notting Hill Carnival* in London, a celebration of Caribbean culture
August	dubbed the *Silly Season* (mainly UK) because Parliament is not sitting and newspapers struggle to find events worthy of reporting; American English use is spotty
September (first Monday)	*Labor Day* (US federal holiday) unofficially the end of the summer season.
October 31	*Halloween* (mainly US); children dress in costumes and go door-to-door, expecting free candy
October (second Monday)	*Columbus Day* (US federal holiday), commemorates Columbus's "discovery" of the New World (October 12, 1492)
October (last Sunday)	*British Summer Time* (UK) and *Daylight Savings Time* (US) end
November (first Tuesday)	*Election Day* (US), for any local, state, and national elections. Not a legal holiday, but usually a school holiday because many schools are used as polling places.
November 5	*Guy Fawkes Day*, also called *Bonfire Night* (UK), commemorating Mr. Fawkes' failed attempt to blow up Parliament in 1605. Public and private bonfires are lit, and effigies of Guy Fawkes are burned.
November 11	*Veteran's Day* (US federal holiday), formerly called Armistice Day in both countries, commemorating the end of hostilities in World War I (1918); in the UK it is now moved to the nearest Sunday and called *Remembrance Sunday*, also *Poppy Day* because everyone wears poppies in remembrance of WWI battlefields
November (fourth Thursday)	*Thanksgiving* (US federal holiday), commemorates early colonial settlers surviving their first year; traditionally spent with family members over a turkey dinner
December 25	*Christmas* (bank holiday in UK; federal holiday in US), visits from *Santa Claus* in the US, and his twin *Father Christmas* in the UK
December 26	*Boxing Day* (UK bank holiday); *Kwanzaa* (US), a recently invented holiday celebrated by African Americans, begins
December 31	*New Year's Eve*, called *Hogmanay* in Scotland.

Bank holidays in the UK are the functional equivalent of US *federal holidays*, also called *legal holidays*; banks and post offices are normally closed and government workers have the day off. Most of them are designed to fall on a Monday. In the UK, most professional workers also have bank holidays off, but not all federal holidays are observed by companies in the US. Days in the calendar above that are not designated as a bank holiday (UK) or a federal holiday (US) are usually not observed as paid holidays.

Traditionally there were four *quarter days* in the UK, dividing the year in quarters and marking the due date of various payments. These are little used any more, though two of them, *Midsummer Day* (June 24) and *Michaelmas* (Sept 29) are still so called in conventional contexts.

Resources

Of the few books concerned primarily with the same subject as this one, namely, the differences between American English and British English, I have found one useful: *British English A to Zed* by Normal W. Schur (New York: Facts on File, 2001). It treats a great many words in British English that I have not included because of their datedness, marginal register, or specialized subject area. It will be of interest primarily to Americans interested in British English. I am aware of no comparable book that treats American English for British readers.

Readers interested in books about English generally are advised to start with *The Mother Tongue* by Bill Bryson (New York: William Morrow, 1990; also a Penguin paperback). It is a popular treatment of the phenomenon of English and its history, with a fairly extensive bibliography that contains most of the standard works to that date. A more scholarly and comprehensive approach can be found in the *Oxford Companion to the English Language* (Oxford: Oxford University Press, 1992); it is indispensable for devotees of English and always repays casual browsing or targeted research. For readers interested specifically in the historical development of American English as a dialect distinct from British, the unsurpassed source is *The American Language* by H. L. Mencken (New York: Alfred A. Knopf, 4th edition 1999).

Other recommended books are divided here broadly into two groups: those published in the US, and thus largely of interest to Britons for the subject at hand; and those published in the UK, and thus mainly of interest to Americans interested in British English.

Books published in the US

The student or devotee of American English has a great many choices in dictionaries at present. It is difficult to say how long these happy circumstances will continue in an electronic age when the whole future of paper publishing is undergoing a sea change, and there are already signs that some paper dictionaries with a long and distinguished publishing history will no longer be maintained as up-to-date products. For now, there are six American college dictionaries, and a few larger ones, all of which come in a CD-ROM version as well as the paper one. The college dictionaries are the ones that most Americans use, and the ones they think of as general reference dictionaries. They are

> American Heritage College Dictionary, 4th edition
> Merriam Webster Collegiate Dictionary, 10th edition
> Microsoft Encarta College Dictionary
> Oxford American College Dictionary
> Random House Webster's College Dictionary (2000)
> Webster's New World College Dictionary, 4th edition

They all have strong points and all of them are assembled by dedicated and professional teams of experienced lexicographers. For the speaker of British English, it is difficult to make a single recommendation, and I could not recommend going to great lengths to obtain one rather than another because they are all good. But if pressed I would point to the *Webster's New World College Dictionary* (Foster City, CA: IDG Books Worldwide, 1999). It has clear and concise definitions, and a user-friendly page layout, and it identifies Americanisms by a small symbol (☆), a useful device for all students of the language. Its CD-ROM, however, does not have many sophisticated features. Those who require the multiple capabilities of a CD-ROM for language research can do no better than the *Random House Webster's Unabridged Dictionary* (New York: Random House, 2001).

There are four works worth consulting in matters of style; not all at once, thank goodness, but as required for the type of language being prepared. A good general authority to follow in the absence of any other one being specified is the *Chicago Manual of Style* (Chicago: University of Chicago Press, 1993), now in its fourteenth edition and unlikely to be supplanted as the final arbiter of proper written American English. For journalism, the *Associated Press Stylebook and Libel Manual* (Cambridge, MA: Perseus Books, 2000) is a reliable authority, though many newspapers have their own guides that are commercially available, notably the *New York Times*. For the presentation of scholarly writing the Chicago guide is reliable, and mostly complementary to the *MLA Handbook* (New York: Modern Language Association, 1999). Finally, for government documents the authoritative source is the *United States Government Printing Office Style Manual*; aside from its intended use, it is a thoughtful and consistent guide to the use of American English. It also has the advantage of being available free and online, as well as for purchase. The URL for the online version is:

http://www.access.gpo.gov/styleman/2000/browse-sm-00.html

If it has moved from here, look for it via the GPO website (www.gpo.gov), which is also the place to go if you want to purchase a copy of the guide.

Books published in the UK

DICTIONARIES

The American seeking a good British dictionary is also spoiled for choice; dictionary publishing flourishes in the UK as in no other Anglophone country. There is no exact counterpart to the American college dictionary in terms of scope and coverage, and the nearest equivalent is a slightly larger, more detailed volume with some encyclopedic information. The main contenders in this category are

Collins English Dictionary, 5th Edition
New Oxford Dictionary of English, 1st edition (corrected)
The Chambers Dictionary, "New Edition" (1998)

Of these, the *New Oxford Dictionary of English* (Oxford: Oxford University Press, 2001) is the best choice: it is up-to-date and based on the exhaustive Oxford English Dictionary; it is been widely and justly praised by ordinary users and professional lexicographers alike.

Lovers of English and researchers into its secrets who want the whole enchilada will eventually succumb to the *Oxford English Dictionary* (OED) in some form. There are microprinted paper editions available, but the online version is the one to go with for research with all the latest technological tools. Subscriptions are hefty for the individual, but many institutions, such as university and public libraries, allow access to their patrons. If your library doesn't, lobby for it. Details are available at www.oed.com, where you can also take a very informative tour of the dictionary.

The *Longman Dictionary of English Language and Culture* (Harlow, UK: Addison-Wesley-Longman, 1998), although it is a learners' dictionary, has many points of cultural interest to the American reader. The *Oxford Guide to British and American Culture* (Oxford: Oxford University Press, 1999), also aimed mainly at learners of English, goes into considerably more detail on points of cultural reference in both countries, detailing more than 10,000 items from history, literature and the arts, places, and institutions. Readers seeking to improve their understanding of the other culture through reading but find that too many of the cultural references are opaque will find this volume useful.

Style and Usage Manuals

No student of the English language generally should be without H. W. Fowler's *Modern English Usage.* The second edition (Oxford: Oxford University Press, 1983) although dated in some respects, is the best one to own because it preserves more of Mr. Fowler's original concise and incomparably witty language. There are fewer general authorities for the style of presentation in British English than there are for American English, and probably more of these imposed at the institutional level. Nearly all British newspapers and broadcasters have their own manuals for the use of their writers. The classic work for copyeditors is *Copy-Editing* (third edition) by Judith Butcher (Cambridge, UK: Cambridge University Press, 1992). A competing work, less extensive and considerably less damaging to the pocketbook is *Hart's Rules for Compositors and Readers* (1983). It is the style bible for Oxford University Press, which publishes it. Equally useful is the *Oxford Dictionary for Writers and Editors* (2000) which also presents the house style of the Oxford University Press. Finally, Michael Swan's *Practical English Usage* (Oxford: Oxford University Press, 1995) is a useful volume for Americans and other "off-islanders" who want to get a fix on the British approach to interpreting proper English.

INTERNET RESOURCES

Language is a moving target and books about it are only snapshots; this one is no exception. Because of the dynamic aspects of language it is essential that any book research into it be supplemented by material that is newer and up-to-date, and for this the Internet is the place to go.

Everyone by now has had the disappointing experience of looking for an website that has vacated its last known address and left no information as to its present whereabouts. In order to spare the reader this frustration, I have kept the number of actual URLs here and throughout the book to a minimum. Here I will focus instead on ways that search engines can be used to find information about American and British English. Before we get to that however, a few sites are worth mentioning because of their great usefulness and interest for the transatlantic English speaker, and their claim to a permanence that it is hoped will at least continue during the present edition of this book.

The top-level government websites in both countries are gold mines for the researcher, whether in the field of language alone or more generally. They provide efficient links and search capabilities for all available government sites and documents. As well as containing a wealth of information that is of interest to overseas visitors, government-published documents exemplify the default rules of usage and presentation in each country and thus are invaluable for gleaning facts about American and British English usage today. The government web portals are:

For the US: www.firstgov.gov
For the UK: www.ukonline.gov.uk

The portals for the fifty US state official sites, which lead to links for many other public and private bodies within each state, follow a formula:

www.state.xx.us

Where *xx* corresponds to the two-letter official postal abbreviation for that state (see chapter 7 "Addresses").

Reading the daily press in either country is an informative and entertaining way of acquainting oneself with the particulars of the other dialect, as well as getting a flavor for the preoccupations and prejudices of the natives. All the major newspapers have good online editions. Some recommendations:

For the US: www.nytimes.com (*New York Times*)
www.washingtonpost.com (*Washington Post*)
www.latimes.com (*Los Angeles Times*)

For the UK: www.telegraph.co.uk (*Daily Telegraph*)
www.guardian.co.uk (*Guardian*)
www.thetimes.co.uk (*Times*)
www.independent.co.uk (*Independent*)

Yahoo (www.yahoo.com) can be used efficiently for finding online English-language newspapers in any country. From the homepage, click on Newspapers, (under News & Media), then By Region, then Countries, and choose your country.

Search Strategies

Doing research on the Internet with a search engine is like looking for a needle in a haystack, with the aid of a magnet: you have a valuable tool to aid you, but you have no way of knowing whether the needle you're looking for is even in the haystack. A great deal of time can be saved by using a search engine with sophisticated filters that enable you to eliminate a large number of "false positives" from the search results; Google (www.google.com) and AltaVista (www.altavista.com) are recommended; start your search on the "advanced search" page, or learn to use the syntax of Boolean operators that are allowed by each site on the main search page. Both engines have help screens online.

The simplest method for eliminating certain results, usable on both AltaVista and Google, is with the + and – signs. For example:

+ "Bill of Rights" – "United States" + England

Would go a long way toward eliminating results from a search containing information or text from the US Bill of Rights, if it is the English one that you were looking for.

Both engines also allow you to restrict your search to a particular domain or to a particular top-level site. This can be very useful for eliminating a huge number of sites that you think will contain only noise. Given the current, less than perfectly consistent division of domains, you cannot eliminate all undesirables in this way, but it is possible, for example to limit your search to UK sites (domain .uk), US government sites (domain .gov), or US educational institutions (domain .edu).

If you wish to limit your search to a more specific domain level, use the "only this host or URL" option on AltaVista, which accepts wildcards; this does not work on Google. For example, if you wish to limit your search to British university sites, enter www.*.ac.uk. For public school and government sites in Kentucky, you can enter the string www.*.ky.us.

Google also allows searches of Usenet discussion groups, where a great deal of unedited, bleeding-edge language and jargon can be found, of great interest to the linguistic researcher if you don't mind wading through wodges of screed. Click on Groups from the Google homepage.

For researching particular words or terminology in various fields, there are two approaches. One is to start through a reference portal that gives access to a number of online dictionaries and glossaries. Some of these were most recently sighted at:

http://www.yourdictionary.com/
http://pssst-heyu.com/dictionarydownloads.html
http://www.deraaij.com/irt/english.html
http://www.uvigo.es/webs/sli/virtual/dicten.htm
http://saussure.linguistlist.org

A second approach, sometimes successful for obscurer purposes, is to locate a glossary online containing the object of your enquiry. For example, the search string + "nolo contendere"+ glossary might be successful in locating definitions for your study. For major fields of knowledge you can also find glossaries using search strings such as "real estate glossary." You can use this in combination with the domain-limiting methods noted above to further refine your results.

Corpus Research

The single most important tool for any researcher of language is a corpus: a large body of language collected in a database, along with software tools that enable the researcher to make queries. Corpora are costly and complicated to assemble; the ones owned by individual publishers are jealously guarded. There are, however, a couple of alternatives for the individual. One is the British National Corpus. Its homepage is

http://www.hcu.ox.ac.uk/BNC/

From here you can query the database and see multiple examples of usage of a particular word or phrase. There is currently in the making an American National Corpus, though it is some time away from completion and it is not known at this point whether free public access will be permitted. You can stay tuned for details at

http://americannationalcorpus.org

Finally, if you wish to use the whole World Wide Web as a corpus, searching for the occurrence of particular words or phrases on websites, go to

http://www.webcorp.org.uk/

This site gives you the option of receiving the output via email in the form of an ASCII file, which you can then manipulate with concordancing software.

About the Author

ORIN HARGRAVES grew up in the mountains of southwestern Colorado and graduated from the University of Chicago. He is a tenth-generation American of almost undiluted British Isles ancestry, and has lived for considerable periods in London. He has worked in lexicography and reference publishing since 1991, making substantial contributions to dictionaries and other reference works from publishers such as Bloomsbury, Cambridge University Press, Langenscheidt, Longman, Merriam-Webster, and Oxford University Press. He is also the author of travel guides including *Culture Shock! Morocco* and *London At Your Door.* He lives in Carroll County, Maryland.

Subject Index

This index contains the subjects and headings under which various areas of vocabulary are introduced and discussed in this book. It also contains numerous entries for words and phenomena that are unique to one or the other dialect or country, pointing the reader to the page where such items are defined or discussed.

Word Index

Indexed here are higher-frequency words common to both dialects that represent particular points of usage difference between British and American English. Orthographic variants, which are treated systematically in chapter 1, are omitted, except for those representing exceptions to various rules.